C. R. GILL
BSc., MPhil.,
UNIT CLINIC
KINGSWAY/
DERBY, TEL

Attribution Theory in Clinical Psychology

THE WILEY SERIES IN CLINICAL PSYCHOLOGY

Series Editor:

Fraser N. Watts
MRC Applied Psychology Unit
Cambridge

Severe Learning Disability
and Psychological Handicap
John Clements

Cognitive Psychology
and Emotional Disorders
J. Mark, G. Williams, Fraser N. Watts,
Colin MacLeod and Andrew Mathews

Community Care in Practice
Services for the Continuing Care Client
Edited by Anthony Lavender and Frank Holloway

Attribution Theory in
Clinical Psychology
Friedrich Försterling

Further titles in preparation

Panic Disorder: Research and Therapy
Edited by Roger Baker

Psychology and Criminal Conduct:
Theory, Research and Practice
R. Blackburn and R. M. B. Tulloch

Health Psychology: Models and Applications
Marie Johnston and Theresa Marteau

Measuring Human Problems
A Practical Guide
Edited by David Peck and C. M. Shapiro

Attribution Theory in Clinical Psychology

Friedrich Försterling
University of Bielefeld
Federal Republic of Germany

Translated by Jonathan Harrow

JOHN WILEY & SONS
Chichester · New York · Brisbane · Toronto · Singapore

Library of Congress Cataloging-in-Publication Data:

Försterling, Friedrich.
 [Attributionstheorie in der klinischen Psychologie. English]
 Attribution theory in clinical psychology/Friedrich Försterling, translated by Jonathan Harrow.
 p. cm. — (The Wiley series in clinical psychology)
 Translation of Attributionstheorie in der klinischen Psychologie.
 Biography: p.
 ISBN 0 471 91604 8 : (U.S.)
  1. Clinical psychology. 2. Attribution (Social psychology)
 I. Title. II. Series.
  [DNLM: 1. Psychological Theory. 2. Psychology, Clinical. WM 105 F758a]
 RC467.F6713 1988
 616.89-dc19
 DNLM/DLC
 for Library of Congress   88-5696
                                                                              CIP

British Library Cataloguing in Publication Data

Försterling, Friedrich
 Attribution theory in clinical psychology.
 (Wiley series in clinical psychology).
 1. Clinical psychology. Applications of
 psychology. Attribution theory
 I. Title
 157′.9

ISBN 0 471 91604 8

Typeset in Palatino 10/12pt by Witwell Ltd., Southport
Printed and bound in Great Britain by Biddles Ltd, Guildford

Contents

Series Editor's Preface

One of the purposes of this Wiley Series in Clinical Psychology is to present coherent and authoritative accounts of topics in clinical psychology where exciting advances are currently being made. The contributions of attribution theory to clinical psychology is such a topic, and Försterling has provided here the first comprehensive review. Like most books in this series, it is authored rather than edited, and for that reason offers an attractively systematic approach to its subject.

The book begins with a clear exposition of attribution theory and its basic assumptions. It then proceeds to examine the emotional, behavioural and clinical consequences of causal attributions. Attributional theories are well-established in abnormal psychology as, for example, in the attributional reformulation of the learned helplessness theory of depression. However, Försterling also reviews recent work extending attributional theories to a wide range of other clinical phenomena from smoking to marital dysfunction.

With this background, Försterling turns to what is the most original and clinically valuable part of the book, a thorough consideration of the modification of attributions in therapy. The theoretical principles of attribution therapy are clearly set out and relevant empirical research is comprehensively reviewed. In particular, Försterling succeeds in conveying the richness and subtlety of attributional therapy in clinical practice. He shows how a clear grasp of the basic principles of attributional theory pays dividends when it is applied in therapeutic work with the individual patient.

Clinical psychology is a field with permeable frontiers. It has close links with many other professions and scientific disciplines. I hope, therefore that the Series will have a broad appeal to all those concerned with the application of psychological knowledge to clinical problems. This particular book will be a valuable resource for the whole spectrum of professions engaged in providing psychological treatment. It will also be of interest to psychologists with a basic interest in attribution theory who will see in this book the growing scope and power of its practical applications.

FRASER WATTS
Series Editor

Foreword

The 1970s was a time of both change and continuity in psychology. Change was very evident in the field of social psychology. Festinger's theory of cognitive dissonance had provided the dominant paradigm or issue for social psychology in the 1960s. Dissonance theory offered a non-common-sense approach to attitude formation and change that was based on the 'fit' between cognitive elements. Inasmuch as attitudes historically have been the backbone of social psychology, and since there was a very conscious desire to progress beyond what was known as 'bubba' (grandmother) psychology, the dominance of dissonance theory can be readily understood. However, by the end of the 1960s dissonance theory had run its course which also is understandable. The many studies that were conducted left others searching for new places to make a contribution. In addition, dissonance was linked to drive theory, but this conception had already been discarded by motivational psychologists. And of greatest importance, dissonance theory was conceptually sparse, so that there were no new directions toward which the theory could turn, new phenomena that could be addressed and incorporated.

A second field of study ready to undergo change in the 1970s was clinical psychology. Academic psychologists had long been suspicious (at best) of the non-empirical stance of psychoanalytic theorists — as though they were not as accountable as other scientists for their pronouncements. While alternative approaches in clinical psychology also were available in the 1960s, including humanistic, client-centered, and behavior-modification therapies, it was evident that clinical psychology also was ripe for new directions. The stimulus for change was constantly fueled by studies apparently documenting that the effects of psychotherapy were minimal, or even worse, non-existent.

There was, however, a constant within the flux of psychology. That constant was the full acceptance of a cognitive psychology, with the conception of an organism who thinks, processes information, makes decisions, judges oneself and others, socially compares, recognizes the self, and so on. The behaviorism of Watson was buried by perhaps all but the behavioral therapists. Hence, cognitive psychology provided the backdrop for social and clinical psychology both during and after the 1960s. Festinger's dissonance theory, which is based on the congruence between cognitive elements, and the growth of ego psychology in the 1960s were consistent with this overriding cognitive context.

This background spawned the direct influences on this book — attribution theory in clinical psychology. Attribution theory first came into being with the writings of Fritz Heider in 1958. However, it fully burst into social psychology in the early 1970s and has dominated this field for the past fifteen years. Why did attribution theory, rather than some other conception, replace dissonance theory? First, it fits within the cognitive context, with the individuals presumed to search for mastery and understanding, asking why events have occurred and inferring the intents of others. Second, it is a psychology that does not rely on the non-obvious — people are accepted as attempting to be rational, guided in their beliefs by informational inputs, and directed in their actions by naive psychological theories. Of greatest importance, it is theoretically rich, providing the conceptual tools to be applied to an array of phenomena in widely disparate areas including personality, educational, organizational, sports, and developmental psychology, to name just a few non-clinical fields of study influenced by attributional approaches.

At the same time that the attribution theory was gaining dominance in social psychology, cognitive therapies were gaining increasing attention in clinical psychology. Sparked by the ideas of Beck, Ellis, G. Kelly, and many others, how clients make sense of the world around them and how these interpretations guide their feelings and actions became a central theme in change attempts. Even behavioral-oriented therapists began to recognize the importance of thought processes, and there grew an influential school of cognitive behavior-modification.

These trends describe the background for this fine book by Friedrich Försterling. Here we have for the first time, in the 1980s, a clear marriage between the vital approaches to attribution theory and cognitive therapy. What could be more natural, more right! Dr Försterling was trained by Albert Ellis, while I had the good fortune to host him at the University of California, Los Angeles, where many attribution theorists are housed. Hence, he is the perfect person to conduct this marriage and preside over the ceremony. And he has performed this union well.

In this book, Dr Försterling first gives a detailed review of attribution theory, including the attributional analysis of learned helplessness. He then turns to attribution training techniques and research, providing a complete survey of the empirical literature. This is followed by a comparison between attributional concepts and change techniques and the thoughts and practices of other cognitive therapies; the comparison highlights the relation between these schools. Hence, one is led to recognize the unique contribution that attribution theory can make to cognitive therapy; it is made evident that basic theory in social psychology can contribute to applied procedures in clinical psychology.

This is a very timely and important book, merging trends in psychology that cry out for connection. These tears need no longer be shed. Dr Försterling has done an important service for psychology and has made a lasting contribution. History, of course, always provides the final verdict. My belief is that this book will have a long life and that this integration will be part of the subsequent history of psychology.

Bernard Weiner
November 1985

Preface

This book has grown out of my interest in two different disciplines of psychology: general psychology, specifically motivational and social psychology, on the one hand, and clinical psychology and psychotherapy on the other. It is guided by the assumption that work in the field of clinical psychology can greatly benefit from research and theory from the area of general psychology. It will be demonstrated that one of the basic general psychological theories — namely attribution theory with its different variants — can be used to make concrete deductions for the clinical practice. In addition, the present book aims to illustrate that the application of basic psychological theories in the field of clinical psychology as well as psychotherapy can be an important field for the testing and development of theoretical conceptions that have originally been formulated in the area of experimental psychology.

Because of the general-psychological as well as clinical orientation of this book, it is also addressed at different readerships: It aims to address both the practicing psychologists as well as the researcher. Firstly, the book has been written for practicing clinical psychologists and psychotherapists who want to consider their work from the perspective of modern psychological theories. As attributional models share many similarities with cognitive behavioral approaches to therapy, it will probably be most advantageous for therapists with these orientations to receive stimulation for their practical work from this book. However, I also believe that attributional processes play a central role in other psychotherapies, such as more traditional behavioral approaches, Rogerian, as well as psychodynamic therapies. It is, therefore, to be hoped that the present book will help to identify and to provide a common language for some processes that might be similar in different schools of psychotherapy.

Secondly, I would also like to address researchers with the present book, specifically those who work in the area of clinical psychology and those who are concerned with basic research in the area of attribution theory. Researchers within the field of clinical psychology may find information about how attributional conceptions can be implemented into this area of psychology, whereas the basic researcher, who is concerned with causal attributions, might be more interested in exploring the range of convenience of this theoretical approach in another area of psychology; namely clinical psychology and psychotherapy.

As attributional research has frequently been conducted in the area of achievement behavior and in the classroom, the ideas presented here are also relevant to educational psychology and to psychologists working in schools. The book should also be especially interesting for psychologists who are concerned with behavior modification in the classroom and with achievement change programs.

I would like to express my gratitude to those persons who have helped me to develop and maintain my interest in general psychology as well as clinical psychology and psychotherapy. I am grateful to Dr Albert Ellis and the staff members of the Institute for Rational-Emotive Therapy in New York City, where I received training in clinical psychology and cognitive behavioral methods. Furthermore, I would like to thank Professor Dr Wulf-Uwe Meyer, University of Bielefeld, West Germany, for numerous stimulating discussions and helpful comments on earlier drafts of this manuscript. I am also greatly indebted to Professor Dr Bernard Weiner for the postdoctoral training I received from him, and for the support and stimulation that he has provided for my work since then. Last but not least, I would like to thank Beate Schuster for many helpful comments and for her kind support on the book.

Friedrich Försterling,
November, 1985

Preface to the English Edition

The present book is both a translation as well as a revised, updated and expanded edition of the German volume entitled 'Attributions theorie in der Klinischen Psychologie', Psychologie Verlags-Union, 1986. Some chapters have been translated directly, others have been changed, and most importantly, new sections have been added and recent literature has been included. For instance, Chapter 7 now contains descriptions of attempts to cast problems of behavioral medicine, preventive health behavior and marital distress in an attributional framework. In addition, Chapter 10 now includes sections that address the problems of attribution assessment, the use of self-handicapping strategies, and mention is made of the influence of emotional processes on cognitive variables. The changes, additions, and inclusion of more recent literature has expanded the references by more than one third compared to the German edition.

I would like to thank Jonathan Harrow for translating the manuscript into the English language. It was a pleasure to work with him and I am grateful for his many helpful comments and suggestions.

Friedrich Försterling
January, 1988

Chapter 1

Introduction

During the past 20 years, no other theoretical approach within the area of social psychology and personality has received as much attention as attribution conceptions (see Harvey, Ickes, and Kidd, 1976, 1978, 1981; Harvey and Weary, 1981; Heckhausen, 1980; Jaspars, Fincham, and Hewstone, 1983; Kelley and Michela, 1980). Attributional models have provided the conceptual tools to cast a vast amount of psychological phenomena within a unified framework, for instance, achievement behavior, social affiliation, helping behavior, organizational psychology, and power motivation. In addition, social psychological phenomena, such as person perception, coalition formation, close interpersonal relationships as well as reward allocations in groups, have been analyzed from an attributional perspective.

Attribution models have also been used for the analysis of phenomena within the area of applied psychology. Within both educational and clinical psychology, many of the dominant approaches have taken an attributional perspective (see Antaki and Brewin, 1982; Peterson and Seligman, 1984; Weiner, 1979, 1982a, 1986). Within research concerning helplessness and reactive depression (see Abramson, Seligman, and Teasdale, 1978; Coyne and Gotlib, 1983) as well as achievement motivation (see Weiner, 1979, 1986), causal attributions have taken a central role.

The present work applies attributional conceptions to phenomena from the area of clinical psychology and specifically to problems of psychotherapy and behavior modification. It will be shown that a relatively comprehensive system of diagnostic procedures and therapeutic interventions can be deduced from attributional premises and research. It will furthermore be demonstrated that this attributionally based model can be used to conceptualize important aspects of currently dominant therapeutic approaches within a unified framework.

The first two parts of the book describe selected topics from basic attribution research. First, the central premises of attribution theory are discussed and compared with basic assumptions of other clinically relevant psychological theories. Furthermore, I discuss the determinants and characteristics of causal attributions as well as possibilities for assessing and

1

classifying them. Finally, a description of theoretical models concerning attributional antecedents is presented (Kelley's covariation principle, Heider's conceptions of equifinality and local causality, as well as research concerning a model of indirect communications of attributionally relevant information as introduced by Meyer and coworkers).

The second part of the book describes models that are concerned with how attributions affect behavior, experiences, and emotional reactions. Weiner's attributional analysis of achievement motivation and the attributional reformulation of Seligman's concept of learned helplessness are summarized. Finally, I describe attempts to use an attributional framework for the understanding of additional behavioral consequences including helping behavior, anger, health related behaviors, and loneliness.

The selection of the basic attribution research that is described in the first two parts of the book is neither representative nor exhaustive. Important theoretical as well as empirical contributions such as Kelley's (1972) causal schemata, theory and data concerning differences between the causal attributions of actors and observers (Jones and Nisbett, 1971), and the theory of correspondent inferences (Jones and Davis, 1965) are either omitted or only briefly described because they are not central for an understanding of the latter chapters of the book. This is certainly not meant to imply that these models are irrelevant for questions of clinical psychology. It also should be noted that the discussion of the basic attributional research in Parts 1 and 2 does not always reflect the latest trends but is instead guided by the desire to enable the reader to understand the following parts of the book.

Part 3 describes, analyses, and summarizes laboratory research that has attempted to apply attributional principles to the modification of behaviors, affects, and cognitive processes. These studies are especially relevant for the purposes of this book as they 'simulate' the central aspects of clinical psychological activities (diagnosis, therapy, and outcome evaluation). In a first step, so-called 'misattribution methods' that are based on the Schachter and Singer (1962) two-factor theory of emotions are described. These programs attempt to ameliorate dysfunctional behaviors by misattributing physiological arousal and can be conceptually differentiated from so-called 'reattribution methods'. Reattribution training is based on the work of Bandura, Seligman, and Weiner. It attempts to favorably influence reactions to success and failure by convincing subjects that their achievement outcomes are due to the causal factor of effort.

Part 4 discusses limitations of attributional change studies. Guided by the ideas that underlie attributional retraining methods, I introduce an expanded model for the application of attributional conceptions in clinical psychology. This model integrates attribution research on the antecedents of causal cognitions (especially Kelley's covariation principle) with attributional research on the consequences of causal thinking. It is based on the premise of attribution theory that individuals are motivated to attain a realistic view of the causal relations in their life space, and that this realistic view enables the person to cope adaptively with and to control the environment. From this postulate I deduce that, under certain circumstances, dysfunctional affects and behaviors can be triggered and/or maintained by unrealistic attributions. Subsequently, it will be demonstrated that a spectrum of dysfunctional behaviors and emotional reactions in addition to those that are addressed by reattribution training (helplessness and underachievement) can be cast within an attributional framework when these premises and deductions are taken into account.

Finally, it will be shown that the attributional approach presented here shares many central assumptions and many specific predictions concerning clinical questions with models of cognitive psychotherapy as introduced by Beck (1976) and Ellis (1962). Both approaches are rooted in philosophy, conceptualize individuals as 'lay scientists', and assume that realistic or 'scientific' hypotheses about personally relevant events have a high functional value. Subsequently, I will present an attributional analysis of some central elements of the theory and practice of cognitive-behavioral therapies and then illustrate that techniques for therapeutic cognitive changes can be derived from attribution theory. Finally, I ask which therapeutic goals can be derived from attribution theory and what the desirable characteristics of a therapist might be from an attributional standpoint.

The present book is not 'only' concerned with the application of knowledge from the area of general psychology to the area of clinical psychology: I assume that the application of general psychological theories to clinical psychology is, in addition, an important 'testing ground' for psychological theories. Bandura (1977a) states

> The value of a theory is ultimately judged by the power of the procedures it generates to effect psychological changes. (p. 4) For this reason, psychological methods are best evaluated on the basis of their effectiveness in changing actual psychological functioning. (p. 5)

In addition to the testing of general theories, their introduction to clinical questions can also assist in their elaboration and refinement. Some of the limits of the theories of learned helplessness, depression, and achievement behavior will be addressed (Chapter 9) when integrating theoretical assumptions and research about attributional antecedents with work concerning attributional consequences.

Although I will arrive at the conclusion that therapeutic interventions in the laboratory that are based on attributional principles are generally successful, I do not want to indicate that there is a comprehensive, clinically established, and empirically tested and evaluated 'attribution therapy'. However, occasionally I shall refer to terms such as 'attribution therapy' or 'attributionally guided interventions' throughout the book to illustrate which concrete diagnostic or therapeutic interventions could be deduced from attributional principles. This is certainly not meant to imply that the respective technique has proven to be the most effective one to ameliorate a certain clinical symptom.

My main goal is to use a theoretical perspective that has already been proven as useful in other areas of psychology for the analysis of clinical phenomena and therapeutic techniques: because of the importance of attribution conceptions in social psychology, motivation, and personality, attribution theorists have developed an elaborated conceptual system and have also conducted many empirical studies and experiments to test attributional hypotheses. As a result of this, attribution theory has developed a vast number of empirical paradigms, and I hope that my attempt to demonstrate the usefulness of the application of attributional principles to clinical questions will also encourage researchers from the field of clinical psychology to use paradigms from attribution theory for their empirical studies. Hence, I also hope to be contributing to an enrichment of clinical methodology.

On a more general level, I pursue — like others (Brehm, 1976; Frieze, Bar-Tal, and Carroll, 1979; Weary and Mirels, 1982) — the question of to what extent contemporary theories from general and social psychology can provide a third alternative for the field of clinical psychology and psychotherapy. The first question is whether the clinical methods that are derived from contemporary psychological theories can be conceived of as an alternative or addition to the more traditional behavior modification approach that is also based on general psychology in that it has applied research concerning classical and operant conditioning to questions of psychotherapy. Secondly, applications of contemporary psychological models can be compared to or contrasted with the vast number of psychotherapeutic schools that have developed independently of experimental psychology, such as, for instance, Psychoanalysis, Cognitive Therapy, Rational-Emotive Therapy, and Rogerian Therapy.

This book is guided by the belief that theories from contemporary general and social psychology actually offer a very promising 'third approach' for the field of clinical psychology, and it aims to outline a segment of this approach. In doing this, it will hopefully soon become evident that this third approach also has many connections to the other (two) approaches, especially to the psychotherapeutic approaches that are already being practiced, and that it not only makes different but frequently also similar suggestions with regard to the methods through which psychological suffering can be ameliorated.

Part One

Characteristics and Antecedents of Attributions

Chapter 2

Basic Assumptions of Attribution Theories

When a theoretical approach is applied to an area of phenomena, the basic assumptions and premises of the theory have far-reaching implications for how the phenomena are viewed, which aspects of them are especially analysed, and which ones are neglected. For instance, it is an important (methodological) premise of traditional learning theory that it is impossible to assess cognitive processes accurately (see Skinner, 1953). As a consequence of this assumption, 'traditional' behavior therapists pay much less attention to their clients' thoughts and images than to their (observable) behaviors. The strong emphasis that psychoanalysts place on the childhood memories of their clients can be traced back to the Freudian assumption that current dysfunctional behavior is determined by early experiences and developments in the first years of an individual's life.

An attributional analysis of clinical phenomena also has implications for the conceptualization of diagnostic and therapeutic questions and problems. It determines how dysfunctional behaviors, affects, and experiences are explained and will also suggest specific therapeutic procedures and decisions; such as which emotional states and behavioral reactions are considered worthy of change, and what type of relationship between client and therapist is considered to be desirable.

As I believe that the basic premises of theories are highly important for subsequent clinical applications, I shall first — following a brief historical excursus — introduce the basic premises of attribution theories and will then compare them with some central assumptions of other clinically relevant psychological theories. In addition, I will point out some of the diagnostic and therapeutic implications that can be derived from central attributional premises. These derivations will also be compared with those from other theoretical approaches (i.e., learning theory, psychoanalysis, cognitive therapy).

7

2.1. A HISTORICAL NOTE

Attribution models are concerned with the formation and the consequences of causal explanations that individuals use in order to 'make sense' of the events in their lives. The analysis of causal explanations has a long tradition in many fields of psychology as well as in different philosophical systems (see Eimer, 1987; Einhorn and Hogart, 1986). In a recent monograph — that largely guides the present 'historical' section —, Eimer (1987) elaborates how these philosophical traditions relate attribution theory and research. The philosophers Hume (1740/1938), Kant (1781/1982) and Mill (1872) were specifically interested in determining how individuals come to judge one event (e.g., lightning) as a cause for another occurrence (such as the burning of a barn).

Hume postulated that there are some basic prerequisites that have to be met before we consider one event as the cause of another: First, the causal candidate must precede the event in time (the lightning has to be present before the barn will start to burn) and secondly, there has to be a spatial closeness between the cause and the event (the lightning has to 'strike' the barn before we would attribute the fire in the barn to it). Most characteristic for Hume's position, however, is that the two events must occur repeatedly before we would identify one event (the lightning) as the cause for the other (the burning barn). We would need to observe several times that, whenever lightning strikes, a fire will break out.

Hume's ideas were elaborated and specified by Mill. Mill points to the fact that we also tend to perceive the non-existence of an event as a cause, for instance, we would say that the absence of a lightning conductor has caused the barn to catch fire during the thunderstorm. This case was not included in Hume's analysis. Mill introduced the 'Method of Difference' as an explanation of how causal judgements are performed. He states: 'If an instance in which the phenomenon under investigation occurs, and an instance in which it does not occur, have every circumstance in common save one, that one occurring only in the former; the circumstance in which alone the two instances differ, is the effect, or the cause, or an indispensable part of the phenomenon' (p. 452). For instance, in the present example we have lightning close to two barns, in one instance the barn does not catch fire (there is a lightning conductor) whereas the other barn (without a lightning conductor) starts to burn.

As the lightning conductor is the only causal candidate that is different in the two cases, it will be held responsible for the event and its non-occurrence. (We will discuss the 'Method of Difference' more closely in Chapter 4.)

Note that it is highly characteristic for both Hume's and Mill's position that causality itself is not a directly perceivable characteristic of events, but is a judgement that individuals need to infer from multiple observations. More specifically, Hume and Mill would argue that there are no 'causal ties' between events that we could 'directly perceive', and that we would not be able to identify the fact that it snows as a cause for the road getting slippery if we had not observed these phenomena before. Our apparent impression that one can 'see' that the snow makes the street slippery is merely an illusion.

This 'empirical' conception of causality has been subjected to criticism. For instance, Ducasse (1926) argued that causality can also be ascribed when the individual makes a single observation (e.g., the person who has never seen lightning before will 'perceive' that the lightning caused the barn to catch fire). In order to ascribe causality, it is sufficient when there is temporal and spatial vicinity of two events, and the potential cause (lightning) is the only event that has changed in an otherwise constant frame of reference before the effect (burning of a barn) has occurred. In these cases, causality is — according to Ducasse — directly perceivable.

Conceptions of causality play a central role in different areas of psychology such as perception (see Michotte, 1946) and developmental psychology (Piaget, 1954). However, they are most explicitly dealt with by attribution theorists. Although attribution theory developed from different paths within psychology such as Schachter and Singer's (1962) theory on emotions and Rotter's (1954) social learning theory, Fritz Heider is considered to be the founder of attribution theory. Fritz Heider, an Austrian psychologist who emigrated to the United States before World War 2, introduced philosophical considerations about causality to the field of psychology while analysing questions in the field of human perception. When Heider applied for his dissertation at the University of Graz (Austria), the philosopher Meinong posed him a puzzle. He asked 'Why do we say that we see a house when, in fact, only the sunlight that is reflected through the house meets our eye?' While trying to answer this question Heider referred to several constructs within the process of perception, two referring to the environment and two concerning the perceiver. With regards to the environment, Heider differentiated (1) the object of perception (the house) and (2) the extensions of these objects which are, for instance, the light waves that are reflected by the house and which travel through space and meet the eye. On the side of the person, the light waves leave (3) a stimulus pattern on the retina, and it is now the 'task' of the perceptual system to (4) reconstruct the object of perception (the house) from the sensory input (the light waves which leave a continuously changing pattern of stimuli on the retina). The reconstruction of the object according to the perceived stimuli is, for Heider, an attribution process. The perceptual system attributes a property ('this is a house') to the sensory input. Eimer (1987) calls this conception of attribution a 'property attribution'.

Eimer (1987) argues that property attributions have to be differentiated from *causal* attributions. For instance, when we say that Object 1 (the lightning) 'causes' Object 2 (the barn) to catch fire, the attributer establishes a causal relation between two objects that have already been perceived in the manner outlined above. In addition to ascribing properties such as color or length to the perceived stimuli (the barn and the lightning), the attributer establishes a (causal) relation between these two objects. The analyses of such *causal* attributions were later in the focus of Heider's interests and constitute the domain of attribution theory.

Even in his early work, Heider pointed to the mechanisms by which one could arrive at causal attributions. These were 'similarity' and 'closeness'. He suggested that one is prone to hold a 'bad' person responsible for a 'bad' act and a 'good' person for a 'good' act, and that one attributes an effect to a cause that is close to and not distant from the effect. This analysis was guided by the analyses of perceptual processes by Gestalt psychologists. In addition, this position is similar to the one described by Ducasse who assumes that causality can be perceived in a singular situation.

However, in his influential book 'The Psychology of Interpersonal Relations' (1958), which to a large extent deals with the mechanisms that lead individuals to causally explain the behavior of others in social situations, Heider introduced for the first time a different conception of causality that was not derived from the psychology of perception. He suggested that, in many cases, it is necessary to observe a 'pattern of data' in order to arrive at causal judgments. For instance, when I want to decide whether a person intentionally tries to hurt me or if the instance in which he did hurt me was accidental, I have to find out whether he will also try to hurt me if situations change (see Chapter 4). This analysis certainly requires the observer to have made several observations — a prerequisite which is not necessary in cases when attributions are made on the basis of closeness and similarities of causes and effects. Hence, in Heider's later writings, a conception of causality akin to Mill's Method of Difference can be detected. The introduction of this has — as will also be illustrated in the following chapters of this book — greatly influenced modern attribution research and theorizing.

2.2. THREE CENTRAL ASSUMPTIONS OF ATTRIBUTION THEORY

Attribution conceptions have been developed within the area of perception and then applied by social psychologists in order to analyse the processes by which individuals explain the behavior of others. However, attribution theory has also influenced many other areas of psychology in addition to social psychology: the fields of motivation and emotion, personality, and clinical psychology. Due to the diversity of different attributional approaches in different fields of psychology, there does not exist a single unified attribution theory in which systematic statements and corollaries constitute a unified theoretical system (see Kelley, 1973). However, thanks to the programmatic work of Fritz Heider and the strong influence of Harold H Kelley's work (1967, 1972, 1973; Kelley and Michela, 1980), there are some basic premises that are common to almost all attribution models: (A) Attribution models assume that causal thoughts, or more generally, cognitions, play a central role for behavior, affect, and experiences. Therefore, attribution conceptions belong to the so-called cognitive models of psychology (see Neisser, 1966). (B) Furthermore, these approaches assume that individuals are motivated to seek a causal explanation for events in their physical and social environment, and they assume that individuals use methods that are rather similar to those used by scientists in order to determine causality. Therefore, attribution theories have been referred to as 'rational' approaches to behavior. (C) Finally, although not as salient as the previous two points, attributional approaches also have a distinctly functionalistic 'flavor'. In such approaches, it is assumed that a causal understanding serves the function of attaining personal goals (Weiner, 1985 a, b, 1986) and ensuring survival: 'The attributer is not simply an attributer, a seeker after knowledge; his latent goal is that of effective management of himself and the environment' (Kelley, 1971, p. 22).

2.2.1. Attribution theory as a cognitive approach

As already indicated, attribution theory is concerned with the causal judgments that individuals use to explain events that happen to themselves as well as others in the social and physical domains of life. Therefore, it is the antecedents and consequences as well as the characteristics of such causal explanations on which attribution research focusses. Such causal attributions are frequently answers to 'why'-questions (e.g., 'Why have I failed the exam?' — 'Because I have not studied hard enough'; or 'Why does the car not work?' —'Because there is no more gas in the tank').

Therefore, thoughts, or, in other words, 'cognitions', are naturally the central focus of attribution research. In this aspect, attribution approaches differ largely from other psychological theories that concentrate, for instance, on the stimulus conditions in the environment and the drive states of the individual in order to predict or to change behavior. As a consequence, attribution conceptions belong to the so-called cognitive psychological theories. Cognitive theories are based on the premise that situations or stimuli (S) do not automatically, directly, or mechanistically trigger reactions (R) such as behaviors and emotions. Instead, they assume that cognitions (C) mediate between stimuli and reactions. This is frequently described as in Figure 2.1 (see Meyer and Schmalt, 1978; Kelley and Michela, 1980; Weiner, 1972).

Cognitive psychological theories specify how individuals select, process, store, recall, and evaluate information about the self and the environment. In addition, while trying to predict behavior, attribution theorists are only

interested in situations or stimuli inasmuch as they provide the individual with
information that influences their cognitive conception of the environment and
themself. It is, however, not assumed that these stimuli influence behavior
directly (see Weiner, 1980a). As a consequence of the assumption that the
cognitive processing of events largely determines how individuals behave and
feel, cognitive psychologists are guided by the belief that an individual's
reactions can be predicted if one knows the person's cognitive representation
of the situation.

$$S \longrightarrow C \longrightarrow R$$

Attribution theory   Attributional theories

Figure 2.1   The basic structure of attribution conceptions (according to Kelley and
Michela, 1980).

Research that is concerned with causal attributions can be divided into two
subfields (see Figure 2.1). First, there are attempts to specify the antecedent
conditions (S) that lead to different causal attributions (C) (S - - -> C). For
instance, such approaches aim to predict under which circumstances a person
attributes success to high ability or the ease of a task. Approaches that address
these antecedents of causal attributions are called *attribution theories*.

The second subfield in this area addresses the question of how attributions
(C) influence reactions (R), such as behaviors, affects, or other cognitive
processes such as expectancies. For instance, research that investigates how
attributions for an outcome affect how individuals feel and behave following
success and failure would be classified in this field. These approaches that are
concerned with the consequences of causal attributions are labelled *attributional*
models.

Attribution and attributional research does not necessarily address all kinds
of cognitions. For instance, whether an event is considered as important or
unimportant, a person is perceived as small or tall, and other cognitions are not
part of attribution research. Instead, attribution models limit themselves to
naive *causal* theories of individuals: Therefore, it is the (naive) *causal* conceptions
of the 'man on the street' that are the subject of the (scientific) inquiry of the
attribution researcher; knowledge of the naive causal theories should then
enable the scientist to predict behavior.

2.2.1.1   *Some implications for clinical psychology*

As cognitions are the central topic of attribution theory and research,
applications of such approaches in the area of clinical psychology would largely

consist of the identification of the *cognitive* determinants of different psychopathological states and behavioral as well as emotional maladaptation. More specifically, the attributional approach to clinical problems would consist of identifying the causal attributions that might possibly be connected with phenomena such as depression, test anxiety, health behavior, excessive anger, or psychopathic behaviors — to name just a few possible areas. In addition, clinical attribution research would also need to specify and analyze the antecedents that lead to the attributions that cause maladaptive reactions and would have to find out how to (therapeutically) change them. Therefore, an attributional approach to clinical psychology and psychotherapy would logically lead to cognitive therapeutic interventions, and 'attribution therapy' would be guided by the question how causal cognitions (and/or their antecedents) that lead to dysfunctional reactions could be changed most effectively.

2.2.1.2. Relationships to other theories

In addition to attribution theory, there are certainly other approaches that deal with the cognitions that mediate between stimuli and reactions, and there are, furthermore, approaches that exclude cognitions from their research programs. As already indicated, traditional approaches to learning, specifically the theories about classical (Pavlov, 1927) and operant conditioning (Skinner, 1953) as well as psychoanalytic approaches, dramatically differ in this respect from attribution theories. Classical as well as operant models do not (or at least *did* not, see Rescorla, 1988) include cognitive variables in their models of behavior; especially because they argue that cognitions cannot be observed scientifically. Therapeutic procedures that are based on the classical and operant conditioning paradigms therefore do not pay much attention to the cognitive processes of their clients. 'Traditional' behavior therapists aim to explain the onset and maintenance of maladaptive reactions exclusively in terms of external stimuli and therefore try to change their clients' maladaptive reactions through systematic variations of external circumstances.

In traditional psychoanalytic approaches, cognitions only play a 'superficial' role. Due to their basic theoretical assumption, that (present) psychological problems are caused by past traumatic experiences that are probably not within the reach of the patients' consciousness, psychoanalysts are especially interested in their patients' dreams, childhood memories, and free associations, and therefore do not regard causal cognitions as crucial. By contrast, within the course of psychoanalytic therapy, it is expected that the client will make progress when they gain a conscious understanding of past traumatic events that occured during childhood.

However, there are other approaches that do stress the importance of cognitions: Examples are — besides attribution theory — Festinger's theory of social comparison (Festinger, 1954) and the theory of cognitive dissonance (Festinger, 1957). In addition, a strong focus on cognitions can be found in personal construct theory (Kelly, 1955), Rotter's (1954) social learning theory, the theory of Rational-Emotive Therapy (Ellis, 1962; Ellis and Grieger, 1977), Beck's cognitive theory of depression (Beck, 1976), as well as Mahoney's (1974, 1977a,b) and Meichenbaum's (1977) approach to cognitive therapy.

All these approaches share the assumption that external circumstances, stimuli, and events do not directly determine behavioral and emotional reactions, but that the individual's interpretation and evaluation of 'reality' directs their responses. In addition, the theories that underlie cognitive approaches to psychotherapy specify the cognitive processes that give rise to dysfunctional emotions and behaviors and suggest that therapy of these dysfunctional emotions and behaviors should address these cognitive processes. Cognitive therapies (e.g., Beck, 1976) try to influence negative emotions such as depression by changing cognitive inferences, interpretations, and evaluations.

However, the models that underlie cognitive therapies differ from attribution approaches in that they focus on the consequences (C → R) of cognitions rather than the antecedents of those cognitions (S → C) that lead to dysfunctional reactions. This makes them more similar to attribution*al* approaches than to attribution models.

2.2.2. The desire to make realistic attributions

It is a basic assumption central to most attribution approaches that individuals generally (but not always) attempt to develop a *realistic* concept of causality with regard to the events in their personal domains. It is assumed that the methods that the 'man on the street' uses to come to causal conclusions have remarkable similarities with the methods used in science. Heider (1958, p. 297) pointed out that 'this (causal) understanding is gained by way of a causal analysis that is in a way analogous to experimental methods', and Kelley (1973, p. 109) suggests that: 'The assumption is that the man in the street, the naive psychologist, uses a naive version of the method used in science'.

Therefore, attribution theorists frequently refer to individuals as 'lay scientists' and assume that they are motivated to use the information available to them for their causal judgment and to weigh this rationally. In addition, it is also assumed that individuals will revise old causal judgments when they come into conflict with contradictory data.

Although attribution theories are guided by a view of humans as basically rational beings and believe that individuals want to be well and authentically informed about the causes of events, much research in the attribution field is directed at the question about when and why humans think and behave 'unscientifically' or 'irrationally' (see, for a summary, Ross, 1977): It is discussed when (and why) available information is neglected, avoided, or incorrectly processed in order to explain why incorrect causal judgments are made and/or maintained. Motivational, self-serving, attention-related, as well as cognitive processes are thought to be responsible for unrealistic causal attributions (see Jones and Nisbett, 1971; Kelley and Michaela, 1980). For instance, attributions may — under certain circumstances — serve the (motivational) function of presenting one's own personal achievements in a most favorable manner (see Försterling and Groeneveld, 1983; Jones, 1980). This can be attempted, for instance, by creating the impression that successes that were objectively due to the help of others were, in fact, caused by the own person in order to be considered as competent by other persons.

Similarly, individuals might come to unrealistic causal judgments because they fear that the 'true' attributions might affect their self-esteem negatively and subsequently cause them to experience negative affects. For instance, failure at an important task that is attributed to chance might be less damaging to one's self esteem and might cause fewer negative affective consequences than failure that is attributed to low ability. In the same way, success attributed to high ability might give rise to more intense positive feelings than success attributed to luck. Therefore, it appears conceivable that individuals might be prone to attribute success unrealistically to their ability and failure to bad luck in order to maximize positive and minimize negative emotions following achievement activities.

Cognitive causes for unrealistic attributions might, among others, include a lack of information. For instance, it has been suggested that a person who works on a task generally knows that they had succeeded at similar tasks in the past. Therefore, it would be quite realistic for this person to attribute the (single) failure to chance. However, a person who observes this sequence might be unfamiliar with the actor and therefore not possess the information that they used to be successful in the past. The observer might therefore come to the (unrealistic) conclusion that the actor is generally unable to solve such tasks (see Jones and Nisbett, 1971).

Furthermore, difficulties in processing available information and to memorizing them at a later point in time might be the causes for unrealistic attributions under some circumstances. For instance, Jones, Rock, Shower, Goethals, and Ward (1968) have demonstrated that successes and failures that stimulus persons experience at the beginning of a series of tasks have a stronger impact on causal attributions (primary effect) than recent outcomes. Stimulus persons who succeeded at the beginning of a series of tasks were judged to be more competent than those who experienced an identical number of successes at a later point of this sequence. This finding might reflect the fact that subjects form causal hypotheses at the beginning of the series of tasks (for instance, success is due to high and failure to low ability) and that later observations (e.g., the success of the initially failing person) are (often mistakenly) adapted to these hypotheses (success of the initially failing person and failure of the initially successful person must be due to chance).

2.2.3. The motive to link events causally

A third basic premise of attribution (al) theories, which is not as salient as the previously mentioned two points, is that it is functional to make causal attributions. Practically all attribution theorists more or less explicitly state that knowledge of why an event has occurred has hedonic and/or survival value. Causal judgments that result from rational, 'scientific' analyses of the events might help the individual to predict the future quite effectively and behave appropriately in a given situation (see Forsyth, 1980). Heider (1958) states that it is 'an important principle of common sense psychology and science in general, that the individual grasps reality that he wants to predict and control by attributing the unstable changeable behaviors to the underlying unchangeable conditions'. Finally, Weiner (1985 b) remarks: 'Once a cause, or causes, are assigned, effective management may be possible and a prescription or guide for future action can be suggested. If the prior outcome was a success, then there is likely to be an attempt to reinstate the prior causal network. On the other hand, if the prior outcome or event was undesired ... then there is a strong possibility that there will be an attempt to alter the cause to produce a different (more positive) effect' (p. 548 – 549).

While gaining a picture of the causal networks of events, individuals can use external events and stimuli — in addition to just registering them — as a source of information with regard to their causal beliefs (attributions). These causal inferences subsequently enable them to behave functionally and appropriately in the environment. It is hardly possible to imagine how life would be if we did not make causal attributions. For instance, one would just register that the car one is using breaks down, but would not know whether to get gas, change the spark plugs, or to take it to a garage. If a person just registered that they failed an examination, without asking *why* failure has occurred, the individual would not know whether to study harder in the future or to change university. It is certainly also beneficial to be informed about the causes of success because it is likely that one can repeat a successful event if one knows why it has occurred in the first place.

Although attribution (al) theories have postulated that it is functional to make causal attributions, there are no clear definitions or hypotheses as to what is meant by 'functionality', or, more specifically, what attributions are functional for. For instance, one can only speculate that Weiner's (1985 b; Wong and Weiner, 1981) definition of functionality implies that attributions are helpful for the attainment of personal goals that are consciously represented in the person's mind ('Causal perceptions are instrumental to goal attainment . . .' Weiner, 1985 b, p. 21). The knowledge that one has failed to attain a subjectively desired goal because of lack of effort could give rise to the plan to invest more effort in the future. This plan and the actual investment of more effort might in turn enable the individual to attain the desired goal. However, if failure was due to inappropriate strategies, additional effort would not be helpful for goal attainment, and it would be more instrumental to try out a new strategy.

However, there are also situations in which the attainment of personal goals has negative consequences for the long-range goals of the individual. For instance, for a man who is in hospital and should stay in bed because of an illness, it would probably be harmful to get up and go for a walk in the town. However, this individual might nevertheless develop the wish to go out for a walk (personal goal). If this person fails to attain this personal goal (for instance, the nurse prevents him from sneaking out of his room), a realistic understanding of the causes of this failure, would help him to realize this personal goal in the future. He might find out that the nurse heard him banging the door and he could therefore be quieter on his next attempt to make an excursion. Attainment of this personal goal, however, would be dysfunctional for his goal of regaining health. The patient may simply not be aware of the fact that the attainment of the personal goal is counter-productive for his long-range goal (health), or he might not even have this long-range goal. It follows from the present example that there is no easy answer to the question of how attributions are functional (see also Försterling and Rudolph, 1988). Attributions could — besides helping the individual to attain personal goals — be instrumental for long-range goals, such as survival or happiness, that the individual might not even be aware of. For instance, realistic attributions might help the individual to select more realistic goals and change some of the previously held personal goals. In our example, it may well be that the knowledge about how 'staying in bed', and 'going for a walk' are related to the development of the healing process cause the patient to change his short-range goal of going for a walk in favor of a long-range goal such as the desire to get healthy sooner.

The assumption that information about causal relations in the individual's life-space has a general, long-range, functional and survival value appears to characterize the work of Heider (1958) and Kelley (1967). These authors talk about the individual's general motive to determine the causal structure of events. This motive is assumed to operate regardless of whether events are immediately related to personal goals; if they are important, unimportant, expected or unexpected. Attributions are believed to generally help the individual to attain cognitive mastery of the world and to control events (see Forsyth, 1980).

2.2.3.1. *Some implications for clinical psychology*

The assumption of attribution theory that individuals tend to ascribe causes to events rationally, and that they use methods similar to those that are used in science in order to understand, master, and control their environment has important implications for questions from clinical psychology and psychotherapy. It can be deduced from these premises that dysfunctional behaviors and emotional reactions can be caused by a lack of causal attributions for events or by unrealistic attributions.

If this is the case, therapy should, at least in part, be concerned with attributional changes. From an attributional perspective, therapy could well consist in fostering the clients' realistic causal understanding, with the gathering of attributionally relevant information, and with disputation and scientific examination of attributional assumptions that are connected with the problems of the client (these points will be elaborated in Chapter 10).

2.2.3.2 *Relationships to other theories*

If attribution theory is compared with other psychological approaches, it becomes evident that many psychological theories neglect 'rational', information-processing aspects of human behavior and largely emphasize hedonic principles, that is, the desire to avoid pain and to maximize pleasure. In this, attribution approaches specifically differ from theoretical conceptions that rely on drive reduction principles.

Festinger's (1957) theory of cognitive dissonance, for instance, is based on hedonic premises: he postulated that humans are motivated to change cognitions that are in a dissonant relationship. It is assumed that such dissonant cognitions (i.e., the belief that it is unhealthy to smoke and the realization that one smokes a lot) result in the experience of negative arousal. This negative state in turn should motivate the individual to reduce cognitive imbalance by — for instance — changing one of the two dissonant cognitions. The resulting reinstatement of a consonant state is then believed to be accompanied by the disappearance of the negative arousal. According to Festinger (1957), it is quite common for individuals to reduce cognitive dissonance by changing realistic insights (e.g., 'Smoking is dangerous') to quite irrational cognitions (e.g., 'As so many individuals smoke, smoking cannot be that dangerous'). As individuals are assumed to tend to reduce cognitive dissonance as effectively as possible, it should be expected that humans should become more and more irrational and detached from reality during their lifetime. Hence, the basic mechanism postulated by dissonance theorists should result in a blurred and biased perception of the self and the surrounding environment (see Herkner, 1980). Naturally, this is an assumption that is diametrically opposed to the basic premise of attribution theorists who assume that individuals strive for a realistic understanding of the self, the environment, and other persons. It is noteworthy that before the inception of dissonance theory, Festinger (1954) had formulated the theory of social comparison processes. This theory — like attribution theory — is based on the premise that individuals tend to compare themselves with other individuals in order to assess their strengths and weaknesses accurately.

A basically hedonic view of human functioning is also characteristic for psychoanalytic theories of personality. In Freud's conceptions, individuals are primarily guided by the desire to satisfy their sexual and aggressive urges. Goal attainment is assumed to be accompanied by pleasurable states ('Lust'), and failure to satisfy the instinctive urges results in displeasure ('Unlust'). Hence, psychoanalytic theory postulates that behavior is basically motivated by the desire to maximize pleasure and to minimize pain.

With regard to questions of clinical psychology, it can be deduced from psychoanalytic theory that the client's absence of tension and pain, goal attainment, and positive emotions should play a central role. Those processes that prevent him or her from reaching these 'pleasurable' states would be 'worthy of therapeutic change' from a hedonic point of view. Hence, successful therapy would consist of reducing tension and dissonance in order to improve the client's well-being.

However, from the perspective of the premise of a 'rational human being', as advocated by attribution theorists, positive emotions and lack of tension would not appear to be the most important goals of psychotherapy. From an attributional point of view, it would be more important to help clients to feel and behave appropriately in accordance with the (realistic) causal interpretations of (problematic) situations. An 'attribution therapist' might possibly consider therapy as especially effective when a client comes to a 'painful' conclusion. For instance, an individual might find out that they lack the ability to reach a goal which is of high personal importance to them. This insight might cause them to feel sad or even helpless for a while. However, the realistic attributions (to lack of ability) and the resulting affects (sadness) may well help the individual to set more realistic goals for the future and, as a consequence, feel better in the long run.

Attribution conceptions are not the only psychological theories that postulate that individuals are motivated to gain a realistic impression of the causes of events in order to behave adaptively. In his personal construct theory, Kelly (1955) assumes that individuals can be viewed as lay scientists who develop 'personal constructs' about the events in their lives in order to predict the future and to act effectively. When a construct fails to perform this task, the emotion of anxiety will result, and the individual has to change their construct while taking into account the new situation and data that were previously ignored.

Although psychoanalysis primarily relies on hedonic mechanisms while trying to explain human action, Freud also introduced the so-called 'reality principle' that accounts for some of the 'rational' aspects of human thought and behavior. The reality principle describes ego functions that help the individual to take into account the possible negative consequences of behavior that is primarily guided by hedonic impulses.

Finally, recent cognitive approaches to behavior therapy that currently dominate (see Smith, 1982) clinical psychology and psychotherapy (i.e., cognitive therapy and cognitive behavior modification) have many similarities with attributional conceptions. For instance, Beck (1976), Ellis (1962, 1984), Frank (1973), Mahoney (1974, 1977 a, b), and Meichenbaum (1977) assume that dysfunctional behaviors and affective states largely result from unrealistic (cognitive) interpretations and evaluations. For these authors, therapy consists of working toward a realistic view of the problematic situations (see Chapter 10). In this process, the therapist should play the role of a 'scientific adviser' who challenges the 'irrational' or 'unrealistic' beliefs of the client. According to Mahoney (1977b), the therapist has to help the client to become a 'personal scientist' with regard to their personal problems. Finally, the relationship between scientific thinking and functional reactions has already been pointed out by Korzybski (1933) in his book entitled 'Science and Sanity'.

2.3. THE RANGE OF CONVENIENCE OF ATTRIBUTIONAL THEORIES

Like all other psychological theories, attributional approaches have a limited range of convenience. Heider (1958, p. 1), the founder of attribution theory, has already indicated that 'Our concern will be with "surface" matters, the events that occur in everyday life on a conscious level, rather than with the unconscious processes studied by psychoanalysis in "depth" psychology'. The fact that attribution theory does not explicitly address phenomena such as slips of the tongue, dreams, or human sexuality certainly does not mean that attribution theorists neglect the existence or importance of these phenomena.

The range of phenomena that is addressed by attribution theorists might not be as diversified as the range of phenomena addressed by psychoanalytic theory. There are naturally many areas of psychology that have not lent themselves to an attributional analysis: for example, problems from physiological psychology, human perception and memory, motor learning, and many aspects of largely physiologically based motive systems such as hunger and thirst.

Even within the field of social and achievement motivation where attributional theories have been particularly influential, attributional approaches have not been applied to all aspects of these motive systems. For instance, Heckhausen and Kuhl (1985) have recently pointed out neglected steps of a motivational sequence ('from wishes to action') that do not appear to be related to attribution processes.

Within the area of clinical psychology there are also quite a few phenomena that have not been analyzed from an attributional framework (for instance, autism, phobic avoidance, psychotic symptoms, schizophrenia) and many of these possibly never will be.

Hence, there are areas of psychology to which attribution models have been applied successfully, others that could be but have not yet been examined from an attributional perspective, and still others that might never be amenable to an attributional analysis. A central concern of the present book is to explore further the range of convenience of attributional conceptions by summarizing and analyzing which phenomena from the areas of clinical psychology and psychotherapy can fruitfully be subjected to an attributional analysis.

Chapter 3

Dimensions of Causal Explanations

Causal attributions are concepts that individuals apply in order to explain events, actions, and experiences (in general: effects) in different areas of life. They are frequently — but on no account always — answers to 'Why questions' (see Weiner, 1979). When dealing with achievement-related activities, we often ask why we have been successful or unsuccessful: 'Why has "XY" failed the examination?' (effect). 'Because he didn't make enough effort' (attribution). 'Why did I get this job?' (effect). 'Because I was lucky' (attribution).

In the field of interpersonal relations, we think about why other individuals show certain forms of behavior: 'Why is Carl annoyed with me?' (effect). 'Because I said something that hurt his feelings' (attribution). 'Why is Betty so friendly to Paul? Because she wants to get to know him.' We also find attributions that are connected to events dealing with power ('Why did we lose the election? Because we did not have the opportunity to give a precise presentation of our election policies.'), and in the field of mental and physical health ('She caught a cold because she didn't dress warmly enough'; 'He is depressed because he's lost his job and, in the past, his parents didn't love him').

Of course, individuals do not ask 'why' questions and undertake an elaborate causal search after every event. For example, we cannot expect causal analyses to be performed if effects are consistent with lasting causal convictions, or in other words, causal hypotheses, causal theories or schemata. We seldom think about why the bus that we take at the same time every day arrives on time, or why we have not won a lottery. Nevertheless, at any time, we would be able on request to describe our causal assumptions about the punctual bus or the loss in the lottery: for example the belief that the bus driver is a conscientious person, and that it would be an extreme coincidence to win a lottery. Without being the object of actual attention, causal attributions (causal hypotheses) nevertheless guide our behavior; we return to the same bus stop and wait for the bus, and we do not gamble away all our money on lotteries.

Only when the course of actions and events is disrupted by occurrences that are contrary to expectation might situations arise in which we consciously analyze our causal assumptions, look for new information that is relevant for an attribution, and revise our attributional conviction (e.g., if the bus does not arrive on time, we may inquire whether the time table has been altered) (see Meyer, 1988; Weiner, 1985 a, b, 1986).

Wong and Weiner (1981) have shown that a search for the causes of success and failure is particularly made when the result of an action is either unexpected or negative (failure) (see Försterling and Groeneveld, 1983; Lau and Russel, 1980). In addition, Försterling and Schoeler (1984) showed that information that is relevant for attributions is more frequently gathered when it is linked to activities from areas of personal importance than when it is linked to areas of low importance.

It should be emphasized that attributions can be conceived of as both 'immediate' answers to 'why' questions as well as lasting cognitive structures, schemata, or convictions that are, at times, barely accessible to consciousness (see Kelley, 1983a).

In addition, Heider (1958, p. 256) points out that: 'Attributions may not be experienced as interpretations at all, but rather as intrinsic to the original stimuli'. Causal cognitions also do not always have to take a verbal form (e.g., 'I was unsuccessful because the task was too difficult'), but can express themselves in visual or acoustic imagery (e.g., 'I had the feeling that the task was like a mountain blocking my path'). When describing the phenomenology of causal attributions, Kelley (1983a) states

> We need no longer rely on answers to our explicit 'Why' questions as our sole source of information about people's causal thinking. With suitable adjustments made, for what is assessed vs. what is believed (no small problem!), naturally occurring arguments can provide useful information about the attribution process. (p. 348)

3.1.   CLASSIFICATORY PERSPECTIVES

The examples of attributions given at the beginning of this chapter make it clear that we can produce an endlessly long list of attributions for different fields of life. As there is such a great number of causal attributions in the various fields of human activity, attempts have been made since the beginnings of attribution research to develop classificatory perspectives for causal attributions (see Heider, 1958).

Taxonomies of attributions are necessary in order to construct meaningful theoretical conceptions about the antecedent conditions and consequences of causal attributions, and to test them empirically. Statements about the determinants and consequences of *single, specific,* causal elements would only possess a low generalizability. For example, the knowledge that a high jumper, after a good performance, increases his expectation of producing higher achievements in the future if he thinks that his original performance is due to the size of his body (attribution), is only significant for the field of high jumping or possibly also for other athletic activities. On the other hand, if we can find laws that apply to an entire class or category of attributions (that are phenotypically different but genotypically identical; see Weiner, 1986), they will have a larger area of validity. Such a large area of validity is given, for example, by the finding that success that is considered to be due to a stable cause (such as ability, body weight, height, or work habits) leads to a subjective increase in the estimated probability of future success (see Weiner, 1986; Chapter 6).

Various taxonomies of attributions can be found in both models of the antecedent conditions of attributions and models that are concerned with attributional consequences. We have reached a stage in which attribution research has produced such a multitude of dimensions that these, in turn, require classification. We cannot discuss all the analyses of dimensions in the present chapter. We shall, therefore, restrict ourselves to those that have proved to be particularly useful and that appear promising for future research.

First of all, attributions can be classified according to *relational* properties, that means, regarding their relation (e.g., closeness or distance, number of connections) to further causal attributions and effects. On the other hand, we can also undertake *qualitative* differentiations of thoughts about causality.

3.2. RELATIONAL DIFFERENTIATIONS

3.2.1. Proximal versus distal

Kelley (1972, 1983a) introduced the distance between a cause and its effect as a criterion for classification. Figure 3.1 illustrates this differentiation through the example of an individual who undertakes an explanation for their depressive mood. The person explains their current state (depression) through a chain of causes that have sequentially influenced each other and differ in their distances from the effect: they grew up as a single child and the parents were socially isolated. These causes are temporarily very distant from the effect (depression) and are thus distal. They lead to a temporally closer cause (proximal) for the effect that is being explained (depression). Due to the experiences during childhood, no friendships could be developed. This leads to a direct (proximal) reason for the depression, namely, the current loneliness.

The theoretical differentiation between proximal and distal causes touches a fundamental aspect of the attribution process. However, it has yet to be taken

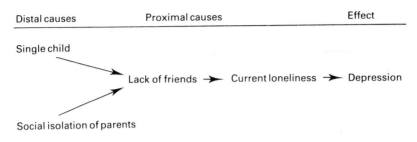

Figure 3.1 Promixal and distal causes of an effect.

up by empirical research. It is the effects of proximal attributions on behavior that have been analyzed most frequently (see Chapters 4 to 7).

3.2.2. Simple versus complex

Causal cognitions can be either simple or complex (Kelley, 1972, 1973, 1983 a). Simple causal structures exist when merely *one* cause produces only *one* effect (e.g., 'He is depressed because he has lost his partner'). By complex causal structures, either several causes or their interaction bring about one or several effects (e.g., 'He became depressed because his wife left him just when he had a lot of stress at work, and she acted because of financial considerations'). Simple causal cognitions are, for example, multiple sufficient causal schemata (see Kelley, 1972, 1973). Figure 3.2a presents such a schema that is characterized by the fact that one of two causes is considered to be sufficient for the occurrence of the effect.

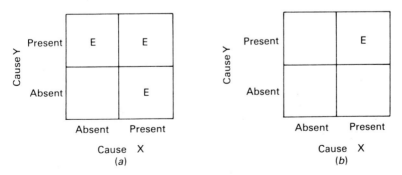

Figure 3.2 (a) Multiple sufficient and (b) multiple necessary causal schemata (from Kelley, 1973).

For example, an effect (E), such as the sadness of a person (P), can be explained by either an external cause (e.g., losing a job) or an internal cause (e.g., a melancholic personality). In contrast, complex causal structures are similar to multiple necessary schemata (Figure 3.2b). Here, several causes have to occur together if the effect is to follow. For example, if an individual (P) is depressed and commits suicide (effect) after losing their job, there will probably be a tendency to include, alongside the external cause (X), one or more further causes (Y), such as a depressive personality structure, in order to explain the effect (E). The presence of merely one cause (X or Y) would not be regarded as a sufficient explanation for the effect.

3.3.   QUALITATIVE DIFFERENTIATIONS

3.3.1.   Internal versus external

Nearly all conceptions of attribution — beginning with Heider (1958) — differentiate between causal factors that lie in the person and those that lie in the environment. For example, if we explain a failure through a lack of ability, we are making an internal attribution. An external attribution is given if we make, for example, the difficulty of the task responsible for the failure. Thus, Kelley (1967) talks about person (internal) and entity (external) attributions and Weiner, Frieze, Kukla, Reed, Rest, and Rosenbaum (1971) introduce, in line with Heider's considerations, the differentiation between internal (e.g., ability, effort) and external (chance, task difficulty) causal explanations for achievements results (locus of causality). Kruglanski (1975) proposed that this dimension should be replaced by a division of causes into endogenous (activities that are carried out for their own sakes) and exogenous (activities that only represent a means to an end). However, this proposal has received little further attention in the literature.

The differentiation of the perceptions of causality into internal and external on the dimension of locus of control can also be found in theoretical conceptions outside of attribution theories. For example, in his social learning theory, Rotter (1954, 1966) differentiated between internal and external locus of control without referring to Heider. In addition, both DeCharms (1968) and Deci (1975) used a division into internal and external causes for actions.

3.3.2.   Stable versus variable

Weiner (Weiner, 1979; Weiner et al., 1971) again referred to Heider (1958) when, in addition to the dimension of locus of control, he differentiated causes according to whether they are perceived as being stable (unchanging over time) or variable (changing).

By crossing the dimensions of 'locus of control' and 'stability', Weiner presented a much-cited taxonomy of causal explanations for success and failure. Table 3.1 shows how, in a 2 by 2 table, we can differentiate an invariant, stable factor (ability) from an instable, variable one (effort) among the internal factors; and the temporarily fluctuating random influences (luck) from lasting, stable, invariant task characteristics (task difficulty) among the external factors. Kelley (1967) labels variable causes such as effort or chance 'circumstance attributions' (see Chapter 4).

Table 3.1   Causal elements and their dimensions in the field of achievement (taken from Weiner *et al.*, 1971)

		Locus of control	
		Internal	External
Stability across time	Stable	ability	task difficulty
	Variable	effort	chance

3.3.3.   Intentional (controllable) versus unintentional (uncontrollable)

Within Weiner *et al.*'s (1971) fourfold table, it is not possible to differentiate whether an individual has not attained a goal because of either a lack of effort or because of tiredness. Both causal explanations would be classified as being internal and variable. Reference was again made to Heider when Rosenbaum (1972) pointed out that a significant conceptual difference between the causal elements has not been taken into account in this connection. Effort can be guided and controlled by the individual, this means, it can be influenced by intention, while, in contrast, tiredness to a large extent evades conscious control by the individual; this means that this factor is mainly uncontrollable or unintentional. Rosenbaum (1972) integrated the dimension of 'intentionality' into the fourfold scheme from Weiner *et al.* (1971) and thus — as we shall see in Chapter 7 — broadened its field of application (e.g., for the field of social evaluations).

Table 3.2 shows that, as well as providing the possibility of a differentiated view of causal elements, this new dimension that was introduced by Rosenbaum (1972) also raises problems. For example, it is difficult to name a causal element that is external, yet, at the same time, can be controlled by the person. In order to fill in this cell in the table, Rosenbaum has to introduce a new observer perspective and gives, as an example of an externally controllable causal factor, a failure for a person (P) that is explained by the lack of effort (controllable) of another person (X) (external). Hence, the dimension of intentionality may not be orthogonal to the locus of control as it might only apply for the internal but not for the external causes (see Weiner, 1986).

Table 3.2   Rosenbaum's expansion of the fourfold table by adding the dimension of controllability (taken from Weiner, (1980a)

	Controllable		Uncontrollable	
	stable	**unstable**	**stable**	**unstable**
Internal	stable effort of self	unstable effort of self	ability of self	fatigue, mood, and fluctuations in skill of self
External	stable effort of others	unstable effort of others	ability of others, task difficulty	fatigue, mood, and fluctuations in skill of others, luck

In his more recent work, Weiner (e.g., 1980a, 1986) differentiates between 'intention' and 'control'. We can intend to carry out an activity (e.g., to pay our bills regularly or to stick to a diet), but might be convinced that we are unable to control or guide our own behavior. In more recent research one can find the term 'intentionality' being substituted by 'controllability'.

3.3.4.   Global versus specific

Within the framework of their attributional analysis of depression and helplessness, Abramson, Seligman, and Teasdale (1978; see also Chapter 6) introduced a further causal dimension, that of generality. This dimension differentiates causes according to the breadth of the spectrum of their effects. At one end of the scale (global), causes are placed that have a broad spectrum of effects, while at the other end, we find 'specific' attributions, that means, attributions that only relate to a narrow, special field. The explanation of a failure through a lack of innate intelligence, for example, would be labeled global, while if the failure is attributed to a lack of special abilities (e.g., a lack of psychomotor skills), we would talk about a specific attribution.

3.3.5.   The dimensional properties of 'strategies'

Recently, Anderson (Anderson, 1983; Anderson and Jennings, 1980) have published interesting research on a causal factor that — similar to effort — is internal, controllable, and variable, yet, in addition, proves to have properties that differentiate it from the factor of effort. This concerns attributions to false (or correct) strategies. If a person attributes failure to this factor, future successes cannot be ruled out (because of its changeability), and they will be perceived as being guidable by the person (internal, controllable). In contrast to the attribution to effort however, attributions to strategy imply that future success is possible without an increase in the application of power, energy, and perhaps even time. If an individual attributes failure to insufficient effort, they might abandon any attempts to attain the goal if, for example, the goal is not very important, yet the effort required to attain it is very large, and, in addition, would involve the withdrawal of time and energy from other fields. From such 'economy perspectives', a goal might be abandoned after failure if this failure is attributed to a lack of effort, yet, if the failure is attributed to an error in strategy, there might be a temptation to 'try again', as it 'doesn't cost anything' (the strategies are present in the behavioral repertoire). However, it is not possible to represent this conceptual difference between effort and strategy in the current taxonomies of attributions.

3.4. THE 'STATUS' OF ATTRIBUTION DIMENSIONS

The above-mentioned attribution dimensions have not been determined empirically, but represent the product of 'logical scientific analyses' by researchers. These are classificatory perspectives that are introduced by scientists to classify concepts from the 'naive psychology' of the 'man on the street'. Weiner (1979, 1982a), when referring to Schütz (1967), talks about second-order concepts. The concepts of dimensions (e.g., stable as opposed to variable) are not assumed to be present in the heads of psychological laypersons ('order must be imposed using scientific terminology that may not be part of the layperson', Weiner, 1982a, p. 167). On the other hand, in the attributional models of behavior, the consequences of causal attributions do not depend on the specific attributions but on their dimensional qualities. These, in turn, are not unchangeable: 'The perceived properties of a cause can vary. For example, mood might be thought of as a temporary state or as a permanent trait' (p. 167). For example, if an individual attributes a failure to bad moods, and in addition believes that these moods are lasting, they would show responses because of the failure which would be similar to those that would be triggered by other stable failure attributions (e.g., lack of ability, task difficulty). Yet, if the moods are perceived as being temporary and unstable, responses should follow that would also be aroused by other variable factors (e.g., chance, effort).

Consistent with the idea that it is not the specific cause but its location on the causal dimension that determines behavior, many attribution studies have recorded the perceived dimensional qualities of causes alongside (or even instead of) the specific causes themselves (e.g., 'How changeable is this cause?') (see Försterling, 1984; Seligman, Abramson, Semmel, and von Baeyer, 1979; Weiner, 1980 b, c).

This consideration, which underlies the operationalizations of attribution studies, presupposes that dimensions are phenomenologically represented in the subjects' minds, although naturally it cannot be expected that, in an unstructured interview, subjects could immediately point out that the common property of effort and ability is their 'internality'.

If these dimensions are represented in the minds of naive persons and, at the same time, they are important for the behavioral effects of attributions, it would seem to be sensible to use multivariate statistical procedures to test whether laypersons and scientists possess different conceptions of dimensions. This possibility is particularly relevant for attribution research because there is no agreement on which classification perspectives are the most important ones for causal attributions.

In addition to the attribution dimensions mentioned in this chapter, we can rank attributions according to other, for example, evaluative aspects. We can, for example, differentiate between whether they are positive or negative, or whether they are important or unimportant. In addition, we can ask whether they alter steadily (like age) or in an unpredictable way (like the weather; see Kelley, 1983 a), whether they are more concerned with the character or with behavior (Janoff-Bulman, 1979), or whether they refer to psychological or to physical concepts.

In recent years, some studies have addressed the task of determining causal dimensions by empirical means (Falbo and Beck, 1979; Försterling, 1980b; J. P. Meyer, 1980; Passer, 1977; Wimer and Kelley, 1982; see Weiner, 1986, for a summary). These studies used statistical methods such as multidimensional scaling (Passer, 1977), factor analysis (J. P. Meyer, 1980; Wimer and Kelley, 1982), or cluster analysis (Försterling, 1980b). As a rule, they used attributions that were given by the experimenter and had to be classified by the subjects. Wimer and Kelley (1982) extended the search for classificatory perspectives for causal attributions to such that were not given by the experimenter, but were freely expressed by the subjects and came from different areas of life.

3.4.1.   An evaluation of the empirical analyses of dimensions

In general, the empirical studies on determining causal dimensions show that the 'scientific' and the 'naive' causal conceptions have a lot in common. Particular support can be found for the differentiated considerations made by Weiner which have been the basis for much research work (see Chapters 5 and 7). In the studies that have investigated achievement-related cognitions, we can find the dimension of locus of control (J. P. Meyer, 1980; Försterling, 1980b; Passer, 1977), stability (J. P. Meyer, 1980), and controllability (Försterling, 1980a; Passer, 1977; J.P. Meyer, 1980) However, the results seem to depend strongly on the data used for the statistical analyses. Wimer and Kelley, who presented a large number of classification possibilities from completely different areas of life, accordingly found more attribution dimensions in the statistical analysis of their data than researchers restricting themselves to achievement causes. This supports the assumption that different dimensions are relevant in different areas of life. Although it may well be true that the most important dimensions have been determined in the field of achievement-motivated behavior, future research will probably be able to identify additional classifications if they are related to other areas of life or to other antecedent conditions and consequences.

Furthermore, the studies have shown that causal elements (e.g., task difficulty) can possess different dimensional features depending on different context informations (e.g., internal: 'The task is too hard for me'; or external: 'Nobody can manage this task'). Therefore, it is important that we do not just discover (or change) the respective, specific attribution, but also its dimensional quality if we want to be able to predict or modify behavior on the basis of attributions.

Chapter 4

Antecedents of Causal Attributions

The main concern of attribution models is to analyze the antecedent conditions of different causal ascriptions. For example, they may investigate when a person attributes their failure to pass an examination to a lack of ability and when they attribute it to an unfair examiner. All the models that are concerned with the antecedent conditions of causal factors are based on the work of Fritz Heider (1958), which they either supplement, systematize, or refine.

Heider (1958) was initially interested in the conditions underlying attributions of 'intent' or 'motive'. His ideas about this were later taken up by Jones and Davis (1965) and Jones and McGills (1976). These authors have put forward the 'theory of correspondent inferences'. We shall not present this theory, as the following chapters only refer to Heider's ideas when dealing with attributions of intent.

The most influential model of the antecedent conditions of causal attributions is the covariation principle presented by Harold H. Kelley (1967, 1973). His work is also based on Heider and systematizes Heider's assumption that persons act like 'naive scientists' by gathering information on the covariations between events and their possible causes in order to make attributional inferences. As we will refer to this model several times in this book, it will be dealt with in more detail here. However, we will not report further developments of this model (see Alloy and Tabachnik, 1984; Hewstone and Jaspars, 1987; Hilton and Slugoski, 1986; Jaspars, 1983; Pruit and Insko, 1980), as, once more, we will not refer to them in the present volume. Likewise, we can only partially repeat the wide-ranging discussions and the multitude of empirical investigations that have been stimulated by the Kelley model.

Finally, this chapter will refer to recent research by Meyer and colleagues that is concerned with the indirect social communication of information that is relevant for attributions (see Meyer, 1982, 1984; Meyer, Bachman, Biermann, Hempelmann, Plöger, and Spiller, 1979), as we will later discuss process within therapy in which such indirect communications of attributions play an important role.

4.1. THE ATTRIBUTION OF INTENTION, EQUIFINALITY, AND LOCAL CAUSALITY

Heider (1958) assumes that attributions of behaviors to the intention of the actor are of special importance in the psychology of the 'man on the street': when we know that a person has intentionally performed a certain act, we will use this behavior as indicative of their character or other stable dispositions. Behaviors that we attribute to the demands of the situation or to chance do not provide us with such information about the person and would not allow us to predict how they are going to behave in the future. Secondly, 'intentions' are according to Heider 'final causes': We typically do not ask further causal questions once a personal free decision to perform an act has been identified as the cause of behavior.

Much of Heider's work, therefore, concerns the antecedent conditions of attributions of intention or motive, or, in other words, the preconditions by which a person attributes the behavior of another individual to their intention or motives. This includes, for example, the question of which are the given conditions by which we either assume that a man who is travelling on the same bus as us has intentionally trod on our foot or accept his behavior as being accidental.

According to Heider, information about equifinality or multifinality and about the presence of local causality are examined in order to decide between intentional (personal causality) and non-intentional (impersonal causality) causes.

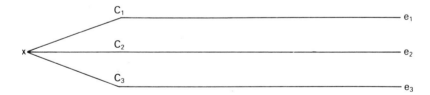

Figure 4.1   Multifinality by personal causality (taken from Heider, 1958).

Figure 4.1 gives a graphic presentation of the state of multifinality that he assumes to be a condition of impersonal causality. Every time the individual shows a behavior (x) (e.g., he gets on the bus), this behavior leads to different effects (e) in different situations or on different occasions (C). If, for example, one observes on different days (C_1, C_2, C_3) that our person (P) gets on the bus (behavior x), and that on one day (C_1) he steps on another person's foot (e_1), on a second day (C_2) he trips over another passenger (e_2), and on the third day (C_3)

he gets on the bus without any difficulties (e_3), we will probably not be inclined to attribute the effect (e_1, that he trod on the other individual's foot) to intention.

In contrast, Figure 4.2 presents the state of *equifinality* that should lead to attributions of intent. Equifinality means that a behavior (x) of a person (P) under different conditions (C_1, C_2, C_3) leads to identical consequences (e_1).

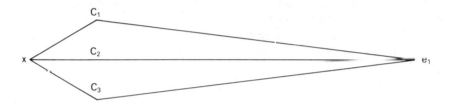

Figure 4.2   Equifinality by personal causality (taken from Heider, 1958).

If our passenger always treads on the same person's (P) foot on different occasions (C_1, C_2, C_3), in other words, under different conditions, we will attribute to him the intent of harming the individual, as the passenger changes his behavior in accordance with the situative conditions in order to achieve his goal (e_1).

However, Heider points out that equifinality can also be observed in physical systems and not just in fields of human behavior. He offers the example of a ball in a bowl. Regardless of the position in which the ball starts rolling (C_1, C_2, C_3), it will always come to rest at the lowest point in the bowl (e_1). In such cases, of course, we do not talk about the ball having a 'motive' or an 'intent' to 'strive' toward the deepest part of the bowl. In this case, the second precondition for the attribution of motives or intents formulated by Heider has yet to be fulfilled: in our example, no local causality is present. The forces that always make the ball stop at the same position in the bowl are not just found in the ball (only then would we be able to talk about local causality), but are a part of the entire physical system. In contrast, local causality is only given if the forces necessary to achieve the goal (e_1) are localized in the person who is performing the activity.

4.2.   KELLEY'S COVARIATION PRINCIPLE

When analyzing the mechanisms by which a person arrives at an understanding of the causal structure of their environment, Kelley (1967) assumes that the 'man in the street' gathers and processes the available (multiple) observations that are relevant for the causal explanations of a certain event in a way that is similar to methods used by scientists. This idea is linked to Heider's (1958, p. 297) assumption that the causal understanding of events 'is gained by way of a causal analysis that is in a way analogous to experimental methods' (Kelley, 1967, p. 194).

As in Heider's work on causal attributions, the Method of Difference as introduced by J. S. Mill is the central construct in Kelley's model. 'Covariation' is understood as the joint occurrence of a (possible) cause and an effect or an event. It is assumed that the effect is attributed to the cause with which it covaries.

> That condition will be held responsible for an effect which is present when the effect is present and which is absent when the effect is absent. (Heider, 1958, p. 152)

We can illustrate the covariation principle with the following example. Every time the electric light is on in the kitchen (the effect is present), somebody has manipulated the light switch (condition, cause). However, if the light is not on in the kitchen (the effect is not present), nobody has manipulated the switch (the cause is lacking). Whether or not the electric oven, for example, is switched on has no bearing on whether the light is on or not. As only the manipulation of the light switch and the burning of the electric light covary and no other events (such as the switching on of the oven), the manipulation of the light switch is made responsible for being the cause for the light being on.

Kelley considers that the causal attributions that are relevant in the field of social psychology can be assigned to the following classes: (1) *Attributions to persons* are present if an effect (e.g., the person is successful with a task) is traced back to relatively stable features of the person (e.g., their attitude to work, ability, or body size). A differentiation is made between such attributions and (2) *attributions to entities* which are applied when the effects that a person generates are traced back to constant factors that lie outside the person (e.g., success with a task is explained by its easiness and not by the individual's ability). From the actor's perspective, both other persons and environmental actualities can be entities. Last, Kelley introduces the concept of (3) *attributions to circumstances (or 'time')*. This covers causes that change across time or different modalities (e.g., tracing back the person's success with a task to chance, effort, assistance from other persons, or mood).

According to the covariation principle, whether an effect is traced back to one of these three causal classes depends on which of these causes the effect covaries with.

Kelley (1967) labels the covariation information on the joint occurrence of effects and persons as *consensus*. Information on the joint occurence of an effect and one or more entities is labeled *distinctiveness*, and *consistency* stands for the circumstances (points in time, modalities) under which an effect occurs.

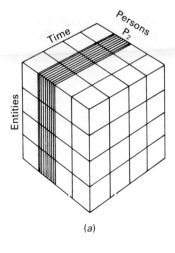

(a)

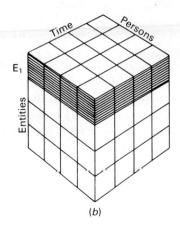

(b)

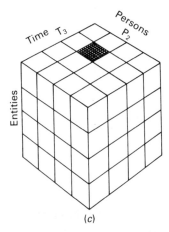

(c)

Figure 4.3 A pattern of covariations that leads (a) to attributions to the person (b) the entity and (c) to circumstances (taken from Kelley, 1973).

Kelley uses a cube that is based on the analysis of variance to illustrate these ideas. In this cube, the effects to be explained form the dependent variables and the possible causes (persons, entities, and times) the independent variables (see Figures 4.3a to c). Figure 4.3a illustrates a covariation pattern which suggests a causal attribution for the effect (e.g., success on a task) to the person (e.g., the person's abilities). In the case illustrated, the effect (E) covaries with the persons (P_1–P_4). The effect is present when person 2 is present and not present by the other persons. Thus, there is a low consensus. In addition, Figure 4.3a reveals that the effect (E) does not vary systematically with different entities (person 2 is equally successful at different tasks); this is labeled low distinctiveness. Finally, the different points in time and modalities in which person 2 works on the task also do not influence the outcome: P_2 produces the same result (success) under all conditions. This is called high consistency. As, in Figure 4.3a, the effect only covaries with different persons and not with timepoints or entities, it is traced back to the person (the continual achievement of success is due to the person P_2, for example, their high abilities).

A covariation pattern that leads to attributions of an effect (e.g., P_2's success on task E_1) to the entity (e.g., the easiness of E_1) is presented in Figure 4.3b. In this example, the effect covaries exclusively with different entities (high distinctiveness), and it makes no difference at all who is working on the task (high consensus) and at what timepoint and under what conditions (high consistency). At all timepoints, all persons are only successful with E_1 and with no other task. This suggests that P_2's success with E_1 is due to features of the task (or the entity) and not to features of the person.

The preceding two examples (Figures 4.3a and b) were characterized by the fact that the effect covaried with only one cause (the person or the entity) and did not covary with the remaining two causes (entity and time or person and time, respectively). The constellation presented in Figure 4.3c, however differs in that the effect covaries with all three possible causes. Figure 4.3c presents a pattern of data that suggests an attribution of the effect to the circumstances. Here, the effect only occurs in connection with one timepoint (T_3, low consistency). No other person solves the task (low consensus, only P_2 solves the task) and the person only solves the specific task under consideration (E_2) and fails to solve other tasks (high distinctiveness).

Table 4.1 Covariation patterns that should lead to attributions to either the person, the entity, or the circumstances (taken from Orivs, Cunningham, and Kelley, 1975).

| | Information | | |
Causes	Consensus	Distinctiveness	Consistency
Person	low	low	high
Entity	high	high	high
Circumstances	low	high	low

Table 4.1 summarizes the different levels of consensus, distinctiveness, and consistency that are supposed to lead to the individual classes of attributions (entities, persons, and circumstances). If these covariation patterns are present, the individual will, with a high degree of confidence, trace the effect back to one of the three causes. Nevertheless, Table 4.1 in no way presents all the conceivable constellations of data. If we assume that covariation information would vary on the levels 'high' and 'low', eight data patterns would emerge —

2 × (consensus) × 2 (consistency) × 2 (distinctiveness). For instance, if the effect only covaries with the timepoint (low consistency) and not with persons (high consensus) or the entities (low distinctiveness), we would come to consider the point of time as the responsible causal factor. Sometimes we attribute the fact that a person achieves success in business to the 'right time', because almost everybody (high consensus) who opened any business (low distinctiveness) at this time was successful. Hence there is covariation only with the points of time and not with persons or entities.

Kelley (1973) also introduces the possibility that one can make an interaction of two or three causes responsible for the effect (see also Figure 4.3c). For example, if P (and only P; i.e., low consensus) is continually (high consistency) unsuccessful at a task (and only this task; i.e. high distinctiveness), one is inclined to make an *interaction* between the person (say, P_1) and the specific task (say, E_3) responsible for the effect. The effect only occurs when both the person (P_1) and the specific task (E_3) are present, therefore, it covaries with both the person and the task but not with timepoints.

4.2.1. The model as an analogy to the analysis of variance

Kelley compares the mechanisms by which individuals arrive at causal attributions with the analysis of variance, a statistical method that is frequently used in the social sciences. In this analogy, the classes of causal factors (persons, entities, and points in time) represent the independent variables and the effects (for instance success and failure) the dependent variables. In a similar way to the analysis of variance, the 'man on the street' uses a (incomplete and often rash) version of this method to compare the variations of the effect that are brought about by the single independent variables. This comparison of the variances that are caused by the single factors is similar to the test statistic of the so-called F-test that is derived from the quotients of one variance (in numerators) and another variance (in denominators). If these two variances differ greatly (there is a high F-value), this increases the confidence that the effect can be traced back to the corresponding cause. On the other hand, if the difference between the variances is slight (resulting in a low F-value), the certainty that a single one of the causes is alone responsible for the effect is also slight.

For the example that we have used in this chapter in which person (P) is successful at task (E), we can deduce the following. If we want to develop a test statistic for our hypothesis that P was successful with E because the task was easy (entity attribution), we have to relate the covariation of the effect that is brought about by the entity with that which is due to the persons and the timepoints. Therefore, in the example given in Figure 4.3b, the distinctiveness (variance due to the entity) has to be divided by the consistency and the consensus. As the variance that is due to distinctiveness is high, while consistency and consensus produce hardly any variation, there is a high value for the numerator and a low value for the denominator, and thus a high value for our test statistic. In this case, the effect would be traced back to the entity with a high level of subjective certainty. On the other hand, if the variances were of a similar size in both the numerator and the denominator, the test statistics would have low values, and the subjective uncertainty about which factor caused the effect would be high.

These considerations make it clear that the processing of covariation information does not only lead to causal attributions but, in addition, determines our certainty about the correctness of the causal attribution. 'Here we deal with the particular aspect of self knowledge that might be described as wisdom.... How does a person know that his perceptions, judgments, and evaluations are correct or true?' (Kelley, 1973, p. 112).

4.2.2. Empirical support

Kelley's model has stimulated a great deal of discussion and research on the question of whether individuals actually use and evaluate the information that is available to them as rationally and systematically as the model suggests (see for a review, Alloy and Tabachnik, 1984; Hewstone and Jaspars, 1987). Also, a large number of studies have been published that specify the conditions when individuals either distort information, fail to perceive it, ignore it, or do not acknowledge it because of motivational biases. To take all this literature into account would go beyond the limits of the present book. Nevertheless, for the present considerations, it is important to note that empirical studies have confirmed that individuals who are fully informed about consensus, distinctiveness, and consistency (see, e.g., Table 4.1) actually reach the attributions predicted by Kelley (McArthur, 1972; Orvis, Cunningham, and Kelley, 1975).

4.2.3. Relationship of causal dimensions of the covariation principle with other taxonomies

Various conceptions of attribution theory have introduced different aspects of classification for causal attributions. It has already been shown in Chapter 3 that, for example, Weiner's internal and stable factor 'ability' represents a 'person attribution' in Kelley's classification, while the internal and variable factor 'effort' represents a 'circumstance attribution' (see also Grimm, 1980). Kammer (1984) points out that the division into specific and global causes made by Abramson et al. (1978; see Chapters 3 and 6) is not to be found in

Kelley's work. However, in a questionnaire study she shows that the generality dimension is closely linked to the antecedent condition of distinctiveness as worked out by Kelley (1967). If we experience failure by many different tasks (low distinctiveness of failure), we will make global factors responsible for the failure (such as a lack of intelligence). If, on the other hand, we only fail to solve one task and are successful in many other fields (high distinctiveness), we will be inclined to apply specific attributions for the isolated negative outcome (e.g., a lack of specific abilities).

4.3. INDIRECT COMMUNICATION OF ATTRIBUTIONALLY RELEVANT INFORMATION

Information about distinctiveness, consistency, and consensus is often not available, and in these cases it is not possible to arrive at causal attributions through a 'rational' evaluation of the covariation information. As we have already mentioned in Chapter 3, in such situations it is possible to use generalized causal schemata (see Kelley, 1973) to make attributions. For example, a person who has to exert much effort to solve a particular task concludes that the task is difficult (although they have no information about the performance of other people on this task).

In recent years, Meyer and coworkers (see for a review Meyer, 1982, 1984) have pointed out that information that is relevant for attributions can frequently be conveyed indirectly in certain social settings. If covariation information is not available, it is possible that we adopt the causal attributions that other persons make about our own behavior: This is particularly the case if we grant the other person a great deal of experience and/or a high level of competence for the behavior in question, and we ourselves have little experience in the corresponding field.

In a series of experiments, Meyer and colleagues have shown that particular interpersonal behaviors, that at first glance appear to be desirable and positive, can, when more closely observed, have negative, attributionally relevant implications for the person toward whom the behavior is directed (see for a review, Meyer, 1982, 1984). Investigations have been carried out for sanction behavior (praise or blame), interpersonal emotions (e.g., anger, sympathy), helping behavior, and the assignment of tasks. As these forms of behavior are also highly significant for therapeutic situations (see Chapter 10), we will now deal with these studies in some detail.

The investigations were a consequence of research findings on the effects of causal explanations for success or failure. The findings had shown that observers differ in their reactions to the actors' successes and failures if different causal attributions are made responsible for the outcome. For example, Weiner and Kukla (1970) confirmed that observers particularly praise success and punish failure if the outcomes of behavior are traced back to effort (one tends to praise success which is due to high effort and to blame failure that is due to lack of effort).

However, if one experiences success because of high ability or failure because of low ability, observers do not make evaluative judgments (provide less praise or blame). In addition, Ickes and Kidd (1976) and Weiner (1980b,c) were able to show (see Chapter 7) that one is particularly inclined to help another person who is in trouble if this person's need for help is attributed to causes that they are unable to control (e.g., someone falls over because they are physically handicapped). However, there is a lower probability that assistance will be given if controllable factors are considered to be the cause of the accident (e.g., someone falls over because they have drunk too much alcohol). Finally, attributional research has shown that the affects that are experienced or shown toward the actor depend on the causal explanations that are made for the actor's success and failure. For example, if one explains an actor's failure with lack of ability, one is inclined to feel sympathetic towards them. However, if the other's failure is explained by a lack of effort, one can possibly experience annoyance (see Chapters 5 and 7).

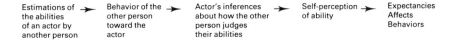

Figure 4.4   Indirect communication of estimations of ability and the inferential process that it instigates (taken from Meyer, 1984, p. 164).

The theoretical considerations and empirical work of Meyer and coworkers are derived from the assumption that a person who is exposed to another person's reaction that is relevant for attributions can, because of the close links between attributions and various social reactions, derive conclusions about how the person making a judgment interprets their behavior. Figure 4.4 graphically shows that actors can derive information on how an observer interprets their behavior from the behavior that the observer shows to them. Under particular conditions, the actor can adopt the observer's attributions for their behavior. These adopted attributions can then guide the future behavior, thinking, and emotions of the actor.

In the following, we will discuss the informative aspects of attributionally relevant behaviors in more detail, and pay particular attention to 'behavior that we usually regard to be positive or socially desirable' (Meyer, 1984, p. 162).

4.3.1. Praise and blame

As already mentioned, we particularly praise or blame an actor if we relate their success or failure to high or low effort respectively. We give praise if we attribute success to high effort, and blame if we attribute failure to low effort.

From this principle one can derive that praise after success informs the actor (indirectly) that the person giving the praise attributes the actor's success to high effort. In the same way, blame should convey the information that the person making the judgment explains the actor's failure through a lack of effort. In contrast, neutral reactions (neither praise nor blame) should communicate the conviction that neither success nor failure are attributed to the factor of effort.

The (indirect) communication of a person making a judgment, for example, that they explain the actor's success through high effort (praise) or does not explain failure through a lack of effort (neutral reaction), contains further information that is attributionally relevant for the person toward whom this behavior is directed. Kelley (1972; see Chapter 2) has pointed out that 'effort' and 'ability' have a compensatory relationship (see also Kun and Weiner, 1973). Especially with easy and moderately difficult tasks, one generally regards the presence of one of these two factors as being a sufficient explanation for success; by contrast the lack of one of these two causes is perceived as a sufficient explanation for failure at difficult tasks. If an actor receives the communication from an observer (through praise) that the observer explains the actor's success through high effort, the actor may infer that the observer considers that they are low in ability, for, if they were high in ability, the actor could solve the task without making an effort, and there would be no reason to grant praise. Furthermore, we can also use this considerations to derive that blame after failure possibly signals to the actor that the observer considers them to have sufficient ability to solve the task, as by applying blame, the observer communicates that they explain the failure through a lack of effort and not a lack of ability. Neutral reactions after failure may, however, communicate to the actor that the observer enlists a lack of ability and not a lack of effort to explain the failure.

It follows from these considerations that forms of social behavior that are regarded as being desirable (to praise someone after success and not to blame them after failure) could contain negative information for the actors about how their ability is perceived. In contrast, less 'friendly' reactions (neutral reaction after success and blame after failure) signal a high estimation of the ability of the person being judged.

4.3.2. Emotions

Similar considerations to those on the indirect effects of praise and blame have also been applied to interpersonal emotions that are related to attributions (see Graham, 1984; Weiner, Graham, Stern, and Lawson, 1982, 1983; Rustemeyer, 1984; Chapter 5). These authors assume that interpersonal emotions that accompany particular causal explanations that an observer makes for an actor's success or failure, such as anger, sympathy, or surprise, also indirectly communicate to the actor how the outcomes of their actions are interpreted. Thus, the hypothesis is that when an observer experiences anger over the failure of an actor, this emotion communicates to the actor that the observer attributes the actor's success to a lack of effort. Due to the compensatory relationship between ability and effort, the 'unfriendly' reaction (anger) should suggest to the actor that they are considered to possess sufficient ability to be successful if they will only make an effort. In contrast, 'sympathy' after a failure (a 'friendly' reaction) signals to the actor that the observer considers their abilities to be comparatively low.

4.3.3. Helping behavior

Like the emotions 'anger' and 'sympathy', behaviors that often accompany these emotions, namely, to help an individual who is in trouble ('desirable' reaction) or to refuse assistance ('undesirable' reaction), may possibly also contain unintended indirect communications about ability perceptions. Meyer and coworkers (see in summary, Meyer, 1982, 1984) demonstrate that persons who receive unsought help when attempting to solve a task feel that they are regarded by the helper as possessing less ability than individuals who receive no help in the same situation.

4.3.4. Assignment of tasks

A further social behavior that has yet to be thoroughly investigated in attribution research is the assignment of easy and difficult tasks. Meyer and coworkers have analyzed the indirect information that is relevant for ability in such behavior (Krüger, Möller, and Meyer, 1983). The research is based on the assumption that a person (the actor) who is assigned an easy task by another individual considers that they are regarded as having less ability than an individual who receives a difficult task.

4.3.5. Empirical support

Many of the studies that have tested the assumptions regarding indirect communications of information that is relevant for attributions (or for ability perceptions) are based on an experimental design that was first presented by

Meyer (1978). In investigations that were initially carried out as simulation studies, two persons (e.g., students) were described who were working on an identical task but experienced different reactions from a judge (e.g., a teacher) though they had both produced the same result. For example, Student A was praised after success and Student B received a neutral reaction from the teacher; Student A was shown sympathy after failure while the teacher was angry with Student B; Student A received unsought assistance while working on the task while Student B did not. Later, this design was extended to laboratory studies. The typical situation in these studies was to have the subject and a confederate of the experimenter working in a room on the same task. After the task had been processed, the experimenter reacted toward the confederate and the subject in a preordained way (praised or gave a neutral reaction, helped or refused help, blamed, showed sympathy or anger, assigned easy tasks to the subject and difficult tasks to the confederate, etc.). After this experimental manipulation of the independent variables (form of indirect communication), various dependent variables that are relevant for ability perceptions and attributions were recorded. For example, how high did the subjects consider the observer to perceive their ability, how well did the subjects think they would do in the next test phase, and so forth.

All of these studies provide very clear findings in support of the hypotheses. Indirect social communications of estimations of ability influence the personal estimation of ability as well as attributions, expectancies, and affects: praise after success, unsought assistance, sympathy after failure, and the assignment of easy tasks communicate to the actor that they are perceived to be relatively low in ability. In contrast, blame and anger after failure, the assignment of difficult tasks, and the omission of unsought help signal high estimations of the actor's abilities.

Part Two

Consequences of causal
attributions

Chapter 5

Achievement Motivation and Attribution Theory

Weiner's attributional analysis of achievement behavior is the most comprehensive theoretical model that deals with the influence of attributions on behavior, affect, and cognitive processes (see Weiner, 1979, 1982a, 1985b, 1986; Weiner *et al*. 1971). This approach has not only influenced research in the area of achievement motivation but also guided the theoretical analysis and empirical investigation of other motive systems and additional psychological phenomena within an attributional framework. In his recent work, Weiner (1980b,c, 1982a, 1986) emphasizes that the model that was originally developed within the area of achievement motivation now serves as the cornerstone of a general theory of motivation and emotion. In fact, the Weiner model has stimulated a vast amount of research and has guided experimental methodology in areas as diverse as helping behavior (Ickes and Kidd, 1976; Reisenzein, 1986; Weiner, 1980a,b), loneliness (Peplau, Russell and Heim, 1979), communication in close interpersonal relationships (Folkes, 1978), and reactive depression (Abramson, Seligman and Teasdale, 1978; Weiner and Litman-Adizes, 1980) (see also Chapters 6 and 7). As the Weiner model has also been used for the analysis of clinical phenomena it will be described here in detail (albeit not 'completely').

One important aspect of Weiner's contribution consists in the systematic application of the attribution principles that had been formulated by Heider and Kelley to issues of achievement motivation research in the 1950s and 1960s. As will become evident in the following, achievement motivation theories at that time were guided by the idea that achievement behavior can largely be explained within an expectancy x value framework. It was believed that the individual's expectancy of future success (subjective probability of success), the incentive for success (valence or utility), and the motive to approach success or to avoid failure determine achievement activities (Atkinson, 1957, 1964; Heckhausen, 1980; Weiner, 1980a). Some of the theoretical explanations of the findings from achievement motivation research that was conducted in this period were reanalyzed and reinterpreted in an attributional framework by Weiner and his colleagues in the 1970s. Now, in the 1980s, a comprehensive attributional theory of motivation and emotion that goes beyond the achievement domain has evolved from these efforts (Weiner, 1986).

5.1. BASIC CONCEPTS OF THE MODEL

The attributional analysis of achievement-oriented behavior assumes that the perception, processing, and interpretation of one's own behaviors is guided by the same mechanisms as the cognitive processing of the behaviors of others. Hence, Heider's and Kelley's conceptions, which were originally developed within the area of social psychology, could be applied to the field of self-perception as well as to motivational questions.

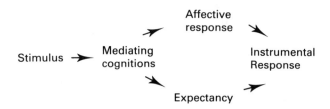

Figure 5.1   The cognitive (attributional) model of achievement behavior (according to Weiner *et al.*, 1971).

Weiner and coworkers (see e.g., Weiner *et al.* 1971; Weiner, 1980a, 1986) assume that following success or failure individuals tend to ask *why* the outcome has occurred. The 'answer' to this 'why-question' (the causal attribution) should, in turn, guide important aspects of subsequent achievement-oriented thinking, feeling, and behavior (see Figure 5.1). As already indicated in Chapter 3, Weiner (following Heider) classifies causal attributions for success and failure according to their dimensional properties. On the dimension of 'locus of control', internal causes such as ability and effort are differentiated from external ones such as task difficulty/ease or chance. On the dimension of causal stability, stable causes (i.e., ability or task characteristics) are differentiated from variable ones (i.e., effort or chance). In this chapter, it will be shown how Weiner and coworkers have conceptually analyzed basic assumptions and variables of the expectancy x value theory of motivation (that is, 'expectancy' and 'goal attainment value') and have reinterpreted empirical findings in this field from an attributional point of view.

5.1.1. Expectancies and causal attributions

When attempting to treat expectancy x value principles within an attributional framework, the first question to arise is 'What do attributions have to do with expectancies?'. It is obvious that the history of a person's successes or failures largely determines whether they expect to be successful or unsuccessful in the future. Success increases and failure decreases the perceived probability of being able to achieve success in the future. On the other hand, expectancies are probably not only reflections of past achievements but will also be influenced by the explanation of *why* one has succeeded or failed in the past.

Weiner argues that the dimension of stability determines which influence a causal attribution will exert on the formation of expectancies following success and failure (expectancy change). From an attributional point of view it can be anticipated that, 'If a particular effect is perceived as determined by a particular cause, and if this cause is anticipated to remain, then the effect should be expected to reoccur. On the other hand, if the cause might change, then the effect is also subject to change' (Weiner, 1986, pp. 94–95). More specifically, success that is attributed to a stable factor should increase the expectancy of being successful at a subsequent similar task to a larger extent than variable attributions. In the same manner, it is postulated that stable attributions for failure decrease expectancies for future success more than the attribution of failure to variable causes. It is also assumed that the mediating influences of stable versus variable attributions are independent of the locus and control dimensions. Hence, the variable elements of 'effort' and 'chance' should lead to identical changes in expectancies when compared with the stable causes of ability or task difficulty. On the other hand, internal (ability and effort) and external (chance and task difficulty) attributions following success and failure should not exert a differential influence on expectancies (see also Weiner, Heckhausen, Meyer and Cook, 1972).

The first experimental study to investigate the hypothesized linkage between the stability of attributions and changes in expectancies was conducted by Meyer (1973). In this study, failures were induced to subjects (high-school students) while working on digit–symbol substitution tasks. Following each failure, subjects were asked to rate their expectancy of being successful in solving the following task within the allotted time. In addition, after each trial they were asked to what extent they attributed the outcome to ability, chance, effort, or task characteristics.

Consistent with the hypotheses derived from Weiner's model, it was found that subjects with a tendency to attribute failure to stable causes (ability and task difficulty) indicated a stronger decrease in subsequent success expectancies than those with a tendency to attribute failure to variable causes (chance and effort).

Many other studies have been conducted that investigate the relationships between the stability dimension and expectancy changes (see e.g., Fontaine, 1974; McMahan, 1973; Rosenbaum, 1972; Valle, 1974; Weiner, Nierenberg, and Goldstein, 1976). These include further correlational studies and laboratory experiments as well as field studies. Summarizing more than 20 articles that address the stability–expectancy relation, Weiner (1986, Chapter 4) comes to the conclusion that a general law has been identified; that is, 'Changes in expectancy of success following an outcome are influenced by the perceived stability of the cause of the event' (p. 114).

However, mention should be made of the fact that other authors (e.g., Heckhausen, 1980; Rotter, 1982) consider that the question about the attributional determinants of expectancy has yet to be settled. It would, however, be beyond the scope of the present chapter to discuss these arguments.

5.1.2. Emotions (incentives) and causal attributions

As already indicated, achievement motivation research in the 1950s postulated that achievement strivings are influenced by the goal attainment value (incentives) in addition to the expectancies. Atkinson (1957) defines the incentives of achievement-oriented activities as anticipated emotional states. He assumes that humans are either motivated to 'approach' success (more specifically, the affect of pride) or to avoid failure (especially the emotion of shame). As a consequence of the important role of emotions in theories of motivation, the attribution approach to achievement motivation has also addressed the phenomena of affects with regard to success and failure.

The original attributional formulation of achievement motivation theory (Weiner et al., 1971) conceptionalized the emotional incentives of success and failure as dependent on the dimension of locus of control. Hence, in the early model, expectancies were regarded as being influenced by the stability dimension, and emotions (incentives) by the locus dimension (see Figure 5.1). It was postulated that internal attributions for success and failure maximize esteem-related emotional reactions (i.e., pride and shame) whereas the (positive as well as negative) incentives of outcomes would be comparatively small when external attributions are made. Success attributed to task ease or failure that is perceived to be caused by bad luck do not give rise to pride or shame about the outcome, whereas one would tend to feel pride about succeeding and shame about failing when the outcome is attributed to internal factors such as effort and/or ability.

Later, Weiner, Russell, and Lerman (1978, 1979) suggested that achievement motivation research had failed to explore the broad range of emotions that is characteristic in achievement-related contexts. They suggested that, alongside pride, individuals experience many additional emotions following success such as joy, happiness, gratitude, and relief. Furthermore, failing is often accompanied by other affective states in addition to shame: for instance, anger, depression, rage, or hopelessness. They further suggested that some of these affective states are obviously stronger when external (rather than internal) attributions are made. For instance, anger is typically evoked when another person prevents us from succeeding at a task, and gratitude is likely to be elicited when another person helps us to attain a goal. In both situations, which lead to anger and gratitude, respectively, external — rather than internal — attributions are made.

On the basis of these observations, Weiner and coworkers (Weiner et al., 1978, 1979, 1982; see for summaries, Weiner 1982b, 1986) conducted a series of studies in order to investigate relationships between attributions and emotions in addition to the locus-pride/shame linkage. As all of this research refers back to an experiment conducted by Weiner et al. (1978), we shall now describe this experiment in some detail.

As a first step, lists of descriptions of affective states were compiled from dictionaries. About 150 emotion words relating to failure (e.g., angry, sad, concerned, depressed) and about 90 descriptors of positive affects (e.g., happy, elated, cheerful) were identified. Subsequently, subjects received scenarios that described hypothetical persons who had succeeded or failed at an important examination. The scenarios furthermore mentioned different causes for the respective outcomes (e.g., ability, effort, chance, task characteristics, personality, or the effort of other persons).

To assess the dependent variables (emotional reactions), subjects were asked to rate on scales how strongly they thought that different affects (that had previously been compiled from the dictionaries) would be experienced by the stimulus person in the situations described.

It is obvious that the study of Weiner et al. (1978) has weaknesses. First of all, rather than assessing 'real' emotions as dependent variables, cognitions about emotions are being assessed. In addition, the fact that subjects were provided with lengthy lists of affects might have caused them to rate emotions which they would normally neither think about nor experience. Finally, the (untested) assumption is made that judgments about cognitions and emotions with regard to others truthfully reflect such judgments about themselves.

Several of Weiner's subsequent studies have attempted to eliminate some of these points of criticism (see for a summary, Weiner, 1982b, 1986). For instance, Weiner et al. (1979) used a 'critical incidence' method that does not provide subjects with emotion labels. Subjects were asked to recall their own successes and failures in the achievement domain that had been caused by certain causal elements (e.g., 'Recall an instance when you failed because of lack of effort'). Then, they were told to write down the dominant feeling that they had experienced in the situation that they recalled. Weiner et al. (1979)

were able to replicate the previous findings from Weiner *et al.* (1978) with this alternative methodology. However, in all these studies only verbal descriptors are used to assess emotional states. So it seems that the replication of these findings using different measures of affects such as facial expression (see Izard, 1977) or vocal parameters (see Scherer, 1986) would be a welcome addition to the consistent findings about attribution–emotion linkages which have been obtained thus far in questionnaire studies.

The results of the studies by Weiner *et al.* can be summarized as follows. Some of the listed affects for success and failure were given high ratings in all attributional conditions. For instance, regardless of the attribution presented, subjects expected the characters to strongly experience emotions such as satisfaction, happiness, and 'feeling good' following successes. Following failures, they were expected to feel displeased or upset and unhappy in all attributional conditions. Weiner labeled these affective states 'outcome-dependent' emotions; 'attribution-independent' affects that are probably triggered immediately following success or failure.

Table 5.1   Attributions for failure and dominating discriminating affects (according to Weiner *et al.*, 1978).

Attribution	Affect
Ability	Incompetence
Unstable effort; stable effort	Guilt, (shame)
Personality; intrinsic motivation	Resignation
Other's efforts; others motivation	
and personality	Aggression
Luck	Surprise

In addition to these outcome-related affects, the authors conclude that there are also affects that are typically 'linked' to different attributions (i.e., emotions that were rated significantly higher under one attribution condition than in the remaining ones). Table 5.1 presents the affects that were discriminative for different attributions following success, and Table 5.2 depicts those that were found to be linked to specific failure attributions.

The authors use these results to conclude that there are certain emotions that are not directly triggered by outcomes (success or failure) but which are guided by causal interpretations of these events.

Consistent with the earlier formulation about attribution–emotion linkages (Weiner *et al.*, 1971), the data from more recent studies that consider a broader spectrum of emotions has revealed that the dimension of locus of control determines self-evaluative emotions such as pride, competence or shame. It has been demonstrated that positive esteem-related emotions are triggered by

Table 5.2 Atrributions for success and dominant discriminating affects (according to Weiner *et al.*, 1978).

Attribution	Affect
Ability	Confidence (competence)
Unstable effort	Activation, augmentation
Stable effort	Relaxation
Own personality	Self-enhancement
Other's effort and personality	Gratitude
Luck	Surprise

internal attributions of success whereas negative self-evaluative affects arise in connection with internal attributions of failure (see Table 5.2).

The findings from the studies of Weiner and coworkers have also revealed that a different type of emotion is connected with the dimension of controllability. For instance, the emotion of guilt is triggered when failure is attributed to internal controllable causes (lack of effort), whereas failure attributed to an internal uncontrollable cause is likely to result in shame. In addition, the emotions of anger and gratitude were also found to be connected to the controllability dimension. One is likely to experience anger when failure is attributed to the (intentional) interference of others (an external cause that can be controlled by the other person), and gratitude is evoked when one attributes success to the help of others (again a cause that can be controlled by another person).

Finally, there are also stability-related emotions. As the dimension of causal stability is related to expectancies of success, Weiner (1986) suggests that emotions 'involving anticipations of goal attainment or nonattainment' (p. 154) will be influenced by this causal dimension. Although systematic research into the emotional consequences of stable and variable causes has not yet been conducted, Weiner (1986) speculates that 'hope' and 'fear' might be related to this dimension: Failure attributed to stable factors implies the (fearful) anticipation that it will reoccur in the future, whereas attribution of failure to variable causes could give rise to 'hope' for the future.

The attributional analysis of emotional reactions that was originally undertaken within the achievement context, and which was limited to the emotions of pride and shame, has now evolved into a general attribution-based model of emotion. Weiner and coworkers have suggested that, in addition to reactions to one's own outcomes in achievement contexts, attributions (about the outcomes of others) also influence how individuals feel toward others in achievement as well as in non-achievement-related situations. Hence, attributional models can be used to analyze aspects of a 'social psychology' of emotions. For instance, Weiner (1980b, c) has investigated how the answer to the question as to why another individual is in need of help influences the feelings toward this individual: The results of the pertinent studies reveal that a need for help that is attributed to controllable factors (e.g., somebody fell over because he drank too much) results in feelings of anger whereas attribution to uncontrollable causes (e.g., somebody fell over because he was blind) produces feelings of pity. In addition, anticipations regarding how an individual will feel in response to an excuse influences the cause that is selected to explain the failure to keep a promise (Weiner, Amirkhan, Folkes, and Verrette, 1987). Individuals are apparently motivated to control (minimize) the anger of other individuals by 'excusing' their breaking of a social commitment by attributing it to an uncontrollable cause (e.g., 'I was late because my car broke down').

A further aspect of the stability dimension has been identified in the context of the studies that relate attributions to interpersonal emotions: Stable attributions for a negative event can increase the intensity of emotional reactions. For instance, one is prone to experience more pity toward persons who fail because of (permanent) blindness than toward persons who have temporary problems with their eyes.

It should be noted that the basic premises of this attributional model of emotions show great similarities to the cognitive conceptions of emotions as introduced by Arnold (1960), Beck (1976), Ellis (1962, 1984), Lazarus (1966, 1984), and Schachter and Singer (1962). However, in contrast to Schachter and Singer (1962), the attributional model of emotion does not implement the concept of arousal. Attributions are conceived of as sufficient antecedents for the experience of emotions (see Chapter 8).

5.1.3.   Attribution and behavior

So far, we have described the attributional antecedents of expectations and emotions. However, we have yet to discuss how attributions, expectations, emotions, or a joint function of these variables affect achievement-oriented behavior in Weiner's model. Obviously, the attributional analysis is not just concerned with a specification of the antecedents of expectancies and incentives (emotions). It also does not assume that behavior is guided by these variables in the same manner that have previously been spelled out by expectancy x value theorists such as Atkinson (1957).

Meyer (1973, p. 150) points out that in Weiner's model emotions do not have the same (incentive) properties as in Atkinson's 'expectancy x value' analysis. Atkinson assumes that individuals are motived by (and respond because of) their expectation (anticipation) of positive or negative affective states. In the Weiner model, however, individuals are primarily interested in finding out 'why' they have succeeded or failed, and different emotions are 'by-products' of differential explanations of failure. No explicit mention is made of whether emotional anticipations (or expectancies) play a role in the motivation process. Moreover, Figure 5.1 postulates a direct path from 'emotion' to 'action', suggesting that the emotion itself — rather than its anticipations determines motivated behavior. We shall now examine how an attributional analysis deals with the explanation of behaviors in achievement contexts.

5.1.3.1.   Task selection

A central question within the study of achievement motivation has been: 'Which tasks will an individual select out of a series of tasks that differ only with respect to task difficulty?' (Atkinson, 1957, 1964; Lewin, Dembo, Festinger, and Sears, 1944).

Guided by the attributional assumption that individuals are motivated to gather information about the attributes of the self, the attributional analysis of achievement behavior (Meyer, 1973; Meyer, Folkes, and Weiner, 1976; Weiner et al., 1971) assumes that task selection is also determined by the desire to gain information. From an attributional perspective, information gain about the self should be highest for tasks of intermediate difficulty. Success at an easy task and failure at a very difficult one will be attributed to task characteristics (task ease or task difficulty) and not to characteristics of the self (e.g., effort or ability). Similarly, attributions to chance are made when improbable results are obtained. Success at a very difficult task will often be attributed to good luck and failure at a very easy task to bad luck. Only when tasks are of intermediate difficulty, can attributions be made to internal factors of the actor (ability and effort).

Empirical studies on task selection have indeed revealed that the majority of individuals prefer tasks of intermediate difficulty to either very easy or very difficult ones (see for a summary, Meyer et al., 1976). In addition, research has been undertaken to investigate whether the preference for tasks of intermediate difficulty is indeed attributable to the desire to gain information about the self (Buckert, Meyer, and Schmalt, 1979; Försterling and Weiner, 1981; Trope, 1975, 1979; Trope and Brickman, 1975). The findings from these studies support the attributional premise that task selection is guided by the desire for information about the self, and they can be interpreted as contradicting the position that task choice is guided primarily by a desire to maximize the expected emotional value of success and failure (Atkinson, 1957).

It should, therefore, be noted that in contrast to traditional expectancy-value theorists an attributional analysis of task choice (behavior) postulates that a different mechanism guides behavior. Task choice is not regarded as a manifestation of the desire to maximize anticipated affects (a hedonistic concern) but rather as an instance of information gain (a 'rational' concern).

5.1.3.2.   Persistence and performance

Compared to the elaborated theorizing and empirical analysis of the attributional determinants of expectancies, affects, and task choice, there are only a few studies that directly assess how attributions influence the motivational indicators of persistence and performance. The first study to address these questions was conducted by Meyer (1973). Performance speed at a digit–symbol substitution task served as a dependent variable. Subjects experienced induced failure while working on the experimental tasks. It was found that subjects who attributed an initial failure to the stable factors of task difficulty and lack of ability needed more time to solve a second task than subjects who attributed initial failure in a lesser degree to stable factors. Similarily, subjects who explained the initial failure with the variable factors of bad luck and lack of effort performed faster than those who scarcely used variable factors to explain the initial failure.

A further series of studies that is concerned with the relationship between attributions and persistence and performance can be labeled attributional retraining studies (see for a summary, Försterling, 1985a). These are studies that attempt to influence motivationally determined performance deficits and lack of persistence 'therapeutically' by changing causal attributions ('the studies best demonstrating the relation of causal attribution to the intensity and the persistence of behavior in achievement contexts', Weiner, 1980a, p. 383). These studies show that persistence can be increased and performance improved when participants are taught to attribute failure to lack of effort (a variable causal factor). These programs will be described and analyzed in detail in Chapter 8.

The data from the study by Meyer (1973) described above suggests that performance quality — probably mediated by persistence — is affected by the dimension of stability: If initial failure is attributed to changeable factors, high expectations following failure can be maintained, and the individual continues to exert effort at the task. This results in a relatively high performance level. By contrast, if initial failure is attributed to stable factors, expectancies of success markedly decrease: One is less inclined to exert subsequent effort, and, therefore, task performance deteriorates.

However, recall that — according to Figure 5.1 — emotions and expectancies are postulated to have a direct influence on behavior. In more recent work, Weiner (1986) postulates that the emotion of guilt (which is effort related) following failure has a motivating influence on achievement activities, whereas ability-related emotions (shame and humiliation) are believed to interfere with subsequent performance. Studies by Covington and Omelich (1984) and Graham (1984) that use path-analytic methods support these assumptions. However, these studies fail to show the influence of expectations on subsequent performance. Hence, the relationship between affects, expectancy, and attributions on the one hand and subsequent behaviors, on the other, has, according to Weiner (1986), still to be determined.

5.1.3.3. *Interindividual differences*

If attributions influence goal expectancies and affects, and if these variables in turn influence behaviors, then interindividual differences in causal attributions for success and failure should also be associated with behavior differences (see Weiner and Potepan, 1970). This is also the logic underlying the experiment concerning the relationship between performance and attributions conducted by Meyer (1973). Achievement motivation research has traditionally been concerned with interindividual differences and has accumulated a large amount of data on behavioral differences between individuals who are either high or low in achievement motivation. Weiner and coworkers attempted to explain interindividual differences in achievement behavior while assuming that the motive groups differ in the way they explain success and failure (Weiner, 1980a, p. 391). It is assumed that individuals high in resultant achievement motivation (when compared to individuals low in achievement motivation) tend to attribute success to internal causes (ability and effort) and failure to variable ones (chance and lack of effort). By contrast, individuals with low resultant achievement motivation should explain success through external factors (task ease and luck) and failure through stable causes (lack of ability and task difficulty). Weiner (1980a, p. 391) concludes that individuals high in resultant achievement motivation:

(1) Approach achievement-related activities (mediated by the attribution of success to high ability and effort thus producing heightened 'reward' for accomplishment).

(2) Persist in the face of failure (mediated by the ascription of failure to lack of effort).

(3) Select tasks of intermediate difficulty (mediated by the perception that tasks of intermediate difficulty yield the most self-evaluative feedback).

(4) Perform with relatively great vigor (mediated by the belief that outcome is determined by effort).

Individuals low in achievement motivation:

(1) Do not approach achievement-related activities (mediated by the relative attribution of success to external rather than internal factors and the exclusion of effort as a causal factor, thus resulting in modulated reward for goal attainment).

(2) Quit in face of failure (mediated by the belief that failure is caused by lack of ability, which presumably is uncontrollable and unchangeable).

(3) Select easy or difficult tasks (because such tasks yield minimal self-evaluative feedback).
(4) Perform with relatively little vigor (mediated by the belief that the outcome is comparatively independent of effort).

It should be noted, however, that some of the interindividual differences postulated by Weiner are based on the mechanism of emotional anticipations which is more typical for the expectancy x value rather than the attributional framework as depicted in Figure 5.1. For example, high achievement-oriented individuals approach achievement activities *because* they anticipate reward affects, and individuals low in achievement motivation are believed to avoid negative emotions with their choices. Other interindividual differences are assumed to be based exclusively on cognitive differences (e.g., the desire to gain information about the self) (see also Meyer, 1973, p. 150).

Chapter 6

Learned Helplessness, Depression and Attributional Style

Attributional principles have not only been applied to questions of achievement behavior. Within the last ten years, attributional approaches have also guided the study of learned helplessness and depression, and hundreds of studies have been published in this area. In the present chapter, I will describe the most important theoretical arguments and empirical studies dealing with the attributional perspective on learned helplessness, however, no attempt will be made to give an exhaustive review of the literature in this field.

6.1. THE ORIGINAL LEARNED HELPLESSNESS MODEL

The phenomenon of learned helplessness was originally discovered during laboratory experiments on avoidance learning (see Overmier and Seligman, 1967; Seligman and Maier, 1967). Dogs that had been placed in. Pavlovian harnesses and thus had no possible means of escaping were subjected to unavoidable electric shocks. None of the reactions that the dogs showed had any influence on the cessation of the negative stimuli.

In a second phase of the experiment, the animals were placed in a cage in which they could avoid the shocks by jumping over a barrier. Seligman and coworkers discovered that the animals that had previously received unavoidable electric shocks still continued to show unusual reactions in the second phase (behavior deficits), even though some time had elapsed since they had been administered the aversive stimuli. These deficits involved the animals' motivation, emotional reactions, and learning (cognitions) and were designated as being characteristic for the state of *'learned helplessness'*.

(1) *Motivational deficits.* Instead of jumping over the barrier in the second phase in order to escape the (now avoidable) electric shock like the animals that had not been exposed to unavoidable stimuli, these animals remained passive, whimpered, cringed, and simply submitted to the shocks. They made absolutely no effort to avoid the aversive stimuli.

(2) *Emotional deficits.*   The dogs that had received unavoidable electric shocks reacted to the following avoidable shocks in an' unemotional, apathetic, resigned manner and showed a reduction in aggressive behavior.

(3) *Cognitive (learning) deficits.* Animals that had been placed in an uncontrollable situation, compared to the animals in the control group, rarely repeated an accidentally performed escape reaction, as they had not 'realized' that the conditions had changed in the second phase of the experiment.

The results of these laboratory experiments were replicated with different kinds of animals (see for a summary, Seligman, 1975). It was also possible to demonstrate the phenomenon of learned helplessness in humans (see for a summary, Wortmann and Brehm, 1975). In the first relevant study (Hiroto, 1974), the participants experienced uncontrollability by being exposed to a loud noise which they were unable to switch off. A control group was also exposed to the loud noise but could cause it to stop by responding in a preordained way. In a second phase of the experiment, in which the participants were then exposed to a controllable aversive stimulus, those who had previously been exposed to uncontrollability were less frequently able to show the reaction that would cause the aversive stimulus to cease than the 'non-helpless' participants who had previously not been exposed to uncontrollability.

The learned helplessness theory uses the concept of an expectancy for uncontrollability to explain the negative effects of experiences of uncontrollability. Figure 6.1 shows how, according to Seligman, an organism that is exposed to uncontrollability can develop the expectancy that it will not be able to control future events (uncontrollability expectancy). This cognitive anticipation is supposed to then lead to helplessness deficits. It is thus apparent that the learned helplessness theory is a cognitive conception (see Chapter 2), as it is not the passive experience of uncontrollability that leads to the deficits, but the expectancy that future events also cannot be controlled. In situations in which organisms are exposed to objective uncontrollability but do not develop the expectancy of not being able to control future events, the described state of helplessness will not arise.

6.1.1.   Helplessness and depression

Seligman's learned helplessness theory has also been applied to explain the phenomenon of reactive depression. It is noticeable that the motivational, cognitive, and emotional deficits that accompany helplessness are also characteristic for reactive depression. In depressives, we can observe motivational deficits that are similar to those of helplessness organisms; such as inactivity and a slowing down of motor reactions. We can also find cognitive learning and recall deficits in depressives, and, in particular, affective deficits, for example, sad and depressive mood states that may be accompanied by anxiety and hostility (see Beck, 1967; Seligman, 1975).

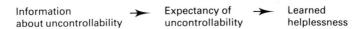

Figure 6.1   The components of the theory of learned helplessness (taken from Seligman, 1975).

Because of the shared properties of learned helplessness and depression one could ask whether Seligman's theory is also a valid explanatory model for reactive depression. If this is the case, depressives should also differ from non-depressives in their expectancies of uncontrollability. After succcessfully completing a task that calls for manual dexterity, depressives' expectancies regarding future success increase less than non-depressives'. They (depressives) respond to success as if it had only occurred 'by chance'.

The attempts to relate the learned helplessness theory to phenomena of human depression and helplessness revealed some shortcomings in this conception (see Abramson, Seligman, and Teasdale, 1978). First, the model does not permit predictions about the conditions under which uncontrollability leads to long-term and/or broadly generalized helplessness symptoms, and when such experiences result in temporary and/or specific helplessness that only concerns a few areas of behavior.

In addition, the original helplessness model has difficulties in explaining one typical symptom of depression. Abramson and Sackheim (1977) point out that it is supposedly characteristic for depressives to experience feelings of guilt and to take on responsibility for negative events (see Beck, 1967). This tendency to feel responsible and take the blame for negative events, however, implies — according to Abramson and Sackheim (1977) — the assumption that they could have avoided the negative event; in other words, they could have controlled it. For this reason, when the learned helplessness model postulates that depressives are characterized by their belief that they are unable to control the events in their lives, it is inconsistent with a characteristic aspect of the depressive syndrome (see Janoff-Bulman, 1979).

6.2.   THE ATTRIBUTIONAL REFORMULATION

In order to rectify the weaknesses of the original model, Abramson *et al.* (1978) presented an attributional reformulation of the learned helplessness theory. At about the same time, Miller and Norman (1979) and Weiner and Litman-Adizes (1980) independently published similar considerations that, however, received little subsequent attention. The basic assumption of Abramson *et al.*'s reformulation refers to Heider (1958) and Weiner *et al.* (1971) and proposes that individuals who experience uncontrollability ask *why* they were unable to control a particular event. The answer to this 'why question'

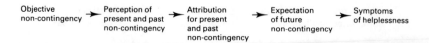

Figure 6.2   The attributional reformulation of the learned helplessness model (taken from Abramson, Seligman, and Teasdale, 1978).

(the causal attribution) should then influence the subsequent expectancy of controllability and thus influence important aspects of either helplessness or depression (see Figure 6.2).

As we have already mentioned in Chapter 3, Abramson *et al.* (1978) classify causal attributions on three dimensions: locus of control, stability, and generality. Each of these dimensions is supposed to be responsible for different aspects of the expectancy of future uncontrollability and to determine different symptoms of helplessness. In the reformulated model, the dimension of locus of control determines whether or not doubts about self-esteem arise in connection with the experience of non-contingency. Abramson *et al.* (1978) introduce the example of a participant in a psychological experiment who is not able to control the occurrence of an aversive noise. If the participant traces this failure back to internal factors, for example, their general inability to solve problems, this can lead to doubts about self-worth, as 'personal general inability' is an internal factor. On the other hand, if the participant manages to convince themself that the experiment involves a problem that nobody is able to solve (an external attribution), no doubts about self-esteem occur, because the participant does not perceive themself as being any less competent than other persons. Helplessness deficits that arise if non-contingency is traced back to internal factors are labeled 'personal helplessness' by Abramson *et al.* (1978). On the other hand, deficits that arise in connection with external attributions for negative events are labeled 'universal helplessness'.

According to Abramson *et al.* (1978), the dimension 'stability over time' determines the temporal duration of helplessness. For example, if an individual attributes uncontrollability (such as losing a job) to stable factors such as own inability (internal) or the (general) economic situation (external), the symptoms of helplessness should last for a long time because our individual does not anticipate any change in their unfortunate situation (personal ability and economic conditions might be perceived as fixed). In such a case, Abramson *et al.* talk about 'chronic helplessness'. If, on the other hand, unstable causes are used to explain non-contingency, for example, lack of effort (internal) or chance (external), the resulting helplessness should be temporary and only last for a comparatively short time. This condition is labeled 'temporary helplessness'.

In addition to the dimensions of locus of control and stability, Abramson *et al.* (1978) introduce the bipolar dimension of generality with the poles labeled 'global' and 'specific'. If non-contingency is explained by a global factor, which is characterized by the perception that it does not just influence the original situation but also a wider range of other situations, the helplessness will consequently spread to a much larger area of life. If, for example, a participant in a psychomotor task experiences failure as being caused by a lack of intelligence (global), helplessness deficits should appear at subsequent dissimilar tasks (e.g., mathematical problems). However, if the failure is attributed to a special psychomotor skill that is only needed for that particular experimental task, there should be no negative effects due to noncontingency in other areas of life or with regard to other tasks. In this case, we talk about specific and not — as in the first case — global helplessness.

Abramson et al. (1978) only speculate about the determinants of the intensity of the symptoms that accompany learned helplessness; such as when a person feels extremely sad or anxious because of the experience of uncontrollability or when these emotions are only weak. They suggest that the 'certainty' with which an individual anticipates future uncontrollability and the 'importance' of the event that they were unable to control influences the intensity of the symptoms. In addition, Abramson, Garber, and Seligman (1980) point out that the importance and the certainty probably do not affect all aspects of helplessness in the same way. For example, it would be conceivable that motivational and cognitive deficits arise if an individual was not able to control a completely unimportant event. However, affective deficits (sadness) would only be anticipated if the corresponding event was high in importance (see also Försterling, 1983, 1984).

6.2.1.   Attributional style as a risk factor for depression

According to Peterson and Seligman (1984), the causal attributions that a person makes responsible for uncontrollability depend firstly on situational and secondly on personality factors. The situational factors that lead to different causal attributions are only briefly and inexactly described as 'the reality of bad events themselves' (p. 349). They introduce the example of the 'reality' of the loss of a spouse which implies 'stability' (the partner will not come back) and 'globality' (this influences many areas of life). They do, however, not identify the crucial aspects of the situations that will lead to different attributions. (We will return to this point in Chapters 9 and 10 where we will discuss it in more detail.)

In the above-mentioned (Chapter 5) attributional analysis of achievement behavior interindividual differences in attributional habits are investigated alongside the situational antecedents of attributions for success or failure. This is also true for the research that was initiated by Abramson et al. (1978). It is assumed that, alongside the 'reality of the events', a personality disposition determines which causal explanation is used by an individual in a particular situation. They describe this personality disposition as 'attributional style' or 'explanatory style'. They postulate that a disposition (an attributional style) that involves the use of internal, stable, and global causal attributions for negative events increases the probability of becoming depressed and helpless after the occurrence of uncontrollable events. Thus, the attributional style is considered to be a 'risk factor' that can lead to depression. (Such a 'depressogenic' attributional style should also include the use of the opposite causal attributions for success; namely external, specific, and variable.) From these assumptions, the authors derive that both the prevention and therapeutic treatment of reactive depression should consist in suggesting to individuals that they should attempt to reduce their use of internal, stable, and global attributions for failure or external, specific, and variable explanations for success.

With the reformulated learned helplessness theory, we can only speculate about the development and antecedent conditions of different attributional styles: Peterson and Seligman (1984) suggest that 'traumatic' events (e.g., the loss of a parent during childhood), information from teachers at school, or vicarious learning could lead an individual to develop an attributional style that predisposes them to react to losses in a depressive manner (see also Chapter 9).

6.2.2.   Empirical tests of the reformulated model

The attributional theory of learned helplessness has stimulated a surprisingly large number of studies designed to test its assumptions (see for a summary, Coyne and Gotlib, 1983; Peterson and Seligman, 1984). Although the model regards the 'expectancy of future uncontrollability' to be the most direct determinant of helplessness, the majority of the relevant research has been concerned with attributional style rather than the expectancies of depressives. It has been tested whether depressives tend more than non-depressives to trace failures back to internal, stable, and global factors and successes back to external, variable, and specific factors. Peterson and Seligman (1984) justify the fact that most of the relevant research has concentrated on the analysis of the attributional style of depressives. They maintain that thus far there are no suitable instruments for assessing expectancies, whereas attributional research has already provided methods for reliably recording causal attributions.

It is obvious that a *direct* test of the attributional helplessness model would involve unethical manipulations. It would be necessary — among other things — to induce highly negative experiences in randomly selected individuals and then to suggest to one group that these events were due to internal, stable, and global aspects of themselves whereas the remainder of the subjects would have to be convinced that the event occurred because of external, variable, and specific causes. Then, the model would predict that only the former group would become depressed. Empirical research that tests Abramson et al's model typically measures the attributions of depressives and non-depressives during laboratory tasks for hypothetical events and in reference to critical life events (Coyne and Gotlib, 1983). The majority of such investigations are correlational studies that relate scores from depression inventories or psychiatric diagnoses to samples of 'attributional' thinking. Hence, most of the relevant studies do not allow conclusions as to whether attributions are causes or consequences of depression or helplessness (see also Brewin, 1985).

Coyne and Gotlib (1983) point out that the first studies that analyzed the relationship between depression and causal attributions refer to Rotter's social learning theory and the Weiner model, and that they were conducted before the (attributional) learned helplessness model was published. These studies generally show that depressives make more internal attributions for failure in laboratory tasks than non-depressives (see e.g., Rizley, 1978).

Studies that are directly concerned with the attributional model of helplessness record causal attributions of persons with varying intensities of depression in a multitude of hypothetical situations and not just for induced failure as in the early laboratory studies (see Peterson and Seligman, 1984). These studies make use of various questionnaries that were designed for measuring attributional style (Anderson, 1983; Peterson, Semmel, von Baeyer, Abramson, Metalski, and Seligman, 1982; Seligman et al., 1979; Stiensmeier, Kammer, Pelster, and Niketta, 1985). These questionnaires describe positive and negative events taken from both social and achievement contexts. The participants have to place themselves in each of these situations and write down the main cause that could have led to the particular result. Afterwards, the participants are requested to rate on scales to what extent the given cause lies within or outside their person, whether it is stable or variable, and whether it is global or specific.

The first study to record the attributional style of depressives was conducted by Seligman et al. (1979) and was performed on college students who, however, were not clinically depressed. It shows that high scores on the Beck Depression Inventory (Beck, Ward, Mendelsohn, Mock, and Erbaugh, 1961) accompany the tendency to make internal, global, and stable attributions for failure. The hypothesis that depressives trace success back to external, variable, and specific factors is less clearly confirmed.

Later studies were able to demonstrate the 'depressive attributional style' in children, lower-class women, and depressed inpatients (see the summaries by Coyne and Gotlib, 1983; Peterson and Seligman, 1984). Recently, Krantz and Rude (1984) have pointed out that in using this procedure one cannot determine whether depressives make different causes responsible for success and failure (e.g., ability as opposed to chance) or whether individuals with varying degrees of depression differ in their perception of the dimensional qualities of the same causes (e.g., ability). (Maybe depressives perceive their lack of abilities as being more stable than non-depressives; see also Chapter 3.)

Studies that demonstrate significant correlations between depression scores and the scores on questionnaires that record attributional style can, of course, not explain whether a particular attributional style leads to depression or whether depression determines the attributional style (see Brewin, 1985). For this reason, investigations have been carried out to shed light on the causal relation between causal attributions and depression. Golin, Sweeney, and Schaeffer (1981) recorded the attributional style and the depression scores of college students at two timepoints. They found that individuals who indicated a depressogenic attributional style the first time they were measured are more frequently depressive at the second measurement point than persons who had made fewer internal, stable, and global attributions for failure. On the other hand, the depression scores from the first measurement do not predict the attributional style at the second time of measurement; a pattern of findings that supports the causal role of attributions in the genesis of depression. Peterson and Seligman (1984) point to further studies that support the belief that attributions play a causal role in the emergence of depression. These are studies that relate individual responses to critical life events (cancer operations, imprisonment, or failures at college) to the causal attributions that the individuals feel to be responsible for these events. The findings from the studies are consistent with the predictions of the attribution theory model. They show that persons with a tendency to make internal, stable, and global attributions for negative events reveal comparatively more depressive reactions and a less adequate coping behavior in connection with the criticial life event than individuals who make more external, variable, and specific attributions. (Naturally it is possible that the negative event independently influenced both causal attributions as well as depression. Hence these studies also do not allow conclusions about the causal role of attributions for depression.)

Furthermore, in recent years, the predictions of the helplessness model have been tested in laboratory studies in which the participants who have made different attributions for success and failure are exposed to induced failure. For example, in agreement with attributional predictions, Alloy, Peterson, Abramson, and Seligman, (1984) demonstrate that, after failure on an experimental task, participants only show helplessness at a second activity that is unrelated to the original task if they had attributed the failure on the original task to global causes.

Chapter 7

Further Consequences of Attributions

Much more recent work has used the assumptions and research paradigms of Weiner's attributional model of achievement-related behavior (see Chapter 5) for the analysis and empirical investigation of various motivational and emotional phenomena in contexts that are not achievement related. Some of these studies also refer to the model from Abramson *et al.* (1978; see Chapter 6); and still others refer to attributional contexts without explicitly mentioning achievement or helplessness theory.

For example, Valle (1979) attempts to use attributional theory to explain the behavior of consumers who are dissatisfied with products that they have purchased. Anderson, Horowitz, and French (1983) and Peplau, Russel, and Heim (1979) investigate the attributions made by persons who complain that they are lonely, Weiner (1980b,c) formulates the attributional conditions of helping behavior, McHugh, Beckmann, and Frieze (1979) are concerned with the causal attributions made by alcoholics, and Eiser, van der Pligt, Raw, and Sutton (1985) investigate the attributions individuals make for attempts to stop smoking. In addition, attributional frameworks have been used to conceptualize test anxiety (Arkin, Detchon, and Maruyama, 1982), the effectiveness of weight-reducing programs (Haisch, Rduch, and Haisch, 1985), and coping with critical life events such as reactions to accidents at work, rape, or illness (see Antaki and Brewin, 1982; Taylor, 1983). Mention should also be made of the analysis of the role of attributions in decisions on setting prison sentences (Carrol and Payne, 1976), of the reactions of hyperactive children to medical therapy (Whalen and Henker, 1976), clinical judgments (Weiner, 1975), medical students' willingness to prescribe psychotropic drugs (Brewin, 1984) (see for a summary, Weiner, 1980a, 1982a, 1986), and to questions of behavioral medicine (see for a summary, Michela and Wood, 1986). Some of these investigations — insofar, as they are relevant for clinical psychology and, in addition, have also stimulated empirical research — will be described in the present chapter.

Although, as a rule, they have not opened up any new theoretical perspectives or research methods in motivational psychology (with the exception of studies on help-giving), these studies demonstrate the utility and the breadth of an attributional theory approach in the field of clinical psychology, and they can be used as examples as to how clinical phenomena can be conceptualized within an attributional framework.

Studies that relate the models from Weiner and Abramson *et al.* to phenomena outside of the achievement area assume that different responses to an event are brought about by the different causal explanations that are made responsible for the event. In the relevant investigations, it is usual to vary the causal attribution for an effect (or it is recorded whether different attributions are made). Then, it is observed whether the responses to the event differ according to which attributions are made.

7.1. HELPING BEHAVIOR

Prosocial behavior is a central research field in social psychology. It is also relevant for problems in clinical psychology as 'psychotherapy' can be regarded as a special case of helping behavior. Numerous studies have investigated the antecedent conditions of helping behaviors toward individuals who find themselves in trouble (see for summaries, Bierhoff, 1982; Hatfield, Walster, and Piliavin, 1978; Weiner, 1986). These studies have investigated completely different determinants of the willingness to help, such as the costs to the helper of providing help or the utility of the help for the person in trouble.

In his attributional analysis of helping behavior, Weiner (1980b,c) assumes that after a person has perceived the individual's need for help, the person asks *why* the individual has got into trouble. The subsequent causal attribution is considered to determine aspects of the helping behavior. The controllability dimension is of particular importance in this (see Chapter 3). A cause is regarded to be controllable if the individual is personally able to guide, influence, or prevent it. For example, 'drunkenness' is perceived as a controllable cause of need for help. Causes that can neither be influenced nor guided, such as a 'physical handicap', blindness, or being crippled, are regarded as being uncontrollable.

Weiner assumes that persons are disposed to help an individual if the causes of their need for help are perceived to be uncontrollable. Yet, help is denied if the individual possessed control over the reason for their need to help. Furthermore, the relationship between perception of control and helping behavior is not direct, but mediated through emotions. He postulates that attributions lead to emotions and that these guide behavior. If the need for help is attributed to uncontrollable factors, the potential helper experiences sympathy and pity. This should lead to the giving of help. Attributions to controllable factors would give rise to emotional consequences such as anger or disgust which — according to Weiner — lead to the denial of help.

This model is supported by data from questionnaire studies in which help situations (e.g., a man falls over on the bus) are described together with their causes (e.g., because he is physically handicapped (uncontrollable) or he is drunk (controllable) (see Piliavin, Rodin, and Piliavin, 1969). The participants are asked to what extent they experienced particular emotions in these situations (e.g., sympathy or disgust) and how probable it would be that they would help the stimulus person.

These studies reveal high correlations between emotions and the rated willingness to offer help: Strong sympathy covaries with the willingness to help and anger with the refusal of help. There are also significant relations between the perceived controllability of the cause of needing help and emotions and the readiness to help. Thinking that the stimulus person has landed in the situation because of uncontrollable causes covaries with both sympathy and the readiness to help. The assumption that the reason for the trouble could have been controlled causes anger and a reluctance to help.

6.2. ANGER

Attention has been paid to the emotion of anger in many fields of psychology. Social psychologists have analyzed the relation between this affect and aggressive behavior, and clinical psychologists have pointed out the possible negative consequences that unsuitably strong anger can have for the physiological, psychological, and social adaption of individuals (Ellis, 1977; Novaco, 1975).

Försterling (1984) was guided by the work of Weiner and coworkers that has already been described in Chapter 4 and in the preceding paragraph on helping behavior (Weiner et al., 1982; Weiner, Russell and Lerman, 1978). These authors illustrated that different attributions for an outcome (such as success or failure or the need for help) result in different emotions for the attributer. Thus, failure that is attributed to a lack of ability (internal, stable, uncontrollable) can be the cause of depressive affects, while attributions to obstruction by another person (external, variable, controllable) can arouse anger.

If external and controllable factors lead to anger reactions, then persons who are frequently and/or intensely angry, in other words, possess a high anger potential, should also show a tendency ('attributional style') to explain negative events as being caused by external and controllable factors. In order to test whether persons with a high anger potential do indeed possess such a characteristic attributional style, Försterling (1984) applied the methods for recording attributional style that were developed in connection with Abramson et al.'s (1978) model (see Chapter 6). A questionnaire was constructed in which the subjects were asked to place themselves in hypothetical situations that could give rise to anger (e.g., 'Imagine that the bus drives off just as you run up to the bus stop'). Then, the participants were instructed to name the main cause for each situation and to rank its dimensional qualities on scales.

As anticipated, the study revealed that participants with high anger scores tended to make more external and controllable causal attributions for negative events than subjects with low anger scores ($r < 0.38$, $p < 0.001$). This finding indicates that in addition to depressive moods, there are other emotional responses or reaction potentials that are accompanied by a typical attributional style (see Chapter 9).

7.3   LONELINESS

According to Peplau, Russel, and Heim (1979), many persons experience loneliness as being extremely negative, and under certain conditions it can lead to clinical phenomena such as depression and alcoholism. The authors define loneliness as a discrepancy between the social interactions that a person desires and those that are achieved (p. 55). Peplau et al. (1979) assume that lonely persons are also motivated to find causes for their undesired situation, and these attributions determine their responses to loneliness; for example, how a person feels about their loneliness and what they do to change the situation.

Thus, they understand 'loneliness' as a 'special case' of (social) failure and assume that the dimensional qualities of the causes that are made responsible for loneliness influence, just as in the field of achievement, the subsequent affects and expectancies (regarding future social successes). They postulate that internal variable attributions for loneliness (e.g., 'I am lonely because I previously haven't made enough effort to get to know people.') lead to active attempts to change the personal situation as, because of the variability of this causal factor, the individual maintains the hope that they can alter the (undesired) situation. In contrast, stable causal attributions for loneliness should lead to the expectancy that the social isolation cannot be altered, and such attributions will be accompanied by social withdrawal and hopelessness.

In a longitudinal study (described in Peplau et al., 1979), college students who regarded themselves as being lonely were asked to weight the importance of various causes for their loneliness. As anticipated, the participants who attributed their loneliness to internal stable factors were subject to more depressive feelings than students who made comparatively variable causal attributions for their social situation. Persons who made variable causal attributions also indicated that they undertook more activities to reduce their loneliness (e.g., going to parties) than individuals with internal stable explanations.

Anderson (Anderson *et al.*, 1983; Horowitz, French, and Anderson, 1982) also points out that an internal stable attributional style for personal loneliness hinders any alteration of this state. He uses empirical findings (Anderson *et al.*, 1983), according to which both lonely persons as well as depressives explain social failures through their lack of personal abilities, to point out that such attributions lead to low expectancies of future social success. Because of these low probabilities of success, the lonely person does not look for opportunities of making social contact (as they anticipate failure), and this (avoidance) behavior leads to the maintenance of loneliness. Even if, objectively, they possess the same levels of social competence, individuals who make variable causes responsible for their loneliness, in contrast, will look for opportunities of making social contact in order to get to know other persons and lose their feelings of loneliness. Hence, they will be more successful socially (less lonely) than persons who attribute social failure to lack of ability.

In addition, Anderson *et al.* (1983; Horowitz *et al.*, 1982) are of the opinion that there is a significant difference between lonely persons and depressives. Depressives distinguish themselves by making internal stable causal attributions in both achievement and interpersonal fields. In contrast, the authors assume that lonely persons will only show a disadvantageous attributional style in the interpersonal field as, despite the social failures that can lead to loneliness, they may well be successful in professional fields.

7.4   ANXIETY

Alongside the phenomenon of reactive depression, the conceptual analysis, measurement, and therapeutic treatment of anxiety is a central concern of research in clinical psychology. This state is characterized by a subjective feeling of unease, is experienced as being aversive, and often has negative effects on the performance and adaption of individuals to the demands of their physical and social environment. For example, highly anxious experimental subjects respond to failure with deteriorations in performance, while the performance of subjects who are not anxious often improves after failure (see Spielberger, 1966). For a long time, cognitive theories have been assigned great importance in the research and therapeutic treatment of anxiety — especially in connection with test anxiety (see Helmke, 1983; Wine, 1982). Nevertheless, attributional theories play a comparatively small role in anxiety research (see e.g., Wine, 1980). The reason why attribution theory has stimulated less research in this field, despite its strong influence on present-day depression theory, may be due to the fact that both attributions and depressive feelings are generally related to *past* events (e.g., losses or failures). In contrast, the emotion of anxiety generally occurs in connection with the anticipation of *future* (dangerous or threatening) events.

Although we are unable to report an elaborated theoretical analysis of the relationships between attributions and anxiety, some empirical research has been conducted to investigate whether anxiety accompanies a characteristic attributional style. Fend *et al.* (1978, quoted in Helmke, 1983) were able to show that subjects high in test anxiety more frequently attributed failure to a lack of ability and less often to a lack of effort than subjects with low anxiety. Arkin, Detchon, and Maruyama (1982) found that low test-anxious subjects make more internal (ability, effort) attributions for success when working on anagram problems than persons with high anxiety scores. Similarly, Arkin, Appleman, and Burger (1980) report that high (social)-anxiety subjects take more responsibility for their failures and less responsibility for their successes in experimental tasks than participants with low anxiety scores.

Arkin and Maruyama (1979) suggest that the relation between anxiety and attributions is mediated through expectancies of success. If an individual traces success back to stable and failure back to variable factors, they can anticipate success in future achievement situations (see Chapter 5). The probability of success for a future achievement behavior is, in contrast, lower if a previous failure is attributed to stable factors and a previous success to variable factors. Furthermore, according to Arkin and Maruyama (1979), high success probabilities lead to low anxiety and low success probabilities lead to high anxiety. In order to test this assumption empirically, the authors recorded both test anxiety and attributions for success and failure in examinations taken by college students during the semester. As anticipated, there was a negative correlation between the stability of success attributions and anxiety scores. However, the anticipated positive correlation between stable attributions for failure and anxiety could not be found.

A further series of experiments points to the link between the emotion 'anxiety' and causal attributions. These are studies that were conducted to investigate the attributions that accompany different levels of achievement motivation. (Recall from Chapter 5 that individuals differing in achievement motivation are also believed to differ in the way they explain success and failure.) In these studies 'test anxiety' was interpreted as a component of achievement motivation. Achievement motivation was conceived as an approach-avoidance conflict in which the approach component was assessed with the Thematic Apperception Test (TAT, see McClelland, Atkinson, Clark and Lowell, 1953), and the avoidance component was recorded with the Test Anxiety Questionnaire (TAQ, Mandler and Sarason, 1952). Subjects were considered to possess a high achievement motive if the approach tendency measured with the TAT was high and anxiety scores were low. Low achievement motivation, on the other hand, was characterized by high test anxiety and a low approach tendency (TAT-score). Therefore, studies investigating the 'attributional style' of individual high and low in achievement motivation more or less indirectly investigate the attributional style of individuals high and low in anxiety. The numerous studies that related achievement motivation scores to biases in causal attribution are summarized by Bar-Tal (1978)

> Individuals high in achievement needs ... attribute their success to their ability and effort, and their failures to lack of effort or external factors ... Individuals low in achievement needs tend to perceive themselves as low in ability, to ascribe their failures more to lack of ability and their success more to external factors. (p. 236)

After considering these studies, Arkin, Detchon, and Maruyama, (1981) postulated that high test anxiety accompanies an attributional style that is characteristic for individuals low in achievement motivation, and that low test anxiety accompanies attributions that are typical for persons high in this motive (see Chapter 5). In a field study Arkin *et al.* (1981) tested these assumptions. At the beginning of the semester, college students completed a test anxiety questionnaire. In addition, their attributions for success and failure were assessed during a seminar. The results show that subjects with low test anxiety more frequently attribute success to ability and effort and less to task difficulty and chance than subjects with high anxiety scores. In the attributions for failure, the subjects with low test anxiety give more significance to the factor of effort than persons with high anxiety. In a similar study, Meyer and Koelbl (1982) found that achievement results that are accompanied by high anxiety are felt to be less controllable than those accompanied by low anxiety.

In summary, we can evaluate the studies on test anxiety (that unfortunately are often only loosely related to one another): High test anxiety accompanies internal stable attributions for failure and external attributions for success. This reveals similarities between the attributional style of depressives (see Chapter 6) and persons with high test anxiety that are probably due to the fact that both responses (anxiety, depression) are characterized by a low concept of one's own ability (see Meyer, 1984).

7.5. INFLUENCES OF ATTRIBUTIONS ON BEHAVIORS RELATED TO HEALTH, ILLNESS, AND COPING

Attributional approaches have been documented as having a wide range of applicability in areas as diverse as achievement, motivation, anger, anxiety, reactive depression, and other clinically relevant phenomena. Therefore, it seems natural that reserachers have also attempted to use attributional principles within the recently growing area of health psychology, behavioral medicine, and psychosomatic dysfunction (see, for a summary, Michela and Wood, 1986; Taylor, 1983): but how could attributions be related to illnesses and health?

Thus far, no attempts have been made to postulate or to investigate empirically 'direct attributional paths' from attributions to certain illnesses that are known to be due to infections or other biochemical causes. For instance, nobody has investigated whether, for example, diabetic individuals have a characteristic attributional style. However, researchers in the area of behavioral medicine have asked whether *behaviors*, *affects*, and *cognitions* that have been addressed from an attributional viewpoint are relevant within the field of health and illness. Recall that emotional reactions to failure and uncontrollability as well as persistence to attain a desired goal have been targets of attributional research. Such outcomes and behaviors are also relevant within the field of behavioral medicine. For instance, motivational questions come into play when we ask under which conditions individuals persist in performing preventive health behaviors such as exercising, giving up unhealthy behaviors such as smoking, alcohol, or drug consumption, or keeping to a diet (primary prevention).

Motivational considerations are also important after the diagnosis of an illness; for instance, when behaviors have to be maintained that are directed toward the reestablishment of health such as compliance with a therapy plan (secondary prevention). Finally, coping with permanent handicaps and illnesses such as spinal cord injuries, diabetes, or cancer can also be analyzed from an attributional perspective (see Taylor, 1983).

Note, however, like all other behaviors or emotional reactions (e.g., achievement motivation, anger, or reactive depression) that have so far been discussed from an attributional viewpoint, health behavior is also overdetermined. This means that we do not assume that attributions explain the major part of the variance regarding — for instance — why people smoke or engage in other behaviors that are damaging to health. Obviously many factors play a role. One may smoke because of an environment that reinforces this habit, genetic addictive predisposition, boredom, or whatever. All of these factors may have nothing to do with attributions. However, it subsequently will be shown that attributions may play an important role with regard to selected aspects of health-related behaviors; for instance, when an individual attempts to stop smoking or keep to a diet and fails to do so. These behaviors can be conceptualized as special cases of goal setting, intention formation, or persistence.

7.5.1. Giving up smoking

Eiser *et al.*, (1985) have pointed out that attributions may play a role with regard to why people keep on smoking. They argue that many individuals are aware of the negative consequences of cigarette smoking and would actually like to quit. However, not all of the individuals who want to give up arrive at the *intention* of stopping because they might lack the confidence that they would succeed if they tried. Hence, 'confidence to succeed' in quitting might be an important variable with regard to who will attempt (and succeed) to quit smoking. Confidence, or expectancy, however, is known to depend on attributions, especially causal stability. Eiser *et al.* (1985), therefore, suggest that individuals who contemplate giving up smoking will think about the possibility of failing and, more importantly, the possible causes of this 'hypothetical' failure. The authors speculate that a person who maintains the philosophy that failure to quit smoking would be caused by stable causes such as 'task difficulty' (e.g., 'It is just too hard') or ability (e.g., 'I am just too addicted') will have little confidence that they might succeed in giving up and will therefore not develop the intention to quit. Conversely, if an individual believes that failure to quit would be due to variable factors such as effort or even chance, expectancies of success should be comparatively higher and should lead to an intention to quit.

Subjects in the study by Eiser *et al.* (1985) were more than 2000 members of the general public who wrote to a radio station asking for information on how to stop smoking. Hence, these individuals probably saw a value in trying to stop. Subjects received a questionnaire asking them — among other things —why other individuals who try to stop smoking fail to do so (e.g., task difficulty, lack of effort, lack of knowledge about how to do it, inability). These perceived causes of the behavior of others were believed to reflect causal beliefs with regard to own outcomes. Subjects were also asked whether they intended to stop smoking within the near future. The authors report a significant correlation between attributions and the intention to quit. Individuals who viewed failure to quit smoking as being caused by unstable causes more frequently intended to give up their habit than those who made stable attributions. In a post-test (1 year later), these subjects were asked whether they had tried to quit smoking. Again, as predicted, more of those people who previously intended to quit smoking gave up their habit than those who did not intend to do so.

Moreover, more of those people who intended to stop actually did cut down their cigarette consumption. Taken together, the data suggest that attributions about failure to stop smoking influence expectancies about whether one is able to give up, and these expectancies determine whether an intention to give up is formed. The intention, in turn, (not the attribution) guides behavior.

7.5.2. Recovery

Little research has been conducted on attributional influences on secondary prevention. Michela and Wood (1986) summarize some studies that indicate that heart attack patients who feel that they were responsible for their having had a heart attack will comply better with medical recommendations than individuals who do not accept their responsibility.

The idea that the attribution for a serious illness affects the individual's adaptation and coping and, as a result, the further course of the illness also receives support in a study reported by Affleck, Tenner, Croog, and Levine, (1987) who analayzed data from men who had experienced heart attacks. These authors report significant (albeit small) correlations between the tendency to blame other individuals or 'stress' (probably external uncontrollable attributions) for the (own) heart attack and the occurence of a second heart attack within the subsequent eight years.

In another recent study, Funke (1987) has applied attributional principles to the recovery from a different illness: tension headaches. The author bases his theorizing on findings that indicate that tension headache patients who attribute their headaches to 'psychological' causes tend to benefit more from biofeedback therapy than those who explain their pain with 'medical' (organic) causes. In a therapy program, Funke induced 'psychological' causes for the headaches to patients. It was expected that patients who learned to attribute their headaches to psychological factors would: (1) show reduced negative emotional reactions to their headaches, (2) increased self-control with regard to headache-producing situations, and (3) improved coping with the headache symptoms.

During 'attribution therapy', Funke provided headache clients with information indicating that their headaches had 'psychological', as opposed to 'physical', causes. He found that (relative to a control group that received relaxation training) individuals receiving attribution therapy: (1) showed an increase of 'psychological attributions' during therapy, (2) had increased expectancies that their treatments would be successful, and (3) had significantly lower depression scores. Finally, he found that the attribution-therapy group reported a (slightly) greater decrease in headache symptoms than the control group.

The results of Funke's study need to be interpreted with caution as the sample is relatively small, long-term effects have not yet been assessed, and it is not clear whether the attributional changes did not include 'unrealistic promises' (see also Chapter 9) to the clients. However, it demonstrates how attributional principles can be applied to problems of illness. First, psychosomatic problems might indeed be a promising field for applying the attributional principles that were described in Chapters 5 and 6 (see also Chapter 8). Secondly, it demonstrates that reactions in response to an 'illness', that is depression *about* the headache, are mediated by attributions. Thirdly, it points to mediating psychological processes that might explain why changing attributions can lead to the amelioration of illness. In this case, the belief that headaches are due to 'psychological' (controllable) causes might make patients more sensitive and more inclined to apply self-control techniques. This, in turn, might actually reduce their headaches.

7.5.3.   Coping with accidents, handicaps, and rape

A further line of research relevant to this chapter is concerned with how individuals cope with and adapt to difficult and/or tragic life events such as accidents, cancer surgery, or rape. In a frequently cited study, Bulman and Wortman (1977) investigated the coping behavior of individuals who had become paralyzed after having received spinal cord injuries during accidents. The authors found that individuals who blamed other persons or other external factors for the accident adapted comparatively less well to their handicaps than individuals who 'blamed themselves' for the accident. (The degree of adaptation was measured through ratings made by the hospital staff.)

Similarly, Taylor (1983) reports that breast cancer patients who believed that their cancer was caused by controllable factors (many of them did!) such as 'dieting' or 'negative attitudes' coped better with their misfortune than those who attributed the illness to uncontrollable causes.

Brewin (1982) reports a similar finding: His subjects were industrial workers who had received minor injuries during accidents at work (fractures and bone damages). As a measure of adaptation, he used the length of time (weighted with the prognosis of medical doctors) that the workers stayed away from their job. It was found that workers who perceived themselves to be responsible (culpable) for the accidents coped better with the injuries (stayed away from work for a shorter time) than those individuals who used factors external to themselves to explain the accident. (Naturally, the operationalization of 'coping behavior' was limited to a very narrow aspect of this phenomenon.)

Furthermore, Janoff-Bulman (1979) has suggested that the (coping) reactions of rape victims are in part determined by their causal explanations as to 'why' they have been raped. The author found that rape victims who attributed their experience to characterological (stable) factors (e.g., 'I have been raped because I have certain personality traits') had more difficulty coping with this negative event than persons who blamed their behavior (e.g., 'I was raped because I walked alone in a dangerous part of town'). It is quite conceivable that persons with characterological attributions had a harder time searching for ways to avoid being raped again, whereas for those who used behavioral attributions, some relatively minor changes in their own behavior appeared to be sufficient to provide future protection.

Hence, there seems to be evidence indicating that the maintenance of a concept of 'control' has positive influence on how individuals cope with the consequences of stressful life events. However, despite the fact that the studies of Brewin (1982), Bulman and Wortman (1977), and Janoff-Bulman (1979) point out that blaming oneself rather than others has a favorable influence on subsequent coping, we are far from definite conclusions in this area (see, for a summary, Michela and Wood, 1986), and the present description is far from being exhaustive. Nevertheless, the studies point to an additional field of clinically relevant attribution-related phenomena —reactions to stressful life events.

7.5.4.   Attributions in distressed couples

As attribution research was originally developed within the field of interpersonal relations (social psychology), it is not surprising that attribution conceptions have also been applied to the study of conflicts (see Kelley, 1979) and distress in close interpersonal relations, specifically in heterosexual couples (e.g., Fincham, 1983, 1985a,b; Finchman and O'Leary, 1983; Kyle and Falbo, 1985). The fact that certain aspects of partner-problems can be cast in an attributional framework is important for clinical psychology and therapy as, according to Kelley (1979) '... in its various manifestations in dating, marriage, cohabitation and romantic liaison, the heterosexual dyad is probably the single most important type of personal relationship in the life of the individual and the history of society (p. 2)'. Hence, attribution theory appears to be relevant for the clinical area of marital and family therapy in that it might offer some tools with which to understand and improve interpersonal relationships.

In an elaborated theory of the 'structure and process' of close interpersonal relationships, which cannot be described here comprehensively, Kelley (1979) has pointed out that causal attributions are among the most important determinants of how we feel and behave toward and interact with closely related persons. He suggests that members of a dyad have a tendency to use their partner's behavior to make inferences about the partner's dispositions. The actor's attribution about the partner's behavior will influence their feelings and evaluations with regard to the specific behavior of the partner and, in addition, the satisfaction that they experience in the relationship. For instance, an invitation to a dinner might be attributed to the partner's lasting desire to please the actor and to be kind and considerate to them. This attribution will probably give rise to more appreciation than a causal explanation of the dinner that it is due to the fact that leftovers need to be used up.

The attribution of the partner's behavior will also guide the actor deciding which 'outcomes' they can expect from the relationship in the future. Knowing that a 'positive' behavior of the partner reflects their lasting desire to please the actor will give rise to the actor's expectation that the partner will continue to help the actor to achieve 'good outcomes' in the relationship. On the other hand, attributions of the partner's positive behaviors to external, unstable factors will not build up the expectation that positive outcomes will be reached in the future. In addition, knowing that a 'negative' behavior reflects a lasting disposition of the partner will lead them to expect (much more than, for instance, external unstable ascriptions) 'bad outcomes' in the future.

Guided by some of Kelley's ideas, Fincham (1985a,b), Fincham and O'Leary (1983), Fincham, Beach, and Baucom (1987) and Jacobson, McDonald, Follette, and Berly (1985) have postulated that there should be differences in how distressed and non-distressed couples attribute each other's behaviors. They argue that non-distressed relationships are characterized by the fact that partners experience a high degree of satisfaction from each other's behaviors, and that they expect this satisfaction to continue in the future. These experiences and expectations are consistent with a tendency to attribute the partner's positive behavior to internal, stable, global, and possibly controllable entities (e.g., 'his personality') and negative behaviors to external, specific, and unstable factors (e.g., 'chance'). On the other hand, 'distressed' couples — who, by definition, do not experience satisfaction from each other's behaviors — should tend to attribute positive behaviors to 'circumstances' (external, specific, and uncontrollable) and thereby minimize their positive impact, whereas they perceive the partner's negative acts to be caused by lasting personal dispositions (internal, global, stable, and possibly controllable): This should maximize dissatisfaction and pessimism regarding future satisfaction from the relationship.

In fact, several empirical investigations suggest that there are differences in how spouses in distressed and non-distressed couples attribute each other's positive and negative behaviors. For instance, Fincham and O'Leary (1983) found that non-distressed couples tend to attribute (hypothetical) positive behaviors of a spouse more to global and controllable factors than non-distressed couples, whereas distressed couples tend to attribute their spouse's negative behavior to global and controllable factors.

Thompson and Kelley (1981) found that a tendency to attribute 'good things' in a relationship to the partner and bad things to the self is associated with high ratings of satisfaction with the relationship.

Furthermore, Jacobson et al. (1985) selected distressed and non-distressed couples for their laboratory experiment. The couples worked on conflict resolution tasks; for half of the dyads, one partner was instructed to act 'positively' (agreeable and cooperative) during the task whereas in the remaining couples, one partner was instructed to act 'negatively' (the partner of the person was not aware of this instruction). Jacobson et al. (1985) found that, in non-distressed couples, positive partner behavior is attributed more to internal factors of the partner (and less to external factors) than in distressed couples. Similarly, negative behaviors are attributed more to internal factors and less to external factors of the partner in distressed couples than in non-distressed dyads.

In addition, Fincham, Beach, and Baucom (1987) asked members of distressed and non-distressed couples to ascribe causes to the partner's positive (for instance 'doing the dishes') and negative (for instance, 'not cleaning the table') naturally occurring, (Study 1) and hypothetical (Study 2) behaviors. When significant differences in the attributions of distressed and non-distressed couples occurred, they were in line with the predictions that spouses of distressed —when compared with non-distressed dyads — make (a) more external, variable, and specific attributions for their own negative behavior than for their partner's negative behavior and (b) make more internal, stable, and global attributions for their own positive behaviors than for their partner's positive actions. These differences were most pronounced on the dimension of generality.

Finally, Fincham (1985b) compared the attributions of unselected couples ('non-distressed') with couples who had just entered marital therapy (presumably 'distressed' couples). These couples were asked what was their major problem in the relationship, and were then requested to list causes for this problem. Again, distressed spouses were more prone to see global aspects of their partner as a source of their marital problems when compared with the unselected group.

In summary, the research presented in this section (and there are more related studies, see, for instance Fincham et al., 1987, for a summary) has generally supported the idea that spouses from non-distressed couples make more 'benign' attributions for their partner's positive and negative behaviors than spouses from distressed couples. Naturally — as the authors of some of the studies (see, for example Fincham, 1985b; Jacobson et al., 1985) acknowledge this — the research presented thus far in this section does not answer the question whether a certain ('benign') attributional style is causal for marital distress or whether marital distress is causal for this specific attributional style (see also Chapters 9 and 10), or whether both factors interact in a specific manner.

In this chapter, it has been shown that attributional principles that have been developed predominantly in the areas of achievement motivation (see Chapter 5), learned helplessness theory (Chapter 6), and social exchange theoretical analyses of close interpersonal relationships (Kelley, 1979) can be used to approach different aspects of clinical and health psychology within an attribution framework. These problems range from anger, anxiety, and coping to rape, loneliness, smoking, and marital distress. The studies clearly do not indicate that attributions are the only determinants of these phenomena and certainly do not suggest that therapy of these states or behaviors should be limited to attributional processes. Furthermore, many of the findings presented here are correlational and do not allow conclusions about the causality of causal attributions. In addition, in none of the studies did attributions account for a great amount of variance. Finally, many of the studies presented here only assess a few aspects (rather than the full range of variables) that are postulated in the Weiner model, the learned helpless-ness approach, or Kelley's (1979) analysis of close interpersonal relations. However, they clearly indicate that systematic, more theory-guided attribution research might be fruitful for an understanding of a wide variety of clinical phenomena.

7.6. EXCURSUS: CRITICISM WITH REGARD TO ATTRIBUTION CONCEPTIONS

Thus far, we have primarily dealt with questions that are concerned with basic attribution(al) research and with the (attributional) explanation and description of some clinical phenomena. In the following two parts of the book, however, we will examine possibilities of applying attribution principles for the analysis of questions related to psychotherapy, behavior modification, and cognitive therapy. We will also introduce theoretical assumptions derived from the analysis of attribution change programs that are based on the principles as presented thus far. Before we present these rather specific derivations from attribution theories that have implications for clinical psychology and therapy, we will look at the criticism that has been voiced toward attribution theories in order to obtain an impression of the limits and the 'soundness' of the foundations on which we will be building our further reasoning.

Criticism of attribution research has been voiced on many levels. On a very general level, for instance, Bindra (1980) has criticized the way in which the concept of cognition is used in so-called cognitive theories. This criticism concerns many other 'cognitive' theories in addition to attribution approaches and addresses several fundamental and philosophical issues of psychological theorizing. It would be beyond the scope of this book to discuss these issues. On the other hand, very specific methodological points of criticism have been directed at attribution research: — for instance — the frequent use of simulational studies and questionnaries to 'assess' dependent variables such as behaviors or emotional reactions. Many of these specific points have already been mentioned in this book and will not be repeated in this section.

Several authors have questioned whether attributions actually occur as often in real life as attribution theorists appear to assume (Krahe, 1984; Kuhl, 1983; Smith and Miller, 1983; Thomae, 1986). For instance, Thomae draws attention to 'the artificial character of many attribution experiments that coerce the subject to make attributions although they usually are not inclined to do so' (p. 6).

The scepticism as to whether individuals spontaneously search for the causes of events can probably be traced back to the fact that most (albeit not all) attribution(al) studies 'force' their subjects to make attributions. Subjects are often explicitly asked what the causes of success or failure might have been or instructed to rate on scales to what degree a certain causal factor has contributed to an outcome. Hence, these studies might have been reactive in that they asked subjects to engage in a process which they 'normally' would not have performed. Naturally, these studies do not address the question of whether (or when) attributions are made without the request of the experimenter.

However, there have been quite a few studies that did explicitly address the question of spontaneous attributional activity. These have recently been summarized (Weiner, 1985a). The studies included in Weiner's review made use of a diversity of methods: coding of written material, thinking aloud, or the recording of thoughts during and after task completion. Weiner summarizes the results of 17 studies: 'All the investigators report a great amount of causal search . . . it appears that the issue of the existence of spontanous attributional activities can be put aside' (p. 81).

Some researchers who might have been unaware of the empirical findings on spontaneous attributional activities have drawn a logically incorrect conclusion from this apparent lack of a demonstration of attributional processes. For instance, Kuhl (1983, p. 69) suggests that attributions must be relatively irrelevant for achievement behavior, as individuals do not exhibit a great amount of causal search following success or failure. However, whether individuals show spontaneous attributional activity and whether attributions guide behavior are two different questions: One can consciously think about the causes of an event 'just for the hell of it' without being behaviorally influenced by the causes (I might spend hours thinking about why banana trees do not grown in Germany but this does not influence my behavior). On the other hand, one's behavior might be strongly influenced by an attribution although the attributer might not consciously reflect upon his attributional script. (One might yell at the boy who threw a banana skin on the street after one has slipped on it): in this example, one would not actively 'search' for an attribution, but just 'perceive' it to be part of the situation ('I slipped *because* he threw the banana skin on the street'). However, we will address criticism with regard to the cognition–behavior/emotion sequence later in this section.

A further point of criticism that has been voiced toward attribution (S → C) theories concerns the assumption that individuals are motivated to gain a *realistic* understanding of the causes of events (see, for example, Herkner, 1980). The assumption that 'the man on the street' treats information 'rationally' while making causal judgments like a 'naive statistician' appears to be especially characteristic for Kelley's (1967; see Chapter 4) covariation principle. However, both common sense and empirical evidence point to the fact that, in everyday life, hardly anybody collects and/or memorizes all the data relevant to an effect in order to analyze it carefully and rationally in a statistical manner before making a causal inference. By contrast, individuals frequently draw causal inferences quickly while neglecting available information or they may underestimate the importance of some information while overestimating other and there are instances in which affective concerns, misdirected attention, limited access to information, or irrational convictions may lead an individual to 'incorrect' attributions (see, for a summary, Ross, 1977).

It is interesting that Kelley (1976) has already pointed to many of these 'shortcomings' of the naive scientist and has suggested several mechanisms that might cause individuals to make 'unrealistic' causal attributions (see also Chapter 10). He also emphasizes (Kelley, 1976) that his 'ANOVA'-model (covariation principle) is not meant to be an exact description of attribution activities in everyday life. Instead, he argues, that the covariation principle can be used to describe a somewhat idealized attribution process, and — possibly more importantly — it can be used to identify and systematically describe the 'exceptions to the rules'. (Note, for instance, that one of the 'attribution errors' that has been discussed in the literature is labeled 'false *consensus* effect'.) Therefore, the 'criticism' that 'individuals are not as "rational" as attribution theorists assume' has stimulated much research and theorizing in the field of causal attribution and should be considered as a stimulating integral enrichment rather than a shortcoming.

A further critical point is more or less of a methodological nature and concerns a premise that guides many attributional studies as well as research concerning other so-called cognitive theories: The assumption that individuals have direct access to the cognitive processes that are believed to guide their behaviors and feelings. In a frequently cited publication, Nisbett and Wilson (1977) have pointed out that many studies within the field of cognitive (social) psychology have reported the expected changes of the dependent variables (behaviors) as a consequence of experimental manipulations. Nevertheless, many of these studies have failed to demonstrate that the cognitive processes that the respective theories make responsible for the behavioral changes, actually had changed in the expected directions. For instance, Storms and Nisbett (1970; see also Chapter 8) gave their subjects who reported difficulties in falling asleep a placebo which was described as producing symptoms similar to those that these individuals experienced while trying to fall asleep (arousal). This 'pill-instruction' should lead the subjects to attribute the arousal that they usually experienced while trying to fall asleep to the pill. As the attribution to the pill should be a sufficient 'non-emotional' explanation of the arousal, subjects were expected to stop worrying and to stop searching for explanations for their symptoms. As a result of this, they should fall asleep more easily. Consistent with this expectation, Storms and Nisbett (1970) report that subjects in the experimental group actually required less time to fall asleep following the (placebo) intervention than individuals in a control group who did not have the opportunity to attribute their arousal to a pill.

However, post-experimental interviews revealed that none of the subjects mentioned thoughts related to the pill or to attribution of arousal as being responsible for their reduced insomnia. In contrast, the subjects explained their 'cure' with causes that were entirely unrelated to the experimental manipulations (for instance, 'I worried less about school'). This indicates that subjects did not have access to the cognitive processes (thoughts about the placebo) that actually caused their behavior to change. Nisbett and Wilson

(1977) suggest that subjects referred to intuitively plausible heuristics that were objectively unrelated to their behaviors in order to explain their behavioral change.

After an extensive review of the literature and own empirical investigations, Nisbett and Wilson (1977) come to the conclusion that individuals are only able to report accurately on the cognitive processes that guide their behaviors under very specific circumstances. In many instance, however, individuals not only do not know which cognitions have guided their behavior, but they even report on cognitions that are entirely unrelated to the cognitive processes that actually guided their reactions. These answers often appear to be generalized heuristics about the relationship between thoughts, emotions, and behaviors.

Recently, Nisbett and Wilson's (1977) arguments have been reexamined, criticized and specified on both, theoretical as well as empirical grounds by Quattrone (1985). Although there is not yet empirical certainty as to whether and/or when individuals have access to their behaviorally relevant cognitions, the arguments of Nisbett and Wilson clearly point to a possible 'danger' when attempting to determine which causal thoughts have influenced an individual to behave in a certain way (a central question for attributional studies as well as for the application of attribution principles to therapy, as will be shown in the following chapters). Instead of reporting on actual cognitive processes, the individual might refer to naive causal philosophies. Indeed, clinical psychologists (e.g., Beck, 1976; see Chapter 10) are well acquainted with the phenomenon that individuals have difficulties in accurately reporting on their thought processes. Therefore, cognitive therapists have developed specific techniques to train their clients in introspection.

As already indicated, Nisbett and Wilson's argument is rather a methodological specification than fundamental criticism of attributional models of behavior. However, other authors have challenged more fundamental premises of attributional models. Unlike Nisbett and Wilson who argue that individuals are often simply unable to report on their attributions, these authors question whether attributions actually determine behavior and affect. In an often-cited article, Zajonc (1980) has reported on literature that suggests that many forms of behavior, especially emotional reactions to a stimulus, occur before cognitive judgments about the stimulus have been made. Hence, Zajonc challenges the basic attributional premise that only the cognitive processing of the stimulus (S → C → R) rather than the ('untransformed perception' of the) stimulus (S → R) causes reactions (behaviors and emotions). For instance, it has been found that subjects already indicated that they preferred certain stimuli to others after having been exposed to them for a period of time which was too short to identify the shape of the stimuli. Zajonc concludes from this type of finding that feeling (in this case 'liking') comes before thinking (in this case description of the properties of stimuli).

The article by Zajonc has given rise to a debate with Lazarus (see Lazarus, 1984; Zajonc, 1984), and, again, it would be beyond the scope of this book to describe this discussion in detail. Nevertheless, two points can be made that are relevant to the contents of this book. None of the experiments reported by Zajonc has addresssed reactions that are — from an attributional perspective — conceived of as attribution dependent. For instance, Zajonc (1980) has addressed 'affective judgments' (especially 'liking'). However, it has yet to be demonstrated that affects like gratitude, pity, depression, or pride or behaviors such as persistence are independent of attribution processes. Nevertheless, Zajonc's arguments clearly indicate that not all reactions are cognitively mediated and that attributional theories should also be concerned with the question of which ones are and which ones are not.

A further, recently growing literature concerns an additional linkage between affects and cognitions. Recall that attributional theories of emotion such as Weiner's model (Chapter 5) or Abramson et al.'s theory (see Chapter 6) postulate that cognitions determine affect (C → R). (This is also a central assumption of cognitive approaches to psychotherapy that will be described and discussed in Chapter 10). However, there is an accumulation of evidence (see, for example, Bower, 1981; Johnson and Magaro, 1987), indicating that the reverse is also true. Feelings or emotions also influence cognitive processes such as memory, information processing, learning, and also the attributions we make (see Brown, 1984). For instance, it has been shown that subjects recall a word list much better when they are in affective states (e.g., happy or sad) which are identical to those that they were in when they learned the list (see Bower, 1981). In addition, there is evidence that the mood state of depression causes individuals to encode and retrieve information congruent with their affective states (see Johnson and Magaro, 1987).

However, attribution theorists do not deny the fact that both processes (from cognition to emotion and from emotion to cognition) 'exist' and that both are worth investigating. Naturally, attribution theorists have thus far focussed on the cognition–emotion linkage and have neglected the emotion–cognition sequence. In my opinion, much interesting research can be expected when 'mood and emotion' are included as independent variables in attribution research.

Part Three

Attributional Change

Chapter 8

Attributional Retraining Studies

Theoretical and empirical advancements in the area of attribution theories have been followed by attempts to use attributional principles to initiate behavioral change and to apply them to the problems of clinical psychology. In 1969, Ross, Rodin, and Zimbardo gave their experiment that therapeutically altered cognitions the heading 'Toward an Attribution Therapy', thus highlighting the potential usefulness of attributional research for psychotherapy. Since then many studies addressing problems of psychological maladaptation from an attributional viewpoint have been published. The pertinent research can be subsumed under the following two categories: misattribution training and reattribution programs. In the present chapter, I shall first analyze how these approaches conceptually differ from each other. Then reattribution programs will be reviewed, analyzed, and evaluated in detail, because they form the empirical base of the arguments, deductions, and suggestions which will be central in the remaining chapters.

8.1 MISATTRIBUTION AND REATTRIBUTION TRAINING

Misattribution studies were stimulated by Schachter and Singer's (1962) two-factor theory of emotion, which maintains that affects result from an interaction of physiological arousal and cognitive processes (see Figure 8.1). More specifically, it was suggested that an individual's appraisal of a situation may lead to physiological arousal (e.g., increased heart rate) and an 'emotional' cognition (e.g., 'the situation is dangerous'). If arousal cannot be readily explained, the individual is expected to search for a cognitive label for the arousal. As a result of the interaction of arousal and thought, the individual is assumed to experience an emotional state. The arousal is thought to be responsible for the intensity, and the cognition for the quality of the effect. Hence the same physiological arousal can give rise to feelings of joy, when the situation is positive, and anger, when the situation is negative.

Reproduced from Attributional Retraining: A Review, *Psychological Bulletin*, **98** (1985), 495–512. © 1985 by the American Psychological Association. Reprinted by permission of the publisher.

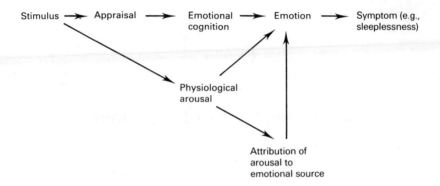

Figure 8.1 Theoretical concepts underlying misattribution studies (adapted from Reisenzein, 1983).

Clinical applications of this theory are based on the derivation that negative emotional states, such as anxiety, can be altered by providing individuals with 'non-emotional' cognitive explanations for their arousal in emotional situations (see Reisenzein, 1983). For instance, Storms and Nisbett (1970) gave insomniacs a placebo and told them that its ingestion produced the arousal that they typically experienced while trying to fall asleep (e.g., increased body temperature). This procedure was designed to change the insomniacs' explanation of their arousal from an emotional (internal) one (e.g., 'I sweat because I'm an insomniac') to an unemotional (external) one ('I sweat because I took an arousing pill'). As expected, Storms and Nisbett (1970) found that individuals who thought that they had taken an arousing pill needed less time to fall asleep than those who took a pill that was introduced as producing symptom-irrelevant arousal (e.g., numbness).

In a second set of relevant studies, a salient non-emotional stimulus (e.g., noise) was presented while subjects were in an emotional situation (e.g., when thinking that they would be shocked). Again, subjects who were led to believe that the noise produced their anxiety-relevant arousal (unemotional cognition) exhibited less fear-related behavior while thinking that they might be shocked than participants who thought that the noise produced symptoms unrelated to anxiety (e.g., itching).

In addition to these classic misattribution investigations, there is a second set of studies in the Schachter and Singer tradition that uses attributional changes for 'therapeutic' purposes. These programs attempt to change cognitions about emotional or behavioral responses. Subjects are led to believe that their undesirable emotional reactions (e.g., depression) are due not to internal causes (their neurotic personality) but rather to external ones. This is attempted in order to ameliorate additional worry and anxiety about the

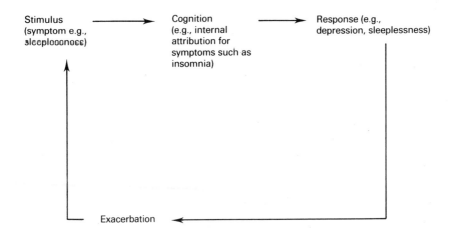

Figure 8.2 Theoretical concepts underlying misattribution-exacerbation studies.

problem, that, in turn, might exacerbate the original symptom (e.g., Nisbett, Borgida, Crandall, and Reed, 1976; see Figure 8.2).

Misattribution studies have addressed a wide variety of clinically relevant phenomena such as sleeplessness (Brockner and Swap, 1983), speech irregularities (Storms and McCaul, 1976), heart phobia (Liebhart, 1978), increasing pain tolerance (Davison and Valins, 1969), drug therapy (Valins and Nisbett, 1971), and depression (Nisbett *et al.*, 1976). Unfortunately, these treatments have not resulted in consistent positive changes of the dependent variables (see, for reviews, Harvey and Galvin, 1984; Reisenzein, 1983; Ross and Olson, 1981). From their analysis of the relevant literature, Ross and Olson (1981, p. 434) conclude: 'Certainly, widespread application of misattribution therapies should await more encouraging data'.

However, there is a second set of attributional change programs that is relevant to clinical psychology and therapy, which can be labeled *attributional retraining*. This research is guided by more recent models of action — namely, Bandura's self-efficacy theory (Bandura, 1977b, 1982), Seligman's model of learned helplessness (Maier and Seligman, 1976; Seligman, 1975) and Weiner's attributional model of achievement motivation (Weiner, 1979; Weiner *et al.*, 1971; see Chapter 5). In contrast to Schachter and Singer's model, these concepts do not make use of the arousal construct. The central assumption is that many behaviors, affects, and cognitions (e.g., phobic avoidance, underachievement, depression, or low expectations of success) are the consequences of the causal attributions one makes about events or behavioral outcomes, such as successes or failures in the domains of achievement and affiliation (see Figure 8.3). These studies typically identify behaviors that are

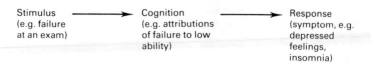

Figure 8.3   Theoretical concepts underlying reattribution studies.

considered to be undesirable (e.g., impaired performance following failure), and that are believed to be caused by specific attributional predispositions (e.g., attributing failures to low ability). In a training period, subjects are taught more 'favourable' causal attributions (e.g., ascriptions of failure to insufficient effort).

In summary, there are several important differences between misattribution and reattribution methods. According to Figures 8.1 to 8.3, misattribution training typically addresses causal cognitions about internal states (e.g., being aroused, depressed, or unable to sleep), whereas reattribution programs try to alter causal cognitions about behavioral outcomes (e.g., success and failure). Furthermore, misattribution studies are mostly guided by Schachter and Singer's work, whereas attribution retraining is based on that of Bandura, Seligman, and Weiner. In addition, misattribution methods focus on the causal dimension of locus of control, that is, whether the causal cognition (about the symptom) can be classified as internal (resides within the individual) or external (is considered to be outside of the individual). Reattribution studies typically differentiate causal cognitions on two further dimensions: stability (how stable is the cause over time) and controllability (whether the individual can influence the cause through intentions) (see Chapter 3).

8.2   ATTRIBUTIONAL RETRAINING PROGRAMS

In this section, I shall review attributional retraining programs. Included are those studies that diagnose undesirable psychological states (e.g., learned helplessness or lack of achievement motivation), attempt to improve these states through the alteration of causal attributions, and finally assess the effects of the interventions. However, if causal attributions are only one among several targets of change, and if the nature of the (design of the) study does not allow for the specification of the independent effects of the attributional change, the study is not included (e.g., Gerling, Petry-Sheldrick, and Wender, 1981).

Table 8.1 summarizes the important aspects of attributional retraining studies. It analyzes the relation of the studies to different theoretical concepts and summarizes the problem areas that the studies address. In addition, the

Table 8.1 Attributional Retraining

Study	Theoretical position/ direction of change	Problem area/ subject selection	Reattribution techniques training duration	Dependent variables/ results
Anderson (1983)	Attributional: Change to effort (strategy) for success and failure	Interpersonal: Selection according to cognitions	Persuasion: One-shot intervention	Increased expectancies, improved motivation and performance (at an interpersonal persuasion task)
Andrews and Debus (1978)	Attributional: Change to effort attributions for success and failure	Circle design, anagrams: Selection according to cognitions	Operant reinforcement (verbal and plus token): Up to 6 blocks (1 block containing 5 success and 5 failure trials)	Increase of effort attributions immediately, 1 week, and 4 months after the training at similar and dissimilar tasks; increased persistence at all different times and tasks; no changes were found in the IAR or the Effort-Ability-Attribution Scale; both methods of reattribution showed similar results
Chapin and Dyck (1976)	Learned helplessness, Attributional: Change to effort for success and failure	Reading performance: selection according to performance (below grade level)	Persuasion (the experimenter verbalized the desired attributions following each outcome): 3 days (with 15 trials each)	Increased persistence (number of sentences with a difficult word voluntarily read aloud)

Table 8.1 *continued*

Study	Theoretical position/ direction of change	Problem area/ subject selection	Reattribution techniques/training duration	Dependent variables/ results
Dweck (1975)	Learned helplessness, Attributional: Change to effort for failure	Arithmetic: Selection according to behaviors (children who were judged to be helpless by their teachers)	Persuasion (the experimenter attributed failure to lack of effort): 15 trials	Increased effort attributions, improved performance (less decrease of correct math problems after failure), IAR scores, test anxiety, and repetition choice tasks were not influenced
Fowler and Peterson (1981)	Learned helplessness: Change to effort for success and failure	Reading performance: Selection according to performance (low reading skills) and cognitions (intellectual achievement responsibility) as well as teachers' judgments	Persuasion (the experimenter stated the desired attribution to the subject) or the subject listened to (recorded) attributions: 3 sessions	Persistence (number of sentences read aloud) increased; no differences were found concerning overall IAR score, but the training influenced effort attributions
Gatting-Stiller, Gerling, Stiller, Voß, and Wender (1979)	Attributional: Change to lack of effort for failure	Academic (intelligence test tasks): Pupils (5th and 6th grade of a German high school) low in achievement motivation	Modeling (A videotaped stimulus person attributed failure to lack of effort, and persisted following failure): One-shot intervention	Persistence at a similar and dissimilar task and generalized attributions were uninfluenced; increased effort attributions at the training task, but not at a dissimilar one

Study	Type	Task	Intervention	Results
Medway and Venino (1982)	Attributional: Change to effort for success and failure	Visual discrimination tasks: Selection according to cognitions (elementary school students with a tendency not to perceive effort as a cause for performance)	Persuasion (the experimenter stated the desired attributions to the subject): 8 blocks with 6 trials each	Persistence (time spent on discrimination tasks and number of tasks completed) improved; attributions were not influenced
Schunk (1981)	Self-efficacy: Change to effort for success and failure	Arithmetic: Selection according to performance (children with low arithmetic performance)	Persuasion (experimenter stated the desired attribution every 5 to 6 min to the subject): 3-session duration (each lasting about 50 min)	Persistence (time spent on division tasks), accuracy, general mathematical abilities, and perceived efficacy were not significantly influenced
Schunk (1982)	Self-efficacy: Change to effort for sucesss at past and future performances	Arithmetic: Selection according to behavior (teachers identified children with low subtraction skills)	Persuasion (experimenter told the subjects that their past performance was due to high effort, or indicated that high effort will be necessary for future success) 3 sessions (each lasting 40 min)	Only linking past outcomes to effort increased performance (subtraction skills) and self-efficacy; persistence (time spent at similar and dissimilar tasks) was not influenced

Table 8.1 *continued*

Study	Theoretical position/ direction of change	Problem area/ subject selection	Reattribution techniques/training duration	Dependent variables/ results
Schunk (1983)	Self-efficacy: Change to ability, effort, or ability + effort for success	Arithmetic: Selection according to behaviors (teachers identified children with low subtraction performance)	Persuasion (experimenter stated the desired attribution to the subject): 3 sessions (each lasting 40 min)	Performance as well as self-efficacy (at subtraction task) improved in all attributional conditions; persistence did not increase
Schunk (1984)	Self-efficacy: Change to ability or effort	Arithmetic: Selection according to behaviors (teachers identified children with low subtraction performance)	Persuasion (the experimenter stated the desired attribution to the subject): 4 sessions (each lasting 40 min)	Performance, self-efficacy, and ability attributions increased as a function of the training; ability feedback yielded superior results to effort attribution training
N. E. Meyer and Dyck (1986)	Learned helplessness, attributional: Change to effort for success and failure	Reading difficulties: Selection according to performance (children with low reading performance)	Persuasion (experimenter stated the desired attributions to the subject): Reading of 10 sentences on each of 8 days	Persistence (number of sentences that were attempted increased). Generalized attributional style (IAR) and a more reading related attribution measure were unchanged

Study	Type of intervention	Task (measure)	Intervention paradigm	Results
Weiner and Sierad (1975)	Attributional: Change to attribution to a pill that interfered with performance for failure	Performance at digit substitution task: Selection with (Mehrabian's) measure of achievement motivation	Misattribution paradigm (Subjects in the experimental condition received a placebo that was described as interfering with the ability necessary for criterion task performance): One-shot intervention	Performance (speed at a digit symbol substitution task) improved for subjects low in achievement motivation in the 'pill' condition
Wilson & Linville (1982; replicated by Wilson and Linville, 1985)	Attributional: Change to variable attributions (informational antecedents rather than specific causes were provided)	Academic (college grades and GRE tasks): Selection according to self-reported dissatisfaction with college, low performance, and worry about performance	Informational (statistical information and fake videotaped interviews indicated that GPAs and general college problems improve over time: One-shot intervention	Improved performance (better GRE task performance immediately and 1 week after training, improved GPA after 1 year); increased persistence (college dropout rate); expectations of better GPAs (in the long run but not in the short run); subjects who were asked to think about attributions, reported better mood during the first week after training

Table 8.1 *continued*

Study	Theoretical position/ direction of change	Problem area/ subject selection	Reattribution techniques/training duration	Dependent variables/ results
Zoeller, Mahoney and Weiner (1983)	Attributional: Change of effort and ability for success, and to lack of effort for failure	Psychomotor coordination: Subjects (mentally retarded adults) who were rated to have motivational difficulties and who had performance decrements following failure were selected	Modeling (subjects watched on a video a peer working on the criterion task; a commentator made attributions) and persuasion (subjects worked on the criterion tasks and received in vivo attributional feedback): 3 sessions (each lasting about 15 min)	Both methods increased performance (time needed to complete the psychomotor task)

Note. IAR = Intellectual Achievement Responsibility Scale. GRE = Graduate Record Exam. GPA = grade point average.

techniques that were used to initiate attributional change are described, and the effectiveness of the interventions on the dependent variables is evaluated.

8.2.1. Theoretical positions and direction of change

One of the most important questions in the area of attributional change is 'What are the desirable attributions and what are the undesirable ones?'. Table 8.1 reveals that most of the attributional change studies have focused on teaching subjects to attribute outcomes in achievement situations to effort. In some of the studies, participants are taught to use effort attributions for success as well as failure, whereas others only include effort attribution retraining for failure trials. In addition, Schunk (1982) differentiated whether past or future performance is linked with effort attributions. The strong focus on effort attributions is guided by the following theoretical models and has different implications within each of these concepts.

8.2.1.1. The attributional approach (Weiner)

Weiner et al. (1971; see Chapter 5) specified in their attributional analysis of achievement motivation that ascriptions of failure to stable (uncontrollable) causes (e.g., lack of ability or task difficulty) decrease subsequent expectancies of success, whereas attributions of failure to internal causes (lack of ability or effort) maximize negative esteem-related affects following the outcome. In contrast, success attributed to stable causes increases subsequent expectancies for future success more than attributions to variable factors (e.g., luck), and esteem-related emotions following success (e.g., pride) are maximized when internal attributions are made. Inasmuch as 'lack of ability' is a stable, uncontrollable as well as an internal cause, attribution of failure to this factor should be particularly detrimental (Meyer, 1984; Weiner and Sierad, 1975). Alternatively, according to Weiner et al. (1971), attributions of success to high ability should elicit pride and increase one's confidence of being successful in the future (see Chapter 5).

Figure 8.4 illustrates that, from the perspective of Weiner's model, different attributions are desirable for success and failure. After success, it would be especially important to make internal attributions (ability and effort), whereas variable causes (bad luck, lack of effort) would appear to be most desirable following failure. However, because Weiner's model of achievement behavior does not postulate a direct link between causal attributions and behavioral consequences (persistence, performance), but includes other intervening variables (affects and expectancies), the conclusions from the model for attributional change programs are somewhat unclear. For instance, as Weiner recently pointed out (Weiner, 1980a), if it is the feeling of guilt following

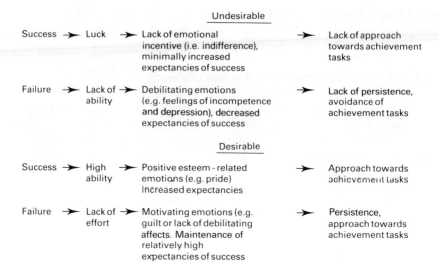

Figure 8.4   Desirable and undesirable attributions for success and failure according to the attributional model.

failure that motivates the individual to try harder in the future, it would be important to train individuals to make 'lack of effort attributions' following failures. However, if it is more important to maintain high expectancies following failure, then both bad luck and lack of effort might be equally desirable attributions.

8.2.1.2.   The model of learned helplessness (Seligman)

Although the attributional analysis of learned helplessness (see Chapter 6) has generated a vast amount of empirical research (see, for a review, Coyne and Gotlib, 1983), attributional change studies guided by the reformulated concept have not yet been published. However, the initial — and frequently cited — training method that attempted to change causal attributions (Dweck, 1975) was based on derivations from the original concept of learned helplessness. Indeed, this study can be considered the first one to combine the attributional literature with learned helplessness research. Dweck and Repucci (1973) found that helpless subjects (children with impaired performance following failure) made fewer effort attributions for their successes and failures than did those who were not helpless. Guided by these findings and by the original model of learned helplessness, Dweck (1975) concluded that helpless individuals should be trained to make the same causal attributions as non-helpless persons, that is, to ascribe success and failure to effort (an internal, controllable factor, see Figure 8.5)

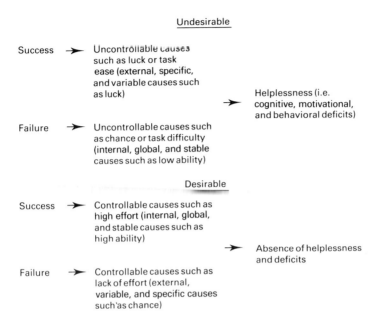

Figure 8.5   Desirable and undesirable attributions for success and failure according to the original and the reformulated (in parentheses) model of learned helplessness.

8.2.1.3.   The self-efficacy approach (Bandura)

In Bandura's self-efficacy theory (Bandura, 1977b, 1981, 1982), causal attributions do not directly influence behavior. However, they may convey information about one's self-efficacy which, in turn, determines important aspects of thought, behavior, and affect. Efficacy expectations denote the perceived probability of being able to perform a certain behavior which is required to produce a certain outcome.

Estimates as to how well one can implement actions influence, among other things, the choice of activities, how much effort the individual intends to invest in goal attainment, and the persistence at a given task. Subsequently, high effort expenditure and persistence usually lead to high performance attainments and effective coping with situational demands (see Figure 8.6).

Efficacy judgments are determined by several factors, and actual performance accomplishments (past success and failures) constitute an especially influential antecedent of self-efficacy estimates. Continuous success gives rise to high self-perceived capabilities, and repeated failures lower these perceptions. However, self-efficacy judgments are not assumed to be a mere reflection of one's past achievements, but are, in part, determined by the perceived causes that have contributed to the respective outcomes.

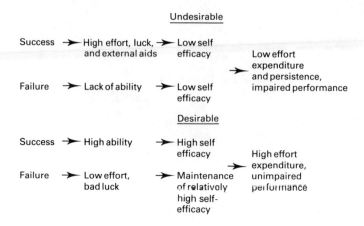

Figure 8.6   Desirable and undesirable attributions for success and failure according to the self-efficacy model.

Bandura did not develop an elaborated theoretical model of how attributions lead to increased or decreased self-efficacy. He stated: 'Successes are more likely to enhance self-efficacy if performances are perceived as resulting from skill than from fortuitous or special external aids', and: 'Success with minimal effort fosters ability ascriptions that reinforce a strong sense of self-efficacy. By contrast, analogous successes achieved through high expenditure of effort connote a lesser ability and are thus likely to have a weaker effect on perceived self-efficacy' (Bandura, 1977b, p. 201).

8.2.1.4.   Criticism and questions

It is important to note that different, occasionally contradictory, hypotheses can be derived from the three theoretical models underlying attributional change. For instance, the original helplessness position (Seligman, 1975) emphasizes personal control. Therefore, success as well as failure could be linked to effort expenditure to establish perceptions of control, because effort is a controllable causal element (Heider, 1958; Chapter 3). However, the attributional model, the reformulated learned helplessness approach, and in particular the self-efficacy concept, could argue that the ascription of success to high effort expenditure implies that the receiver of such feedback is perceived to be low in ability. Kelley (1973) pointed out that, especially for easy tasks and for those of intermediate difficulty, multiple sufficient causal schemata are used to explain success. This means that either ability or effort is perceived as sufficient for success. Therefore, leading a person to attribute success (especially at an easy task) to high effort might at the same time foster a conclusion of low ability. This belief, however, is extremely undesirable according to the self-efficacy, attributional, and the revised learned-helplessness model.

Table 8.1 indicates that the studies under consideration do not investigate what differential effects certain attributions might have depending upon whether they are made for success or for failure. Only a few studies even include differential attributional feedback for both possible outcomes. Zoeller, Mahoney, and Weiner (1983) taught subjects to attribute success to both ability and effort, and failure to lack of effort. The remainder of the studies attempted to induce effort attributions for both success and failure (Anderson, 1983; Andrews and Debus, 1978; Chapin and Dyck, 1976; Fowler and Peterson, 1981; Medway and Venino, 1982; N. F. Meyer and Dyck, 1986; Schunk, 1981), failure only (Dweck, 1975; Gatting-Stiller et al., 1979), or even for successes only (Schunk, 1982, 1983, 1984).

Furthermore, it would appear consistent with the attributional model and the reformulated learned helplessness concept to teach subjects to attribute failure to bad luck, as this external, variable attribution would not negatively affect self-esteem or subsequent expectancies. However, for the original learned helplessness model, bad luck would be considered an undesirable attribution because of its uncontrollability.

None of the studies were designed as a crucial experiment to differentiate between different underlying theoretical concepts for attributional change. To design training studies to test different theoretical models, it would be important to examine those deductions that are dissimilar for the different theoretical assumptions, and not those that are similar. In most studies reviewed here, the attribution of failure to lack of effort is the dominant direction of change; however, all three theoretical models argue similarly that effort is the most desirable attribution for failure. Hence, support for this hypothesis does not help to decide between theories.

The results of studies that attribute success as well as failure to effort (or lack of it) cannot be meaningfully compared with research that fosters effort attributions for failure only. If attributions of success to effort should be ineffective or even harmful, these effects could be compensated by the attributions of failure to effort during the next trial.

More recent attributional training studies depart somewhat from the strong focus on effort attributions. Wilson and Linville (1982, 1985) argued that for the problem area addressed in their study (being discontent with one's academic achievements), it may also be disadvantageous for subjects to attribute their failures to lack of effort. This attribution might give rise to feelings of guilt which, in turn, could be detrimental to future performance or which might lead the student to drop out of school. Guided by this assumption, they informed their subjects that most college students' performances improve over the first year. It was anticipated that this information would increase subjects' expectancies for future academic improvements and reduce negative affects about the present situation. In a similar manner, Anderson (1983) tried to convince (some of) his subjects that failure at the criterion task was attributable to variable (as opposed to stable) causes. They were told that either effort or 'wrong strategies' were responsible for the outcome. Note that attributing failure to wrong strategies implies that one can probably correct them (use different strategies; i.e., a variable attribution). However, there is an important difference for effort attributions in that the effort requires energy, whereas a change in strategy might be a rather effortless way to future success (see also Chapter 3).

8.2.2. Problem areas and subject selection

Table 8.1 summarizes the areas of behavior to which attributional retraining methods have been applied as well as the procedures for the selection of subjects (diagnoses). Although basic attributional research has been conducted with many clinically relevant variables, such as depression, loneliness, hyperactivity, and drug therapy (see Antaki and Brewin, 1982; Weiner 1980b, 1986; see Chapter 7), most of the retraining methods appear to be designed as tests of hypotheses derived from the attributional analysis of achievement motivation. Therefore, problems of intellective functioning predominate as target behaviors. A diversity of phenomena has been addressed within this field. Dweck (1975) and Schunk (1981, 1982, 1983, 1984) used arithmetic tasks, Chapin and Dyck (1976), Fowler and Peterson (1981), and N. E. Meyer and Dyck (1986) conducted research on reading performance, and Wilson and Linville (1982, 1985) investigated general academic performance (grade point average, GPA) and their subjects' college drop-out rates and dissatisfaction with academic achievements. One study investigated performance at psychomotor coordination tasks (Zoeller et al., 1983), and Medway and Venino (1982) studied persistence at visual discrimination tasks, whereas Anderson (1983) assessed persistence, expectancies, and motivation in an interpersonal persuasion task.

Table 8.1 also indicates that, during a pretest or diagnostic phase, it was determined which subjects might benefit from the treatment. For this purpose, one of two procedures has been used. First, behaviors believed to result from certain 'undesirable' attributions (e.g., performance decrements following failure which are thought to be the result of ascriptions of failure to low ability) are assessed, and those subjects who show a high incidence of these are selected for the training program. Second, cognitive diagnoses are made by assessing cognitions or personality variables, such as achievement motivation, that are assumed to be antecedents of the target behaviors under consideration. For instance, Anderson (1983) measured his subjects' attributional dispositions with a questionaire; Andrews and Debus (1978) and Medway and Venino (1982) selected only those subjects who infrequently made effort attributions during the pretest, and Weiner and Sierad (1975) and Gatting-Stiller *et al.* (1979) selected subjects who had low scores in achievement motive measures. However, some studies (see Table 8.1) used cognitive as well as behavioral indicators to select subjects. For instance, Wilson and Linville (1982, 1985) used a variety of measures including subjects' self-reported worry about their academic performance, their GPA, and whether they believed they had the ability to do better at college than they had done previously.

Studies that relied on behavioral indicators for the selection of their subjects also did not proceed uniformly. Sometimes export ratings of the subjects' behavior were used. Dweck (1975), for instance, asked school teachers to identify 'helpless' pupils. Other studies included only subjects who actually scored high on the target behaviors during the pretest; Chapin and Dyck (1976), for example, assessed reading performance and included only children with reading skills below their grade level.

8.2.2.1. Criticism and questions

Some of the studies that are discussed in the present chapter attempted to influence behaviors that have been proven to be closely linked to causal attributions, such as persistence following failure. Other studies, however, used indicators that are only weakly related to causal ascriptions, such as GPA (Wilson and Linville, 1982). It has frequently been pointed out that measures such as GPA are overdetermined (see also Weiner, 1980b). Therefore, it would not seem surprising if attribution retraining should prove to be ineffective on such measures. As tests of attributional models of behavior, variables such as persistence, resistence to extinction, or performance decrements following failure, which have been documented to be more sensitive to causal ascriptions, appear to be more defensible dependent variables for attribution retraining studies.

8.2.3. Reattribution techniques

There is considerable variability in the techniques used to initiate attributional change. Some studies used operant methods, others persuasion, and still others provided their subjects with attribution-relevant information. Finally, in one study (Weiner and Sierad, 1975), a misattribution paradigm was used (see Table 8.1).

An operant method was used, for instance, by Andrews and Debus (1978). They requested children to make attributions for the outcomes of the training task by pressing one of four buttons corresponding to effort, ability, task, and chance attributions. The experimenter subsequently verbally reinforced only effort attributions. Most of the training programs, however, relied on persuasion. Without receiving a specific reason or rationale, subjects were told that a certain cause was responsible for an outcome. Persuasive methods were used via modeling procedures or *in vivo*. For instance, Zoeller *et al.*, (1983) had mentally retarded adults in a workshop setting watch a video film that depicted an actor (a peer) working on the criterion task (screwing nuts on bolts). Following each success and failure of the actor, a commentator verbalized the desired attributions. In addition to this 'modeling persuasion' procedure, Zoeller *et al.* (1983) included an '*in vivo* persuasion' group in their experimental design. Participants in this group worked on the criterion tasks themselves, and, after each success or failure, the experimenter verbalized the desired attributions to them. In a similar manner, Anderson (1983) informed some of his subjects that outcomes at the criterion task (calling people on the telephone and trying to convince them to donate blood) would depend on stable factors (character dispositions and ability). Other subjects were led to believe that outcomes were caused by variable factors (effort and strategies).

Wilson and Linville (1982, 1985) used informational methods: They provided their subjects with antecedent consensus and distinctiveness information (Kelley, 1967), which was designed to lead to the desired attributions. They told their participants, who reported anxiety about their academic performances as freshmen, and who thought that they could have performed better, that most students have fewer academic problems and better grades in their upperclass years than they do as freshmen. It is assumed that this information would change subjects' attributions for their academic problems from stable to variable causes.

Finally, Weiner and Sierad (1975) used a misattribution procedure. They gave their subjects, who were low in achievement motivation, a pill that was introduced as interfering with the ability to solve the experimental task. This was done to reduce subjects' attributions of failure to lack of ability which are believed to give rise to debilitating emotions.

8.2.3.1. Criticism and questions

As there are many different methods used in attribution retraining programs which vary considerably in duration (see Table 8.1), it clearly would be interesting to have data on which might be the most effective methods of attributional change. However, the minority of the relevant studies included different reattribution techniques and assessed their relative efficacy: In Zoeller *et al.* (1983), one group of subjects was placed in a 'modeling persuasion' condition (they watched a filmstrip, and a commentator verbalized the desired attributions for the outcomes of the actor), and another group was in an *in vivo* condition (the trainer verbalized the desired attributions for success and failure to the subjects while they actually worked on the task). The two methods were equally effective. In addition, Andrews and Debus (1978) varied whether subjects received only social reinforcements for making the desired attribution or a token in addition to the verbal reinforcement. Again, the two methods did not yield any significant differences on the dependent variables.

However, the techniques that were compared with each other in these two studies are much more similar (two different operant and two different persuasion techniques) than are the techniques used between different studies (e.g., operant as opposed to informational). Therefore, the most effective reattribution technique remains to be determined.

8.2.4. Dependent variables and results

One of the most important messages of Table 8.1 is that reattribution methods influence a variety of dependent variables (cognitions, behaviors) in the expected directions. With one exception (Schunk, 1981), all training programs reported very promising results. Concerning cognitive changes, the most crucial question is whether the training programs actually attain the intended attributional goals. The results of the studies that used the Intellectual Achievement Responsibility Scale, IAR (Crandall, Katkovsky, and Crandall, 1965) suggest that highly generalized beliefs about causal attributions are not significantly influenced by the programs (Andrews and Debus, 1978; Dweck, 1975; Fowler and Peterson, 1981; N. E. Meyer and Dyck, 1986). However, some of these studies (as well as Gatting-Stiller et al., 1979) clearly revealed that attributions for success and failure at specific tasks that were similar to the training tasks were significantly changed in the expected directions. This pattern of results does not seem surprising, as the situations depicted in the IAR are very dissimilar to the training situations. There is no reason to expect that subjects change very general causal beliefs after, for example, having been trained to attribute failure at a block-design task to lack of effort.

A second set of cognitions that was assessed in the programs was expectancies of success, changes of expectancies following failure, and self-efficacy expectations. The general finding is that reattribution training influenced these cognitions favorably. Consistent with an attributional position, Anderson (1983) found that subjects who believed that task outcomes were determined by variable causes (effort, strategy) had higher initial expectancies and less decrease following failure than did those who were led to believe that success or failure were caused by stable attributes (ability). Also, Wilson and Linville (1982, 1985) found that subjects who had received attributionally relevant information expected to have better GPAs in the long run than controls. Finally, Schunk (1982, 1983, 1984) assessed an expectancy-related measure, perceived self-efficacy ('how certain are you that you are able to solve the task?'). He found that subjects who had their past achievements attributed to effort showed increased self-efficacy expectations.

To ascertain behavior change, performance and persistence have served as the most important indicators in reattribution training studies. For both measures, there is a clear tendency to be influenced favorably by the training procedure. For instance, Anderson (1983) found that subjects who were led to believe that the outcomes at the task on which they were working (calling up students and trying to persuade them to donate blood) were determined by unstable causes persuaded more students than those subjects who were told that outcomes depended on stable causes. In the same way, actual performance increments were found in Dweck's study (1975); training subjects solved more arithmetic tasks correctly per minute than controls. Schunk (1982, 1983, 1984) improved subtraction skills and Wilson and Linville's (1982, 1985) training improved college students' GPAs and their performance at GRE-type tasks. Zoeller *et al.* (1983) reported that their mentally retarded adult subjects who experienced severe performance decrements following failure at a psychomotor coordination task before the training actually improved their performance following failure after the attributional training. Finally, Weiner and Sierad (1975) improved their low-achievement-motivation participants' performance speed with their misattribution procedure.

Significant changes in the expected directions were also reported for persistence as a result of attributional retraining: Wilson and Linville (1982, 1985) found that trained subjects had a lower college dropout rate than controls one year after the training program (however, see Block and Lanning, 1984, for a critical reanalysis of this data); Chapin and Dyck (1976), Fowler and Peterson (1981), and N. E. Meyer and Dyck (1986) reported that trained subjects tried to read aloud more sentences with difficult words than controls. Medway and Venino's (1982) participants worked longer on the post-experimental tasks and solved more problems than did subjects without attributional feedback, and, finally, in the Andrews and Debus (1978) study, retrained subjects spent more time on unsolvable perceptual reasoning tasks (i.e., increased temporal persistence) and attempted to solve them more frequently (resistence to extinction) than did controls. In contrast, Gerling-Stiller *et al.* (1979) were not able to increase their subjects' persistence.

Unfortunately, very few studies assessed affective change in connection with their training. Wilson and Linville (1982) included a mood scale among their dependent measures. The only significant finding was that subjects who were asked to think about causes for their failure ('reason analysis') reported feeling more positive during the first week after the training. Furthermore, Dweck (1975) administered a test anxiety scale before and after the training procedure, however, the training did not cause significant changes on this measure.

8.2.4.1. *Criticisms and questions*

Attributional models of behaviour, such as Weiner's theory of achievement motivation, do not postulate a direct link between causal attributions and behaviors, but include additional intervening variables such as affects and expectancies. As already mentioned, lack of effort, which is considered to be the 'desirable attribution' for failure in Weiner's model, also influences both affects and expectancies. However, to investigate whether attributions, affects, expectancies, or their joint effects influence dependent measures such as persistence or performance, both intervening variables need to be assessed. In addition, it would be helpful to assess the intervening variables that the models define to be important (e.g., self-efficacy perceptions and affects following failure) for testing different models of behavior.

None of the studies reviewed here have assessed and investigated these different links. In the studies that assessed both changes in expectancies and affective states following the training, several conceptual and methodological difficulties immediately become apparent. Weiner (e.g., 1979) specified predictions of the relation between specific emotions (e.g., guilt) and behaviors (e.g., persistence). However, Wilson and Linville (1982) used a very global indicator of emotions (positivity as opposed to negativity) which is unsuitable as an operationalization of affect in Weiner's model. In addition, it is also not (theoretically) clear at what point in time affects should be assessed. Some of the studies reviewed in the present chapter investigated long-range effects of their program (up to 1 year, e.g., Andrews and Debus, 1978). As it appears unlikely (as well as undesirable) that the participants who were subjected to the respective training methods felt guilty throughout the whole year, one would need further theoretical specifications on when the experience of guilt might guide behavior, or, further, whether the anticipation of experiencing it again after a subsequent failure determines performance and persistence. In addition, it appears that more differentiated methods of emotional assessment are needed to answer these questions.

Furthermore, an alternative interpretation of the positive results of the studies could come to mind. The experimenters' attribution of their subjects' failures to lack of effort might have been perceived by the participants as an instruction to try harder. Hence, subjects' increased persistence following the intervention could merely reflect a compliance with the instruction (i.e., to try harder) rather than attributional change. However, there are some arguments against this point. First, some of the studies used long-term follow-ups with altered tasks and a different experimenter to eliminate this possibility (see Andrews and Debus, 1978). Second, some of the studies did not instruct subjects to try harder (at least not directly) and still found the expected results. For instance, Anderson (1983) instructed his subjects that failure was due to ineffective strategies, and Wilson and Linville (1982) merely conveyed to their participants that current problems were due to (unspecified) unstable factors.

Third, most of the studies reported that subjects also changed their attributions in the expected direction in addition to showing changes in the main dependent variable (persistence).

Nonetheless, the present training programs have not yet demonstrated (e.g., via internal analyses) that behavioral changes are actually mediated by attributional changes. In fact, one study has found behavioral changes that were uncorrelated with the attributional changes (e.g., N. E. Meyer and Dyck, 1986). However, it would be beyond the scope of the present chapter to speculate as to whether this lack of correlation is due to the possibility that subjects have insufficient access to their cognitive processes (see Nisbett and Wilson, 1977) or other factors that might shadow the relationship between thought and behaviors (see Quattrone, 1985; Chapter 7).

Part Four

Attribution in Therapy

Chapter 9

Foundations of a Taxonomy of the Attributional Content of Dysfunctional Reactions

It has been demonstrated in Chapter 8 that attributional retraining studies have consistently yielded the intended cognitive and behavioral changes in a diversity of areas ranging form persistence at anagram tasks in the laboratory to gradepoint average and the success rate of individuals who try to recruit volunteers to donate blood (see also Försterling, 1985 a). These studies, therefore, indicate that short, economic, cognitive interventions deduced from contemporary experimentally based psychological theories can be used effectively to modify behavior in 'therapy-like' situations. Reattribution studies constitute controlled experiments that stimulate the central aspects of modern psychological therapies. First, a problem is identified (diagnosis), second, a theory-guided intervention is performed (therapy), and third, the efficacy of the intervention is evaluated. These promising results give rise to the question of whether attribution retraining could be applied in a more comprehensive way to further areas of behavior change and psychotherapy, in addition to problems within the achievement domain. In order to shed light on this question, we shall first analyze the research findings on which attributional training studies are based.

9.1. THE PRINCIPLES OF ATTRIBUTIONAL RETRAINING

Attributional change programs are based on general psychological findings as well as on findings concerning interindividual differences. The first necessary (general psychological) finding was that different attributions for successes and failures lead to different behavioral and emotional reactions following the outcomes. For instance, it was shown that attributions of failure to lack of ability (a stable causal factor) lead to less persistence following failure than attributions to lack of effort (a variable causal element; see Chapter 5). On the other hand, variable attributions for failure maximize subsequent persistence (see Weiner et al.,1971). These findings then led researchers to search for individual differences. It was found that subjects who exhibited reduced persistence following failure tend to attribute negative outcomes to stable factors, whereas persons with a strong tendency to persist attribute failure to variable causes. On the basis of these (two) findings with regard to general principles as well as interindividual differences, questions can be derived that are relevant to the area of clinical psychology: How can individuals who are prone to give up easily following failure be helped to become more persistent? To what extent does a change in the tendency to attribute failure to internal stable factors (e.g., lack of ability) and the fostering of effort attributions influence changes in task persistence. It is precisely the latter question that attributional retraining studies investigate. Naturally, it would also be possible to design attributional change programs exclusively on the basis of knowledge about interindividual differences. However, this procedure is not characteristic for the presented attributional change studies; possibly because psychologists generally tend to analyze interindividual differences only after the 'general rules' are known.

9.1.1. Limitations of the programs with regard to dysfunctions

Following the arguments presented above, it would appear quite plausible to design attributional training programs that address additional dysfunctional behaviors for which general rules and interindividual differences in the use of attributions have been established. However, the attributional training studies that have been conducted thus far have only addressed a small segment of the phenomena which meet the requirements that are needed before attributional changes can be attempted; that is, lack of persistence and underachievement. However, attributional research has dealt with numerous additional phenomena that are clinically relevant; especially depression, anxiety, anger, and loneliness (see Chapters 6 and 7). For instance, research that has been conducted to test hypotheses derived from the attributional analysis of learned helplessness and depression as advocated by Abramson et al. (1978; Chapter 6) suggests that individuals react with depressive affects when they attribute failure to internal, global, and stable causal elements (a finding from general psychology). Correlational studies have also demonstrated (see, for a summary, Peterson and Seligman, 1984) that depressive persons tend to explain their failure with internal, stable, and global factors to a greater extent than their non-depressed peers (a finding concerning interindividual differences). Hence, it would appear quite reasonable to design attributional retraining programs that would attempt to change depressives' attributions (for failure) from internal, stable, and global to external, variable, and specific.

With regard to a different affect, namely anger, Weiner, et al. (1982) have reported that this emotional state is triggered in situations when attributions for the negative behaviors of others are made to factors that are controllable by the other (a general psychological finding). For instance, one tends to get angry about a person being late for an appointment (event) when one believes that they did not try to be on time (attribution to a controllable cause). However, different emotional states will probably arise when the negative event is attributed to factors that are beyond the other person's control. For example, if we believe that the other person did not show up on time because they had an accident, we would tend to experience pity and concern.

Guided by this general psychological finding, Försterling (1984) looked for corresponding interindividual differences in the attributions of persons who differ in their proneness to anger. It was found that individuals who had high scores on an anger questionnaire also tended to attribute the potentially anger-provoking events described in an attributional style questionnaire (e.g., one fails to reach the bus on time) to external and controllable causes (e.g., that the bus driver did not feel like waiting) to a greater extent than persons with low anger scores.

These findings provide the necessary data and requirements for designing attributional retraining methods to modify inappropriate anger reactions. Analogous to the attributional retraining methods that have been described in Chapter 8, such programs would select subjects who suffer from excessive anger and would teach them to make fewer controllable attributions for the undesired behaviors of others. An 'attribution therapy' for anger problems would be concerned with different types of events and different types of attributional changes than the training methods that were described in Chapter 8. The behaviors of other persons (and not successes and failures of the own person) would constitute the relevant events, and the attributional changes that would need to be attempted would not consist of teaching subjects to reduce attributions of failure to low ability in favor of ascriptions to effort. From an attributional perspective, individuals who suffer from excessive anger would need to be taught to make fewer attributions to controllable factors for the negative behavior of others.

9.1.2. Limitations of the programs with regard to the effects

Research that is concerned with the investigation of 'therapeutic' attributional changes has only dealt with two classes of events: success and failure (reattribution training) and (negative) internal arousal states (misattribution training). However, as already indicated, one would have to include an additional class of events in order to extend the range of applicability of the attributional change programs to the problems of anger, rage, and aggression. The attributions that appear to be typical for individuals who are prone to experiencing anger do not only differ in their dimensional properties from those that have been found to be characteristic for depressed people. In addition, the angry persons' attributions and the attributions that appear to characterize distressed couples also concern different events; namely, the behavior of other persons and not just their own successes and failures.

Because different emotional reactions and behaviors are linked to attributions about different types of events, it follows that it is not sufficient for therapeutic applications of attributional principles only to ask which attribution or attributional dimension is responsible for certain reactions. In addition, it has to be determined for which classes of effects these attributions are made. It is plausible that reactions following success and failure, such as task persistence following failure or joy about success, are connected to the causal explanation of success and failure. Moreover, reactions to internal arousal or pain will probably be influenced by how one thinks about these phenomena. Whether one feels angry, anxious, or indifferent about a sudden pain or whether one starts stuttering as a response to internal arousal may well be determined by how one explains the pain or the internal arousal. Finally, it can be assumed that behaviors and emotional reactions toward other people largely depend on how we explain and evaluate other's deeds (see also Harvey and Galvin, 1984).

9.2. LIMITATIONS OF THE PROGRAMS WITH REGARD TO ATTRIBUTIONAL DIMENSIONS

As attributional training methods (see Chapter 8) consider different attributions as desirable and worthy of change, the question arises: 'which direction of change leads to the most beneficial results for the participant in the training?'

It has been shown in Chapter 8 that the major goal of reattribution training has been to improve persistence and performance by increasing attributions of failure to lack of effort and by decreasing attributions for failure to lack of ability. By contrast, misattribution training seeks to modify maladaptive behavior by changing attributions for physiological arousal from internal to external. A possible explanation of the inconsistent results of these two different approaches to attributional change may lie in the different dimensional changes that they attempt. It is possible that reattribution training is more effective than misattribution approaches because the changes that misattribution training attempts are primarily on the dimension of locus of control. It may be that changes on the stability and controllability dimensions, which are typically attempted by reattribution trainings, would also be more effective for the problems that are commonly addressed by misattribution training (problems that arise from cognitive interpretations of arousal). When stable causal elements are used to explain negative internal states, it is implied that the negative condition is expected to continue in the future. This anticipation might in turn give rise to resignation and fear, and these emotions could then exacerbate the original symptoms.

The case of a young man who moves into a new apartment might serve as an example. Upon moving into the new home, this individual finds out that he has severe difficulties in falling asleep (effect), and he explains this phenomenon with the fact that there is too much traffic noise (an external attribution). In addition, he believes that he will be unable to change the apartment within the forseeable future (the cause of the insomnia is perceived as stable). This person could now develop anxiety and depression in connection with his assumption that he will not be able to sleep well in the future. On the other hand, his depressed and anxious feelings about the insomnia might be ameliorated if he would change his attribution to an internal, variable, and controllable one; an attributional change which is favored by reattribution training. He could reach the conclusion that his insomnia is due to temporary nervousness that could be overcome by relaxation training. Hence, it is possible that misattribution approaches could be equally effective as reattribution training if they would only aim for attributional changes to internal, variable, and controllable factors instead of changes on the locus dimension (from internal to external).

However, even if the hypothesis that changes to 'variable and controllable' attributions would lead to more effective results than changes from internal to external ones holds for some behavioral and emotional problems, it seems likely that there would be many other problem areas that would require a different direction of attributional change. This has already been demonstrated for the example of rage and anger. However, there seem to be other dysfunctions in addition to excessive anger that would require alternative attributional changes to those suggested by the models that underlie attributional retraining (that is 'away' from lack of ability). It is even conceivable that some dysfunctions are characterized by the absence of attributions to lack of ability, and that, as a consequence, therapy should consist of training the individual to decrease attributions of failure to lack of effort and to increase attributions to lack of ability.

The possibility of a pathology of a concept of high ability has already been pointed out in the literature. (Försterling, 1980a; Försterling and Rudolph, 1988; Janoff-Bullman and Brickman, 1982). It is also easy to find many examples in which the attributional change (away from lack of ability) that is typically attempted in attribution retraining programs does not appear appropriate and might even lead to negative consequences. Individuals who pursue unreasonable (i.e., unrealistically high) goals in the areas of work or social affiliation, overwork themselves, and damage their health, might attribute repeated failures to reach their high goals to a lack of effort. Under certain conditions, for instance, when the objective abilities of the individual are low, this attribution to lack of effort might be extremely dysfunctional, because it might prevent the individual from setting more realistic goals.

Individuals who appear to be prone to heart attacks (Type A personalities) typically set very high goals for themselves, are extremely persistent in the pursuit of these goals, and unwilling to accept that they are unable to attain their level of aspiration without ruining their health. These individuals could benefit from giving up their need (and perceived ability) to control all events in their environment and from accepting the limits of their abilities (see Grimm and Yarnold, 1984). This cognitive change could be the basis of a healthier life style. In addition, manic depressive individuals also appear to overestimate their own abilities during manic states and exhibit the accompanying external variable attributions for failure. This frequently leads to dramatic and unwanted consequences; for instance, they invest all their property in risky enterprises or gambling while believing they have the ability to succeed.

Finally, there is anecdotal evidence that recovery from alcoholism and other drug problems is frequently connected with an acceptance of low abilities and with giving up the belief that one can control one's behavior in all respects. For instance, Alcoholics Anonymous teaches its members that they will never be able to achieve controlled drinking, and it seems that this acceptance is helpful and necessary — at least for many alcoholics — if they are to give up their dysfunctional habit.

9.3.   THE FUNCTIONALITY OF CAUSAL ATTRIBUTIONS

When comparing different maladaptive emotional reactions and behaviors (e.g., lack of persistence, depression, and anger) and the attributional approaches to modify these reactions (e.g., helplessness theory, self-efficacy theory), it becomes evident that an attribution that is considered desirable from one perspective could be considered as the cause of a problem from a different perspective. Sometimes different theoretical positions suggest different attributional changes for identical problems (see Chapter 8). According to the attributional reformulation of learned helplessness theory (Abramson et al., 1978), it would be quite logical to teach a client who is depressed about a failure at school because he attributes this failure to his lack of intelligence (internal, stable, and global) to change this attribution to an external, variable, and specific one, such as the moodiness of the teacher. However, according to the attributional analysis of the emotions of rage and anger, it would be expected that the client might very well become less depressed, but that these feelings might change to strong emotions of anger and possibly inappropriate rage toward the teacher. These emotions could then interfere with the goal of having a good relationship with the teacher. In the same manner, there also could be negative consequences from teaching our hypothetical student that he failed the test because of lack of effort, a typical change that has been attempted in attributional retraining programs. This attributional intervention might cause the student to feel guilty about not having tried hard enough, and thus only add a new aspect to his depression.

The uncertainty about the conditions which dictate when a specific attribution is desirable and when a causal ascription is worthy of change can possibly be traced back to the fact that attributional retraining programs have mostly been guided by the attempt to reduce a certain problematic behavior (e.g., lack of persistence). However, they have not fully analyzed the behavioral and emotional consequences of the 'new' attributions. It was assumed that the target reactions, for instance, lack of persistence, depression, and anger, would be reduced in frequency or intensity when the causal thoughts that presumably triggered these reactions were changed. It was apparently neglected that these attributional interventions could result in 'new' attributions which in turn might also trigger reactions such as guilt or anger, which could have other negative consequences for the individual.

In order to conceptualize other clinical problems in addition to lack of persistence and depression within an attributional framework and in order to design attributional retraining interventions for these dysfunctions, a theoretical model is needed to predict under which conditions a certain attributional change is desirable and when it is not desirable. Thus far, applications of attributional principles to clinical problems, such as attributional retraining methods or the learned helplessness model, have based the decision as to whether or not a causal explanation is worth changing entirely on the behavioral and emotional consequences that the causal ascription leads to. An attribution was labelled as worthy of change when it led to certain reactions — such as lack of persistence, anger, or depression —that were defined a priori as maladaptive. With this emphasis on the behavioral and emotional consequences of attributions, these approaches are entirely based on attributional models (C → R). However, the strategy of determining the appropriateness of an attribution in a given situation on the basis of its consequences violates the basic premise of attribution theories that are concerned with the formation of causal perceptions. These theoretical conceptions are based on the assumption that antecedent information about covariation determines the attribution that an individual selects in a given situation. Behavioral and emotional consequences only play a very minor role in the formation of attributions in these approaches.

In addition, attribution theories have also postulated that individuals are motivated to (and generally will) arrive at realistic causal judgments that reflect the available (salient) antecedent information about covariation, and that realistic attributions lead to functional behaviors (see Chapter 2). In fact, this assumption distinguishes attribution theory and attributional models from other psychological theories in that they emphasize the rational aspects of human thought and behavior and deemphasize hedonistic mechanisms (see Weiner, 1980a, 1986).

It follows from the previous arguments that a more comprehensive application of the premises of attribution theory to questions of clinical psychology and behavior modification should be based on the assumption that realistic attributions generally (however, not necessarily always) lead to functional reactions. Hence, attributional interventions should be guided by helping clients to make correct attributions. Whether attributions are veridical or not, however, cannot be determined through their emotional and/or behavioral consequences. The fact that one is afraid of a person and therefore runs away from this person certainly does not prove that the person has the intention to do us harm. In order to decide whether the person has negative intentions or not, we would need to examine how the person has behaved in the past and how they are behaving now. That is, in order to determine the veridicality of an attribution, we would have to look at the antecedent conditions of this attribution (e.g., the other person's past behaviors) and not at the reactions that the attribution causes (our anxiety and running away).

9.3.1. The processing of antecedent information as a precondition for realistic attributions and functional reactions

We now wish to broaden the perspective with which considerations from attribution theory are applied to problems in clinical psychology by linking models concerning the role of antecedent information for the formation of attributions ($S \rightarrow C$) to models that are concerned with the behavioral and emotional consequences of causal ascriptions ($C \rightarrow R$). To do this, we take up the basic assumption of attribution theories that states that individuals are motivated to develop an accurate view of the causal structure of events, and that they generally wish to be exactly informed about their personal attributes and abilities. In addition, we adopt the premise of attribution theory that attributions have a high functional value for the individual and should therefore lead to situationally appropriate behaviors and emotions. In other words, attributions should give rise to actions and feelings that are effective for the realization of important goals and survival (see Chapter 2).

From the premises that: (1) individuals tend to make realistic attributions, and (2) that attributions should lead to functional reactions; it can be deduced that (a) realistic attributions should generally lead to functional reactions, and (b) unrealistic attributions increase the probability of dysfunctional reactions (see Försterling, 1986). Figure 9.1 presents these hypotheses schematically.

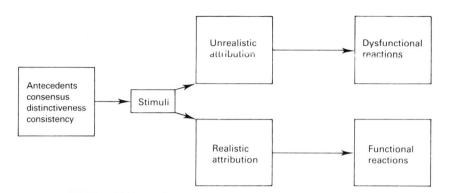

Figure 9.1 Schematic descriptions of the assumed relationship between the veridicality of attributions and the functionality of reactions.

By realistic attributions, we mean those that are neither the product of wishful thinking nor an attempt to gather causes for an event that result in the most positive emotions or reduce negative emotions after failure. Whether or not an attribution is veridical can only be determined from its antecedents. In this connection, we particularily draw upon Kelley's (1967; see Chapter 4) model. We define an attribution as realistic when: 'the effect is attributed to the cause that is present when the effect is present and which is absent when the effect is absent' (Kelley, 1967, p. 22). For instance, if only the individual, x, and no other person (low consensus), fails at a task (effect) at different times (high consistency), and if they also fail at different tasks (low distinctiveness), attributions of failure to stable factors of person x (e.g., lack of ability) can be considered to be quite realistic, because in this example the effect (failure) only covaries with the person and does not covary with the remaining two causal candidates (times and tasks). On the other hand, it would be quite unrealistic to attribute the effect (failure) to the characteristics of the task, as the effect is often absent (for instance, other people do not fail at the task) when this causal candidate is present. However, when failure covaries with the specific task (the person only fails at this specific task and succeeds at others, high distinctiveness) and not with a specific person (everybody fails at this task, high concensus) or points in time (they always fail at this task, high consistency), task difficulty attributions would appear realistic and attributions to lack of ability would be unrealistic. Note, however, that this definition does not imply that information about consensus, distinctiveness, and consistency always leads to clear decisions about the causes of an event (see also Chapter 4), and that there are no other informational categories that might determine whether an attribution is realistic or not.

Let us now consider different reactions that might occur in these two situations that are characterized by different covariational structures.

Attributional research has demonstrated that attributions of failure to stable properties of the self lead to feelings of resignation and to giving up the expenditure of effort on the respective task, whereas attributing failure to external (unstable) causes can give rise to feelings of anger and to persistence (Weiner, 1985b, 1986). An integration of attribution and attributional research that is based on the assumption that it is functional to make realistic attributions would predict that either of the two attributionally guided reactions (giving up or persistence) is only functional when the attribution that 'triggers' the behavior realistically reflects the antecedent information about the situation in which it occurs. That is, being angry and persistent will be functional when failure covaries with the (changing) task that has been assigned by a teacher (and not stable aspects of the self), and giving up will only be functional when failure covaries with stable aspects of the person (and not the changing task). In contrast, it should be dysfunctional to give up when failure clearly covaries with a (changing) task and to keep on trying when failure is caused by a stable cause.

The assumptions that are depicted in Figure 9.1 and that have been illustrated by the example of the students who reacted to exams have already been articulated by Heider (1958). Heider also appeared to believe that there is a relationship between the processing of antecedent information, the resulting attributions, and the functionality of the reactions that are guided by these attributions. He gave the following example 'A man walks in a valley and notices that stones hit the ground in his vicinity. He comes to the conclusion that another individual is intentionally trying to hurt him, gets angry, and defends himself. We can now ask what might have been the antecedent information for this man, who walks in the valley, in order to come to the conclusion that the stones were thrown at him by a person who has the bad intention of hurting him.'

Heider (1958; Chapter 3) suggests that a person's behavior is attributed to his intentions when there is equifinality, that is, when the person uses different means under different situations (variability of means) to always reach the same goals (invariance of the goal). (In Kelley's terms, the behavior would occur with high consistency over times and modalities, and it would be highly distinct.) In our example, we would talk about invariance of the goal when the stones were only directed at the man — regardless of his position —and at no other person or object. Moreover, variability of means would be inferred when different methods were used to direct the stones at our character as a function of the different situations or positions he adopted (for instance, stones could be thrown, pushed, or misdirected).

Furthermore, attributional research has specified that attributions of negative events to factors that can be controlled by other persons give rise to the emotion of anger. The character in Heider's hypothetical situation clearly traced back the falling of the stones to such controllable aspects within another person: Because of the information about the invariance of the goal and the variability of the means, he came to the conclusion that stones were thrown at him intentionally and had not just fallen by chance. Finally, research in the area of human emotions (see Averill, 1983; Izard, 1977) has demonstrated that the emotion of anger activates the individual and serves their self-defence.

In the situation presented in Heider's example, the emotion of anger appears to be a very helpful and functional reaction that is triggered by the (realistic) cognitive analysis of the situation. However, suppose the present situation is not characterized by equifinality and controllability, and the man only accidentally got caught up in a landslide. In this case, attributions to controllable factors, the resulting anger emotions, and looking for an aggressor would be extremely dysfunctional for our individual because: 'I can get out of the danger area and get shelter. The stones will not change their paths in order to find me behind the shelter' (Heider, 1958, p. 101).

This example once more illustrates that the precise processing of available information (equifinality) leads to realistic causal attributions (ascriptions to intentions). These attributions, in turn, give rise to reactions (anger) that may be extremely functional for the individual in the given situation (see Figure 9.1). It also demonstrates again that the appropriateness of a specific reaction largely depends on the situation in which it occurs.

Heider's example can also be used to illustrate the implication of Figure 9.1 that unrealistic attributions increase the probability of dysfunctional reactions (this is the reverse conclusion to the premise that realistic attributions generally lead to functional reactions). Suppose, in our hypothetical story about the man who walks in the valley, that the stones had not been thrown intentionally at him by an individual but were, instead, caused by a landslide. In this case, attributions to controllable factors and the resulting. emotions (anger) and behaviors (defending oneself against an aggressor) would not be functional or helpful for the individual. A person who fails to search for shelter during a landslide and, instead, spends their time looking for an aggressor (who does not exist) has probably reduced chances of survival. In the same manner, however, it would also be dysfunctional not to experience anger and to ignore the dangers of an attack when there is equifinality in a given situation.

9.3.2. Realistic attributions, functional reactions, and clinical problems

Obviously, different emotional and behavioral reactions are functional in different situational contexts. This also implies that 'maladaptive' emotions do not always necessarily have to be negative ones such as anger, depression, or anxiety. In certain situations, positive emotions can also be inappropriate or maladaptive; for instance, when a person reacts with joy to an unwanted failure at an important task or when someone experiences pride after success at a task of chance (for instance a lottery) and subsequently anticipates future success at this task. In the same manner, the absence of negative emotions can also be dysfunctional according to our present framework, for instance, when a person does not fear an objectively dangerous situation and behaves as if the situation were not dangerous at all.

The present arguments should have demonstrated that it is not reasonable to define certain reactions *a priori* as maladaptive or inappropriate. Only when an individual who is in a situation that calls for a certain attribution (C_1) (e.g., there is neither equifinality nor variability of means, and attributions to uncontrollable factors would follow logically) behaves as if another attribution (C_2) would be veridical (e.g., attributions to bad intentions which would lead to anger and which would prevent the individual from looking for shelter) would it be reasonable to label these reactions as 'inappropriate'.

It is not difficult to find further examples which demonstrate that realistic attributions lead to favorable reactions in the long run, whereas the attributional changes (namely, away from lack of ability) that have been favored by attributional change attempts thus far (see Chapter 8) might have disadvantageous consequences for the individual when they are unrealistic. Unrealistic (under- or over-) estimations of one's attributes can lead to an over- or underestimation of the dangers that are involved in a situation. Suppose one were to overestimate one's own knowledge, ability, and available strategies with regard to traffic situations: Reckless driving can easily lead to accidents, injuries, and even death. On the other hand, unrealistically low estimations of one's abilities possibly can cause the individual to choose tasks that are too easy and therefore lack challenge (see Meyer, 1983, 1984). This, in turn could possibly lead to discontentment because the individual does not fulfil their potential.

However, in the short term, unrealistic attributions may well help to decrease negative emotional reactions following unwanted events as well as to increase positive emotional reactions following successes. Many attribution theorists have suggested that (unrealistic) attributions of failure to external factors and of success to internal ones have positive affective consequences (see, for a critical summary, Ross, 1977). However, Carlston and Shovar (1983) provide data that suggest that individuals who exhibit this 'hedonic motivational bias' have to expect immediate negative reactions from others; observers perceived them as less likable and less modest than stimulus persons who attributed failure internally and success externally. Hence, hedonic misattribution might have some short-range positive but also negative consequences.

A recent empirical study that investigated how subjects perceive and evaluate stimulus persons who attribute failures realistically and unrealistic-ally, (Försterling and Rudolph, 1988) yielded results in favor of the hypothesis that realistic attributions render positive consequences. These authors described a character who failed at an exam and indicated that this failure had occurred under antecedent conditions (consensus, consistency, and distinctiveness; according to Kelley) that typically should lead to person or circumstance attributions respectively. Cross-cutting these two experimental conditions, subjects were furthermore informed whether the stimulus person attributed failure to circumstance or to personal factors. Hence, attributions to both causes were realistic in one condition and unrealistic in the other. Consistent with the assumptions presented in Figure 9.1, subjects indicated that they perceived stimulus persons who made realistic attributions as more likely to be successful in the long run, more likable, and more successful in social situations than those who made unrealistic attributions.

Within the field of clinical psychology, we can find further examples for the assumption that 'hedonic' attributions result in negative long-term consequences when they are unrealistic (see also Chapter 7). Patients who recover from heart attacks might benefit highly from the insight that they were themselves partially responsible for the state of their health, and they might learn that giving up dysfunctional habits such as overeating or smoking and other changes in the way they structure their lives would positively influence their well-being in the long run. It probably would not be very helpful for these individuals to insist on the assumption (which might be favored by misattribution trainings) that external causes (such as a demanding environment) were responsible for their health problems, although these (external) attributions might well prevent these patients from feeling guilty about not having exercised or about having overeaten in the past.

In the same way, a person suffering from manic depressive episodes may also profit from the insight that their mood swings are — at least in part —determined by biological (and not external, environmental) factors. This attribution might form the basis for them to allow others to protect them during the manic phase and could also help the individual to maintain self-acceptance and to avoid feelings of guilt when the manic phase is over.

Both the assumptions that are presented in Figure 9.1 and the arguments presented in this chapter are based on the premise that cognitions influence or determine emotions in a sensible and functional manner. These assumptions are in opposition to psychological traditions which consider that the relationship between emotions (emotio) and cognitions (ratio) can best be characterized as an eternal conflict (see, for example, Dewey, 1895). By contrast, the hypotheses presented here are based on the premise that there is not a discrepancy between thoughts and feelings, but that there is 'reason in emotion' (see Ellis, 1962; Zimmer, 1981). Thoughts and feelings are conceptualized as distinctively different entities that are related to each other in a highly functional manner. Tomkins (1962, p. 112) neatly describes these assumptions as follows: 'Out of the marriage of reason with emotions there issues clarity with passion. Reason without emotion would be impotent, emotion without reason would be blind'.

Similar assumptions about the relationships between thoughts and feelings can be found within the schools of humanistic psychology. Maslow (1954), for instance, postulates that connotative, cognitive, and affective processes are —for the healthy person — well coordinated rather than antagonistic processes.

In summary the arguments presented in this chapter suggest that therapeutic, clinical applications of attributional principles in general and attributional retraining in particular should attempt to foster functional emotional and behavioral reactions by altering unrealistic attributions to realistic ones. In order to determine which attributions are realistic and which are not, models about the antecedents of attributions can be used (see Chapter 10). The following examples describe clinical cases in which it has been documented that changes from unrealistic to realistic attributions can cause therapeutic changes.

Example, 1.   Attributional changes from external, variable, uncontrollable to internal, variable, controllable for a causal explanation for an inner state (from Davison, 1966; quoted in Brehm, 1976)

A 44-year-old client who had been diagnosed as schizophrenic complained about pressure sensations above his right eye. He insisted that these sensations were caused by a ghost (an external, uncontrollable attribution). The therapist suggested that a different attribution might be responsible for his complaints. He taught the client that the sensations above his eye covaried with feelings of tension that he was experiencing; they became stronger when the client felt tense and they disappeared when he felt more relaxed. As a consequence, the client started to attribute the uncomfortable sensations to his own tensions (an internal, and partially controllable factor) instead of a ghost. Subsequently, the client felt relieved to have a 'completely normal' explanation for his 'problem'.

Example 2.   Attributional change for an interpersonal failure from internal, global, stable to external, specific, variable

A female client who started to feel anxious and depressed after she was left by her partner (social failure) began to avoid social contacts and, as a result, felt lonely. An analysis of her explanations of the fact that her partner had left her revealed that she attributed this 'social failure' to an internal, global, and stable factor; she said that she was convinced that she was entirely unable to maintain social relationships. In addition, she agreed with the therapist's analysis that her anxious and depressed feelings and her avoidance of social situations were caused by this attribution.

A systematic analysis of the attributionally relevant (covariation) information indicated that her causal conclusion did not find much support. Firstly, she realized that many other persons had been left by their partners (consensus information). Secondly, she came to the conclusion that she was more successful in many other relationships (distinctiveness information). Finally, there were no indications that she would be left by every partner she would have a relationship with (consistency information). The client agreed that this pattern of information clearly did not support her causal hypothesis, and that an attribution to 'circumstances', 'chance', or the characteristics of the former partner would be equally plausible.

This attributional change helped the client to feel less depressed and anxious about the fact that her partner had left her. She also came to the conclusion that she might do better in relationships with other men, and therefore started to devote more time to social activities.

In the following chapter, we will present additional examples of how attributional principles can be implemented in therapeutic practice.

Chapter 10

Therapeutic Interventions Derived from Attribution Theory

So far, we have applied attributional conceptions mostly to theory-related questions in clinical psychology. In the present chapter, we will extend our considerations to aspects of clinical and therapeutic *practice*. First, we will describe Beck's Cognitive Therapy (Beck, 1976; Beck, Rush, Shaw, and Emery, 1979) and Rational-Emotive Therapy (RET) as introduced by Ellis (1962, Ellis and Grieger, 1977; Wessler and Wessler, 1980) in order to then show that attributional analyses of clinical phenomena show strong similarities to those of cognitive therapies, and that cognitive therapy theories can be supported and enriched by attribution research.

10.1. FOUNDATIONS OF COGNITIVE APPROACHES TO THERAPY

During the 1950s, the psychiatrist Aaron T. Beck and the clinical psychologist Albert Ellis independently developed cognitive therapy procedures. Both authors, who had previously worked with psychoanalytic methods, postulated that neurotic disorders such as anxiety and depression do not arise directly because of external stimuli, but depend on how these stimuli are processed and evaluated. In their analysis of cognitive processes that lead to neurotic disorders, both authors took completely different paths. Beck concentrated on the empirical analysis of the cognitions of patients suffering from reactive depression, while Ellis related a wide range of 'maladaptive' emotions and behaviors to principles that had been introduced by different schools of philosophy (the Stoics, Bertrand Russell), and did not restrict himself to a particular form of disorder. He takes up the basic ideas of Epictetus (see edition 1984) and Marc Aurel (see edition 1937), who proposed that, 'Men are disturbed not by things but by the views they take of them' (see Ellis, 1962, p.54).

Despite their different ways of analyzing the cognitive processes that underlie dysfunctional responses, both Beck and Ellis arrive at similar conclusions. They assume that neurotic states arise through and are maintained by biased, unrealistic, 'antiempirical' (Beck), or so-called 'irrational' (Ellis) thoughts. These dysfunctional cognitions are supposed to depend on a lack of information or the unscientific, inexact, or illogical processing of information. Thus the goal of therapy is to analyze the unrealistic and irrational cognitions 'scientifically', and to suggest realistic or rational thoughts to the individual that will lead to functional responses.

10.1.1.   Beck's cognitive therapy

In his analysis of the cognitive determinants and consequences of reactive depression, Beck (1967, 1976) uses the following constructs: the cognitive triad, cognitive schemata, and faulty information processing. By 'cognitive triad', he means that tendency of depressives to carry out unrealistic negative observations of their own person, the situation, and the future. The self is regarded to be inadequate and worthless (e.g., 'I'm a failure'), the situation and the environment are perceived to be unfair and bad (e.g., 'Everything is terrible'), and the future is interpreted as being unalterably negative (e.g., 'Everything is hopeless').

Beck uses the concept of the cognitive schema to explain the fact that depressives maintain this unrealistic view of their own person, the situation, and the future despite contradictory positive information. Under cognitive schema, he understands relatively stable cognitive representations of previous experiences (e.g., the conviction that one has to perform exceptionally well if one wants to be liked by other people) that cause environmental information to be processed erroneously and in a way that generally disfavors the depressive. These inflexible cognitive schemata then give rise to systematic thinking errors or erroneous information processing, and this leads to the maintenance of the cognitive triad and the cognitive schemata. Examples of erroneous information processing are the reduction of complex affairs to black-and-white terms, in other words, the tendency to think in extremes ('My work is either completely good or absolutely bad') or 'overgeneralization', that means, global negative consequences are drawn from specific single events ('The fact that my fellow worker doesn't like me shows that I don't have any real friends'). Arbitrary inferences — a further thinking error of depressives — describes the tendency to extract single aspects from events and then to draw a negative conclusion ('Because my boss was unfriendly to me today he must be planning to fire me').

10.1.2.   The theory of rational-emotive therapy (RET) developed by Ellis

Unlike Beck, who is mainly interested in the cognitive aspects of depression, Ellis (1962; Ellis and Grieger, 1977) is concerned with the identification of beliefs that lead to a wide range of different psychopathological ('maladaptive') responses. These include anxiety, excessive anger responses, marital problems, and achievement disorders. He takes the view that dysfunctional emotions and behaviors are determined by so-called 'irrational beliefs'. By 'irrational', Ellis understands absolutistic, rigid evaluative rules or premises such as the assumption that it is not only extremely desirable to be competent and capable of high achievement, but that *it is absolutely necessary*. Another example is that because a person feels that it is very important to have satisfactory social relationships, they again consider that they are *absolutely necessary*. These irrational cognitions (e.g., 'I absolutely must or should be competent') show certain similarities to Beck's cognitive schemata. These are also relatively permanent cognitive structures that are rigidly maintained despite conflicting information and are not adjusted to fit new observations.

Ellis further assumes that irrational premises are accompanied by a number of unrealistic conclusions (see Försterling, 1980c, 1983). If a person thinks about important goals in an irrational manner (e.g., 'I really must be successful at my work'), they will tend to regard a non-attainment of such a goal as being 'disastrous' and 'terrible' (and not just as being very unpleasant). Furthermore, 'irrational philosophies' are supposed to lead to doubts about the value of the self and a low frustration tolerance. Self-worth problems can arise if the personal evaluation or the self-definition are made on the basis of single events or performances (e.g., 'This failure shows that I'm a loser'). A low frustration tolerance means that the significance and consequences of unpleasant events are unrealistically strongly weighted (e.g., 'Because failures are unpleasant, I cannot cope with failure'). These derivations are again similar to Beck's cognitive triad, as they also concern negative aspects of the person, the situation, and the future.

As already implied, Ellis contrasts irrational thoughts that lead to dysfunctional responses with so-called 'rational' cognitions which are supposed to result in appropriate (functional) emotions and behavior. According to Ellis, rational cognitions are subjective preferences (e.g., 'I would like to be successful and have satisfactory social relationships') and not absolutistic demands as is characteristic for irrational thoughts. Furthermore, rational thoughts should be characterized by recognitions of reality (e.g., 'It would certainly be nice if I was treated fairly at work, but at the moment they are not treating me fairly'), and, unlike irrational thoughts, they are not rigidly maintained across changing conditions (e.g., 'Because I *have to be* treated fairly, person x cannot be unfair'). If we evaluate an important goal rationally, we should, according to RET, arrive at realistic conclusions when we do not achieve our goal and desires remain unfulfilled. This means, for example, that failures are regarded as being unpleasant and disappointing but not as the end of the world, that abilities are estimated realistically and not evaluated globally as being negative, and that although the consequences of failure are certainly regarded as being disturbing, they are not considered to be unbearable.

Like Beck, who regards the cognitions that lead to depression as being false perceptions of reality or thinking errors and therefore as violations of the scientific processing of data and logical inference, Ellis does not just base his definition of irrationality and rationality on semantic aspects (e.g., 'must' as opposed to 'would perfer to'). It is characteristic for irrational thoughts that they are rigidly maintained despite conflicting data and not subjected to scientific testing. According to Ellis, irrational cognitions take the status of dogmatic, absolutistic statements that — rather like Beck's schemata — are inflexible and maintained in the face of contradictory experiences and observations. This includes, for example, the conviction that failure is unbearable (although the individual may continually experience failure and has thus proved that it is in no way unbearable to be unsuccessful). In contrast, rational thoughts have the status of hypotheses. Whether the hypothesis is 'correct' or 'incorrect' is not decisive for the definition of 'rationality'; what is important is that it is tested. According to RET theory, rational cognitions are evaluative hypotheses that are maintained as long as they agree with observations and experiences (e.g., an individual's assumption that it is pleasant and therefore desirable and important to be professionally successful), but which are revised or relativized in the presence of conflicting data (e.g., after retirement, it might be more pleasant and therefore more important for this individual to have a beautiful garden than to be professionally successful, as to carry on in professional life would be too exhausting).

10.1.3. The relationship between cognitions and emotions in cognitive therapy models

According to Beck, unrealistic cognitions can lead to maladaptive emotions (especially depression) and behavioral deficits. In contrast, realistic thoughts about oneself, the situation, and the future accompany appropriate responses. Similarly, Ellis assumes that rational and irrational cognitions determine different emotional states and forms of behavior. Irrational thoughts about an important goal are supposed to trigger disproportionately strong affects that may prevent individuals from attaining their goals (e.g., anxiety) or prevent them from adequately coping with failures (e.g., depression or excessive anger). RET assumes that rational cognitions lead to emotions that help the individual to achieve important goals (e.g., suitable concern or fear should activate the individual to defend themselves from dangers) or help them to cope adequately with failures (e.g., by experiencing disappointment and sadness and consequently communicating to one's companions that one is very upset by a loss).

Both Beck and Ellis assume that the modification of unrealistic cognitions can be carried out through a 'scientific' testing of these thoughts. In Beck's therapy, for example, clients are assigned 'homework' in order to collect 'data' with which to test their dysfunctional thoughts. In addition, cognitive therapy analyzes whether the conclusions that clients draw from their observations are logical or not. In RET, the therapist should carry out a Socratic dialogue with the client in order to analyze the irrational thoughts that lead to inappropriate emotions. In addition, behavioral exercises are developed with the clients in order to collect counterproofs to the irrational beliefs; for example, to do exactly that which an individual believes (falsely) themselves to be unable to do, or to go without things that the individual thinks they must have.

10.2. SHARED FEATURES OF COGNITIVE THERAPY THEORIES AND ATTRIBUTIONAL MODELS

The cognitive therapy models described above reveal that, in important points, they share many features with attributional analyses of clinical phenomena (see Försterling, 1986; Chapter 9). Both approaches are concerned with cognitive models of human behavior and emotions (see Chapter 2); it is not stimuli but their cognitive processing that guide behavior and emotions. Furthermore, both attribution theory and the cognitive clinical approach assume that unrealistic and biased cognitions may lead to dysfunctional responses, while realistic 'scientific' thoughts have functional consequences that enable an individual to have an appropriate interaction with the environmental actualitites (see also Chapter 2).

According to attribution theory, veridical cognitions (attributions) about the causes of events are arrived at by using a 'scientific method' (the covariation principle). In cognitive therapy, it is exactly this method that is applied to analyze, test, and revise unrealistic cognitions, and to encourage rational and realistic thoughts. At a later stage in the present chapter we will show that the therapeutic interventions of Cognitive Therapy and RET can be largely described and explained by the covariation principle.

As well as sharing basic assumptions, attribution approaches and cognitive therapies also address similar areas of research (forms of disorder). Both attribution research and cognitive therapy theories analyze the cognitive determinants of *neurotic* states, for example, anxiety, anger, or feelings of guilt, and not the determinants of *psychotic illnesses*. Among the neurotic disorders, reactive depression has been investigated most thoroughly in all models. Beck, Ellis, and attributional analyses arrive at matching statements on the cognitions that lead to depressive moods (see also Seligman, 1981). The cognitive triad that Beck considers to be responsible for reactive depression, in which the depressive perceives their person, environment, and future negatively, has the same meaning as the tendency to make internal, stable, and global attributions for failure. The tendency of depressives to make internal attributions for failure is characteristic for their negative view of themselves; the stability of the attributions for failures causes the future to also be perceived as hopelessly negative, and the globality of their causal thinking reflects the fact that they regard many aspects of their situation negatively. Ellis similarly postulates that depressives regard themselves as failures and consider that they will not be able to master and cope with their difficulties in the future.

Cognitive therapies and attributional models not only show similarities in their analysis of the cognitive content of reactive depression, but also arrive at matching statements about other emotional states; for example, Ellis and Abrahms (1978) point out that individuals who are either frequently or inappropriately excessively angry often attribute (unrealistically) harmful intent to other persons (external, controllable attributions). As a consequence, RET attempts to clarify the situative determinants of other persons' behaviors to such clients (external, uncontrollable attributions), by, for example, instructing them to adopt other persons' perspectives. The similarities between the attributional analysis of learned helplessness and depression and the analysis of this disorder by cognitive therapy theories caused Seligman (1981) to consider that cognitive therapies can be completely treated within an attributional framework:

> Cognitive therapy and indeed cognitive theory, which can be seen as unsystematic and diffuse, receives systematic and parsimonious underpinnings ... cognitive therapy and rational-emotive therapy boil down to a variety of tactics of attribution retraining and resignation trainings. (p. 129)

However, an explanation of the theories and techniques of cognitive therapies that uses the reformulated model of learned helplessness — as assumed by Seligman (1981) — is only applicable to the analysis (and not even the therapy) of reactive depression. For cognitive therapies — and not Seligman — go beyond the thought content of depression and specify the determinants of many further psychological disorders such as anxiety, feelings of guilt and anger (Beck), or sexual dysfunctions, procrastination, and drug dependency (Ellis, 1973; Ellis and Knaus, 1977). Further, a central aspect of cognitive therapy theories is the provision of possibilities for the therapeutic change of cognitions. These are also not specifically derived by Seligman from his model. We consider, in contrast, the ideas presented in Chapter 9, that analyze the phenomena that are addressed by cognitive therapies with attribution theory, to be more promising. They can open up ways to an attributional analysis of further disorders and can be used to derive hypotheses about the formation of and about possibilities of changing dysfunctional thoughts. In the following, I wish to do this by using models of the antecedent conditions of attributions (Kelley, 1967) in order to cast some aspects of the conceptions of cognitive therapies introduced by Beck and Ellis in attributional terms.

10.3. WHEN CAN ATTRIBUTION INTERVENTIONS BE MADE?

Before we concern ourselves with the possibilities of attributional change, we wish to circumscribe when we consider such changes to be of value. Due to the similarities between cognitive therapies and the attributional analyses of clinical phenomena, we assume that attributional interventions can be applied to disorders in which cognitive therapy procedures have proved to be successful. Accordingly, it would seem to be appropriate to investigate the effectiveness of attributional changes in *neurotic disorders* such as reactive depression, phobias, anxiety, addictions, psychosomatic illnesses, and excessive anger. Previous experience has shown that psychotic and neurological or cerebral disorders cannot be treated with cognitive methods (see Ellis, 1962; Beck, 1976). This restriction of the validity of attribution theory to 'neurotic' disorders is also reflected in the choice of clinical phenomena that we have previously analyzed in Chapters 7 and 8, where we also only dealt with neurotic and not psychotic disorders. However, it appears quite probable that there are circumstances when individuals with psychotic symptoms could benefit from cognitive changes (cognitive therapy). This could, for instance, be the case when a psychotic person has a ('secondary') neurotic problem about their psychotic symptoms: Although it cannot be expected that the psychosis could be influenced directly by cognitive methods, it can be expected that any neurotic symptoms accompanying (e.g., depression about having hallucinations) could be ameliorated through cognitive methods.

The first precondition for the use of attributional interventions is therefore — as in other therapies — the presence of a dysfunctional (neurotic) response (see Figure 10.1). The question of when a response is neurotic (dysfunctional or maladaptive) has evoked numerous controversies in the literature and cannot be solved in the present work. We simplify and assume that events that are traditionally the object of investigation of clinical psychology or psychopathology (see Davison and Neale, 1978; Schulte-Tölle, 1975) are actually worth changing. With reference to the basic assumptions presented in Chapters 2 and 9, we can also regard behaviors and affective reactions that prevent an individual from staying alive as long as possible or achieving self-determined goals as being 'inappropriate' from an attributional perspective. In this sense, not only can the 'classical' psychopathological states (e.g., depression and anxiety) be described as maladaptive, but also — under certain conditions — the absence of negative emotions, for example, when somebody who is

Attribution

	Realistic	Unrealistic
Functional	A	B
Dysfunctional	C	D

(Reaction)

Figure 10.1   Preconditions for the use of attributional interventions.

unjustifiably handicapped in their interests by others does not become angry and protect themselves (see Chapter 9).

The responses that would only be worthy of change from an attributional perspective will not be discussed further here as they go beyond the frame of the present work. In our further attempts to relate attributional frameworks to problems in clinical psychology, we shall start with the situation presented in Figure 10.1 in which an individual is suffering from a dysfunctional response that psychopathology has shown to be disadvantageous (requiring therapy; Cases c and d). In order to be able to use attributional interventions, however, an unrealistic attribution must also be present alongside the dysfunctional response (Case d).

For example, a person is suffering from depressive emotions (dysfunctional response) *because* they *unjustifiably* trace a failure back to a lack of ability (unrealistic attribution). As a rule, attributional interventions cannot be justified by unrealistic causal attributions alone (Case b), because unrealistic attributions may often have no negative influence on behavior and emotions. For a person for whom sporting activities are absolutely unimportant, it may well not matter whether they assume that they do not have enough talent or use the false strategy to explain a particular bad performance in sport. As the personal importance is low, this person will not feel depressed after the failure. In fact, there is some evidence that there may be cases when unrealistic attributions could lead to better adaptation than realistic ones. For instance, Taylor (1983) suggests that (breast)-cancer patients who (unrealistically) attribute the occurrence of their cancer to controllable factors may cope better with their disease than those who (more realistically) assume that the cause for their own and other people's cancers are basically still unknown. In the meantime, however, Taylor (1983) points out that unrealistic attributions that might lead to functional reactions are extremely vulnerable to disconfirmation.

For instance, the cancer patient might learn from either experts or literature that their attribution is false.

Under other conditions, however, particular (unrealistic) attributional biases can represent risk factors which, though at present harmless, can lead to future dysfunctional responses (see Abramson *et al.*, 1978). A mother who has no difficulties in raising her children anticipates that possible future difficulties with their upbringing would depend on her inability to raise children properly. Although, under present circumstances, she feels fine, she might well suffer from emotional complaints as soon as difficulties with her children arise (as she would attribute them to her inability). One could suggest to this woman within the framework of 'prevention measures' that variable causes would be responsible for future difficulties in this area. However, changes in attributions in the absence of dysfunctional responses should only be carried out in exceptional circumstances. Otherwise, one would run the risk of deriving techniques from theoretical models as an end in themselves without testing whether they reach the defined goals (an easing of symptoms).

Case c in Figure 10.1 indicates a further context in which attributional change might be problematic. An individual shows dysfunctional responses, becomes somewhat depressed after being diagnosed as being incurably ill, yet makes completely realistic attributions; namely, that the reason for the length of the illness lies within them and will influence many areas of life (internal, stable, global). They subsequently expect to experience lasting negative conditions. In this case, changes in attributions cannot be carried out, unless one wants to lie to the patient and tell them that they are going to get well again so that they will feel better. In this case, therapeutic procedures that do not require the changing of attributions would be more preferable. In fact, there is a literature indicating that under certain conditions, depressives might process negative information more realistically than non-depressives who appear to exhibit a 'self-serving' attributional bias (see Alloy and Abramson, 1979; Alloy and Ahrens, 1987). This has led Alloy and Abramson (1979) to suggest that depressives might be 'sadder but wiser'. Again, attribution therapy based on mechanisms to foster realistic attributions might not be applicable (may not even be desirable) for the attributions of such 'depressives'. Note, however, that there is no indication that mildly depressed college students would consider their state as inappropriate or worth changing (these were the subjects of the respective experiments) and it is also not clear whether a 'total lack' of depressive symptoms is indicative of adequate psychological adaptation (see Chapter 9). Hence, this research does not indicate that the therapy of reactive depression generally needs to involve changing realistic cognitions for unrealistically optimistic ones.

Finally, one naturally does not want to alter attributions when they are realistic and lead to functional behaviors and emotions (see Case a in Figure 10.1).

10.3.1. Diagnostic issues

Before we describe techniques for attributional change, it seems necessary to consider how attributions can be assessed and diagnosed. Although the question of how to gain access to cognitive processes has raised several debates in the literature (see Section 7.2.), we shall largely neglect these theoretical controversies and focus on 'practical possibilities' for the 'attribution therapist' or researcher to assess the causal cognitions of a client or a research subject. Again, these considerations will not be exhaustive, and the reader can refer to several other sources to complement these questions (see, for summaries, Krampen, 1988; Taylor and Fiske, 1981; Weiner, 1986).

Two fields of a range of literature can be used to obtain suggestions about how attributions can be assessed: (1) basic attribution research including attributional retraining studies (see Section 8.7.2.), and (2) the methods described by cognitive and rational-emotive therapists.

When turning to attribution research, we find that the predominant techniques for the assessment of attributions (in research studies) consist of rather simple 'paper and pencil' methods. The majority of attribution experiments use respondent methods, that means, subjects are asked to rate on scales the importance of different attributions that were provided by the experimenter. This procedure is used for hypothetical as well as 'actual' events.

A therapist who wants to find out how a client causally explains an event (for instance a recent social rejection) could proceed in an analogous (respondent) manner. The therapist could present the client with a list of attributions and ask them about the relative importance of each of them (this could be done in writing or orally within an interview). This procedure is simple and economic and has proven helpful in many attribution studies. It has the advantage that the therapist can obtain information about attributions that they believe — according to their theoretical model — to be relevant to the client's problems (i.e., the therapist can 'test' their attributional hypotheses). However, it has several disadvantages. First, the therapist can only present a limited list of attributions which might not include the ones that are important to the client. For instance, the therapist might ask a client whether they attributed a social rejection to their character or to chance. However, the client might attribute the rejection to their looks, an attribution not tapped in the presented list. In addition, this procedure might tempt the client to think of attributions which they normally would not think about, and they may mistakenly agree to the suggestions of the therapist. Hence, attributions gathered with this method might contain artifacts.

A further method used in research is simple open questioning (an operant method). The subject or client is simply asked how they explain an event causally. This method has the advantage that the client's attribution is not an artifact of the attributional choices presented by the clinician. However, it is possible that a client might not 'remember' what they thought in a specific moment while they might have recalled their thoughts if the therapist used a respondent method. In addition, as we have already mentioned in Section 7.2., this procedure has the disadvantage that the client might refer to plausible heuristics — rather then their actual causal explanations — because they have difficulties in accessing the cognitive processes that actually caused their behavior in the respective situation. Finally, this method *forces* individuals to make attributions (just like the respondent methods). Hence, the therapist or researcher using this method might tempt the client to report on cognitive processes that did not take place.

However, there are also ways to assess attributions in a more indirect fashion. For instance, a client can be asked to 'think aloud' about a certain event while being instructed to report 'everything that comes to mind'. Part of the client's reported cognitions might then be recognized as attributions. In the same manner, the client can be instructed to write down what they think in certain problematic situations. Using this method, the therapist can then score these 'thought protocols' for attributional content.

Thinking aloud and the coding of written material (thought protocols) have the advantage of non-reactivity; however, they also have several disadvantages. Again, the client might actually have causal theories about an event but might not be aware of them or might not consider them worth mentioning. Further, the client might report a lot of material that is irrelevant for therapy, and the therapist might spend too much time scoring long protocols in a search for attributional content.

Attributional research has also made use of scales designed to measure generalized attributions, or co-called attributional style questionnaires (see Kammer and Stiensmeier-Pelster, 1988). Again, the clinical psychologist can make use of these questionnaires. For instance, before beginning attribution therapy with a depressed client, the therapist might want to determine whether the client actually has a generalized tendency to attribute failure to internal, stable, and global causal elements, as is suggested by attributional models of depression (see Chapter 6). These scales have the advantage that psychometric analyses are available, and the client's attributional style can, therefore, be compared to social norms. In addition, attributional style questionnaires do not only assess the individual attributions that subjects made for a hypothetical event, but they also assess the dimensional meaning that the attribution has for the client. However, they have the disadvantage that they only concern hypothetical events and do not address the attributions made by a client for a problematic event.

Attribution retraining studies point to an additional possibility for 'diagnosing' attributions; that is, not to diagnose them. Some attribution retraining studies (see Chapter 8) only diagnose the assumed behavioral consequences of a certain attribution and assume that the subject who behaves in a way consistent with that attribution actually cognizes in this manner. Hence, 'therapeutic interventions' are made without reassurance that the target for therapy actually exists. For instance, subjects who easily give up following failure are selected. It is assumed that they give up easily *because* they attribute failure to lack of ability. Consequently, they are trained to attribute failure to causal elements other than ability. Again, attribution therapy can likewise be conducted on the basis of hypotheses derived from attributional research. For instance, the therapist could hypothesize that the client who feels resigned following failure attributes failure to lack of ability, whereas the client who reports feelings of guilt attributes failure to lack of effort.

I will now present some of the methods for diagnosing cognitions that are suggested by Cognitive as well as Rational-Emotive Therapy (see also Kendall and Korgeski, 1979). *In vivo thought sampling*, a client can be asked to record their thoughts in diaries, either with regard to specific events or at random occasions (see also Klinger, 1978). These 'thought-protocols' can then be used in the therapy session in order to analyze them for their attributional content. Although this method is less economic than asking the client what they had thought in a specific situation, it assures that 'actual thoughts' rather than 'recollections of thoughts' are being recorded. However, a possible disadvantage of this method is that the client might list many thoughts that are irrelevant to the problem and hence, time is wasted.

A method that might combine the advantages of verbal report with those of direct questionning is *imagery*. In the session, a client could be instructed to imagine an event relevant to his problems (e.g., approaching a feared object). The therapist could then ask the client specific questions about his attributions in the respective situation.

Although the different techniques described above demonstrate that the attribution therapist has quite a few possibilities at hand for diagnosing causal cognitions (each with its unique advantages and disadvantages), mention should be made of some of the problems in connection with the assessment of attributions. First of all, we have neglected the fact that attributional models make predictions with regard to the behavioral consequences of attributional dimensions rather than the specific attributions. However, most of the measures of attributions described above do not explicitly address causal dimensions. However, recent research has demonstated that there is a high degree of agreement within and between different cultures as to the dimensional placement of different causal attributions (Schuster, Försterling, and Weiner, in press). Hence, the clinician might be quite optimistic that the dimensional meaning that both therapist and his client ascribe to a specific cause is similar. However, there are also coding devices in order to assess the dimensional meaning of individual attributions (see Russell, 1982).

It is probably more significant that we have limited ourselves in this section to the diagnosis of the 'C' within the S-C-R sequence and have neglected the

'S' as well as the 'R'. With regard to the 'R', the clinical attribution researcher would not need specific diagnostic tools other than the ones used in clinical psychology (e.g., the clinical interview; diagnostic instruments such as the Beck Depression Inventory). However, if we want to stay true to our suggestion that the necessity for therapeutic attributional interventions should not only be evaluated on the basis of attributional consequences, we shall also require methods for assessing attributional antecedents (information about covariation). As the gathering of information about attributional antecedents is a central part of the attributional change techniques to be discussed next, we shall not elaborate how to assess attributional antecedents in this section.

10.4. TECHNIQUES FOR CHANGING ATTRIBUTIONS

If the previously discussed preconditions for attributional interventions are fulfilled, we next have to face the question of techniques for the therapeutic alteration of causal attributions. These can be derived from either attribution research or the theory and practice of cognitive therapies. Attribution theories specify the antecedent conditions of causal perceptions (see Chapter 4), and reattribution training describes concrete techniques for altering causal explanations (see Chapter 8). In addition, the literature on cognitive therapies also describes methods for changing cognitions. Through an analysis of these sources, we arrive at three possible ways of changing attributions: (1) Through *information*. Work on the antecedent conditions of attributions suggests that causal attributions can be changed by gathering and reevaluating information. (2) Furthermore, *operant methods, persuasion, and vicarious learning* can be used to induce change, and (3) the studies described in Chapter 4 show possible ways of influencing causal attributions through *indirect communication*.

10.4.1. The alteration of unrealistic causal attributions through information

The basic assumptions of attribution theory (see Chapter 2) suggest that the use of information is the most obvious method for the alteration of attributions. The therapist can attempt to change the client's unrealistic and dysfunctional attributions by — similar to Beck and Ellis — testing them against reality. In order to do this, the therapist can make use of scientific methods comparable to those used for testing a hypothesis in an empirical investigation.

It can be assumed that there are (at least) two possible ways by which individuals arrive at unrealistic attributions. First, the client may not possess important information; in which case 'therapy' must consist in obtaining this information. Second, the client may already know the attributionally relevant data, but make mistakes in the 'analysis' and interpretation. In this case, the client must be taught 'methodological' skills in the processing and interpretation of data. In both cases we again refer to the Kelley model (see Chapter 4) for the further systematization of attribution alterations, and assume that the testing of dysfunctional attributions can be carried out using the informational dimensions 'consensus', 'distinctiveness', and 'consistency'.

Consensus information. Indications of how other persons behave who find themselves in similar situations to the client are important for deciding whether a certain way of responding is due to oneself or due to the situation or circumstances. If, for example, one thinks that one is the only person who suffers from anxiety, sexual problems, or unemployment, one could develop feelings of inferiority or depression *about* one's problem (in the sense of symptom stress). It is often the case that individuals are insufficiently informed about the behavior and experience of others in 'taboo areas' of life such as sexuality and emotionality; perhaps because it is not usual and/or embarrassing to exchange information relevant to these areas. A liberal exchange of information in, for example, self-help groups or therapy groups can encourage persons to change their attributions on the basis of new consensus information. Women who enter therapy groups with the 'problem' that they do not experience 'vaginal orgasms' and consequently consider that they are inferior, are frequently relieved to hear that many other women do not experience orgasm during intercourse (high consensus). This information may lead the woman to no longer make personal deficits responsible for her 'anorgasmy', which may also encourage her to express her sexual desires to her partner. This can, in turn, lead to an improvement in the sexual relationship between the partners.

Naturally, the realization of *low* consensus can also bring about positive attributional and behavioral changes. A mother experiences that few people take such good care of their children as she does and, therefore, decides to use more of her time to pursue her own interests.

Unrealistic attributions that are due to insufficient information can be tested by obtaining consensus information through, for example, telling clients to ask other individuals how they feel and behave in particular situations. Specific therapy groups that are made up of members with similar problems are particularly suitable for the mediation of problem-related consensus information. In a young parent group one can find out that it is not just one's own children who are aggressive but other parents' children as well. In a 'weightwatchers' group one can learn that it is also difficult for other persons but, however, possible to eat less. In a self-help group one can experience that other individuals are also not contented with their relationships with the opposite sex.

Occasionally psychologists and therapists are 'professional' conveyers of consensus information. Clients may well experience relief when the therapist informs them that other people have had similar problems and were able to overcome them. For someone who has emotional difficulties because of a lack of consensus information, it might also be a good suggestion for them to read literature about this particular area of life in order to obtain relevant information (some sex-therapists suggest to their clients that they should read the Hite Report; see Ellis, 1984).

Consistency information concerns the common occurence of an event with different timepoints (consistency across time) and in different situations and circumstances (consistency across modalities). In contrast to consensus data, clients generally have more consistency information about their behavior than the therapist. This is why it is difficult to convey completely new consistency information in therapy that clients can use to change their causal thoughts. For example, a client who wishes to give up smoking may say that they *cannot* give up, and justify this attribution by indicating that they have smoked for several years and in almost all kinds of situations (consistently). They take this as proof that they *cannot* stop smoking.

It might be a goal of therapy to suggest to this client that they *can* stop smoking if they make enough *effort* and is prepared to accept a period of discomfort. In this case, it would be possible to introduce new consistency information by either imagining or practising new situations. Thus in cognitive therapy procedures, smokers who say that they cannot stop smoking are sometimes asked if they could manage to do without cigarettes for one day if they were paid 10000 dollars, or whether they would die if they did not have any cigarettes. The realization that they would not smoke under every single circumstance may suggest to smokers that they previously did not *want* to stop smoking, but they *could* do it if they wanted to.

New consistency information can further be gathered by trying out different kinds of behavior. Someone who believes that they 'cannot' stay alone by themselves (because they have always become anxious when alone) could be assigned the homework of having to do that which they believe they cannot do (e.g., go away on holiday by themselves). In the cognitive therapy for depression, homework is assigned with the goal of collecting new data for personal hypotheses (Beck *et al.*, 1979):

> Repeated successes generally undermine the patient's belief that 'I can't do it'. As the patient continues to master each problem, his attitudes such as, 'I can't do anything' or 'It is all meaningless' are gradually eroded. (p. 134)

Alongside the possiblity of providing a client with new consistency information in therapy by, for example, carrying out experiments, one can also investigate whether available consistency information is being processed realistically. Beck *et al.* (1979) demonstrate the 'thinking error of selective abstraction' (from a series of available information, only one negative piece of information is used to reach a conclusion) with the following example: a female client who had eaten sweets while on a diet arrives at the attribution that she has absolutely no self-control (internal, stable, global). The following therapeutic dialogue is aimed at realistically acknowledging consistency information (see Beck *et al.*, 1979, p. 68):

P: I don't have any self-control at all.
T: On what basis do you say that?
P: Somebody offered me a candy and I couldn't refuse it
T: Were you eating candy every day?
P: No, I just ate it this once.
T: Did you do anything constructive during the past week to adhere your diet?
P: Well, I didn't give in to the temptation to buy candy every time I saw it at the store.... Also, I did not eat any candy except that one time when it was offered to me and I felt I couldn't refuse it.
T: If you counted up the number of times you controlled yourself versus the number of time you give in, what ratio would you get?
P: About 100 to 1.
T: So if you controlled yourself 100 times and did not control yourself just once, would that be a sign that you are weak through and through?
P: I guess not — not through and through (smiles).

In this therapeutic dialogue, the client is shown that she unrealistically weights available consistency information. She makes an attribution as if low consistency was present (that in the past she had not kept to her diet and thus does not possess any ability to control herself), although she had shown the desired behavior with a high consistency (she had generally managed to deny herself sweets) which points to a high self-control ability. An important aspect of cognitive therapy consists of uncovering and correcting such logical thinking errors. Furthermore, Beck and coworkers (1979) consider consistency information with their clients who expressed depressogenic cognitions such as 'Nothing works anymore', or 'Nothing makes me happy'. Between therapy sessions, they let their patients record when they had felt happy and when they had been successful.

Thus, scheduling activities and rating each for mastery and pleasure provides data with which to identify and correct cognitive distortions. (p. 128)

Distinctiveness information refers to the common occurence of effects with similar and dissimilar entities with which an individual interacts. Attributions that lead to dysfunctional behavior can also be tested with distinctiveness information in the same way that consensus and consistency information can be obtained or reevaluated in therapy. For example, a student feels depressed after failing an important class examination because he thinks that he is completely ungifted (internal, stable, global attribution). If we want to replace this global attribution with a specific one (e.g., being ungifted in this particular subject), we can test distinctiveness information.

We could ask whether the student (as a rule) is also unsuccessful in other subjects (low distinctiveness) or is more successful at other tasks (high distinctiveness). High distinctiveness would be inconsistent with his global attribution, and it might help the student if he were to recall that he is more successful in other areas. Such a procedure would be consistent with the practice of cognitive behavior therapy which often assigns the homework of making a list of those areas of life where one can chalk up a success in order to counteract overgeneralizations of negative estimations of a lack of ability after failure.

Distinctiveness information is not always already available as in the previous example but, from time to time, has to be obtained first. A woman without external or premarriage experience of sex is not content with her sexual life and asks herself whether this is due to her or her partner. If she has only had sexual problems with her partner and not with other men (high distinctiveness), her discontent could be explained with either her partner or special circumstances. However, if she had difficulties with other men (low distinctiveness), then an attribution to her own behavior or characteristics would be more realistic.

In this case, it could well be impossible or inappropriate to obtain distinctiveness information as this would mean suggesting to the client that she should make sexual contact with other men. This could in turn lead to difficulties in her present partnership. Under other circumstances, the collection of distinctiveness information would not entail any problems; for example, a man thinks that he is completely worthless because he is professionally unsuccessful and feels depressed. It would probably, without any doubt, be sensible to suggest that he should take up other activities such as hobbies. Success in other areas of life could help him to build up a more positive self-image.

In order to counteract negative self-evaluations after failures, Rational-Emotive Therapy according to Ellis frequently applies a technique with which distinctiveness information that is already available is reevaluated. Clients who label themselves as 'complete' losers after being unsuccessful (global attributions), and as a result experience feelings of inferiority, are shown that they generally use randomly chosen disadvantageous (distinctiveness) information to define themselves and neglect other more positive information. The diagram in Figure 10.2a is sometimes used in RET to demonstrate to the client that they simply enlist one out of many distinctiveness informations when they label themselves a global loser because of one single unsuccessful event. Furthermore, it should show clients that a more differentiated view of

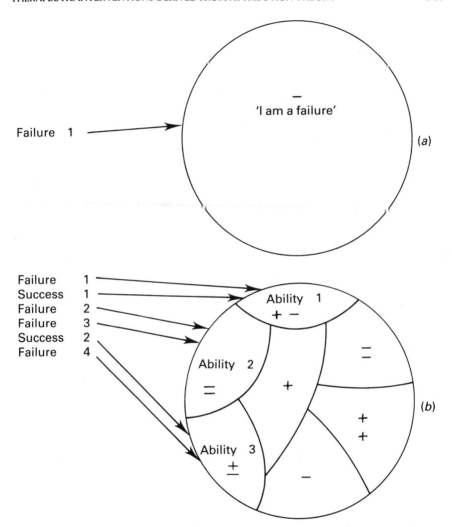

Figure 10.2   Graphic illustration of an overgeneralization (a) and a differentiated (b) evaluation of aspects of the self.

previous successes and failures usually leads to less generalized estimations of personal abilities (Figure 10.2b). Instead of globally labeling themself a loser, it would be more sensible and more realistic for the client to judge their abilities separately across a wide range of different activities.

Similarly, Beck (see Beck *et al.*, 1979) points out that depressives often describe themselves as being 'totally disturbed' (a global attribution for their problems) because they have difficulties in some areas of life. He proposes that the therapist should first of all discuss with the client which areas of life are problematic and which are not (distinctiveness information) in order to relativize the depressive's negative view of their personal situation.

It should be noted here that by using the covariation model from Kelley (1967; see also Chapter 4) it becomes possible to systematize some of the therapeutic interventions of cognitive therapies, and that the model is suitable for the derivation of 'attribution therapy' techniques. Furthermore, it can also be used for the specification of information that can be used to change attributions, and for the specification of new information that has to be obtained and applied, and provides indications for which information is being perceived in a distorted manner or are being falsely weighted. By using the methods of cognitive and behavior therapy, it is then possible to obtain or reassess covariation information in the therapy session.

The following therapy transcript from a Rational-Emotive Therapy Session (taken from Wessler and Wessler, 1980) additionally illustrates the relevance of attributional processes in cognitive therapies and how regular therapeutic interventions within cognitive therapies can be casted in an attributional framework. The dialogue shows how, with the help of the Kelley information (consensus and consistency), an internal and controllable attribution (his own cognitive evaluation of the group) is suggested to a client who sees his problem (speech anxiety) as being caused by external and uncontrollable factors:

T1: Do you know others who are not so anxious in group?
C1: Yes, I guess I do.
T2: Doesn't that indicate that it's not the group but how we view the group that creates anxiety?
C2: It means they've been successful. People like them. They have a lot of confidence. I don't.
T3: Were there times when you weren't so anxious about speaking up in groups?
C3: Yes, when I was in high school.
T4: What is different between now and then?
C4: I guess I wasn't so concerned then about their liking me.
T5: And now you are. You see, then you didn't think of it as being so important, but now you believe it is crucial.
T6: Are there times in group when you don't feel so anxious?
C5: Yes, sometimes it doesn't seem to bother me so much.
T7: Can you think of anything that is different about those times?
C6: Well, sometimes I'm really tired. I say "The hell with it". I just want to go home.
T8: Yes, and you're thinking something else when you are anxious (pp. 74–75).

In this reattribution attempt, the therapist concentrates on testing the consensus and consistency informations that the client has already collected and relating this information to his conclusions. First of all, consensus information is investigated with the therapist's question (T1) whether the client knows other persons who have less anxiety in front of groups than he does. The client states that hardly any other people except him are anxious before groups, in other words, that there is low consensus. This suggests that it is not the group but properties of the client that are responsible for the anxiety (T_2). If the client had maintained the hypothesis that there was high consensus and a lot of people are anxious about speaking in public, one could test this statement by, for example, asking others whether they also suffer from speech anxiety. It emerges that the client attributes other individuals' low anxiety to their high 'self-confidence' (possibly the client regards this attribute to be stable and uncontrollable). In order to analyze the stability of this attribution, the therapist tests consistency information. He asks whether the client always had anxiety in front of groups. This reveals low consistency: At school he was not anxious about talking in front of groups. This suggests that the speech anxiety is not caused by lasting features of the client's personality, because if this was the case, he would also have experienced anxiety in the past. Next (T_4), the therapist asks what had been different about the past, and in this way shows the client that his anxiety covaries with thoughts about others. In order to strengthen this insight, he asks to what extent the client's emotional response is consistent across modalities (T_6), namely, whether there are situations in which he is less anxious. The client replies that he would be less anxious if he assigned less importance to the group (e.g., when he was feeling tired). In this therapy transcript, distinctiveness information is not consulted. However, if the client had expressed that he was 'totally neurotic' (global attribution), it would have indicated that the therapist should ask whether he was only anxious in front of groups (high distinctiveness) or whether he was also anxious in other situations (low distinctiveness).

Variations in the obtaining of information. Sometimes it may be difficult to obtain new information to test unrealistic attributions. It is often not sufficient only to receive relevant data verbally from a professional, and personal changes in behavior are necessary for the 'data collection'. For example, a man is afraid of mice and avoids situations in which he anticipates meeting mice because he assumes that he would be unable to cope with the negative emotions that the sight of a mouse would give rise to. It is possible that, from a cognitive perspective, a 'flooding'-procedure would be the most 'effective' method for bringing about an attributional change. By performing the behavior that the client thinks he cannot show (such as taking a mouse onto the palm of the hand), he obtains an effective counterproof to the dysfunctional attribution (see also Bandura, 1977b). As in the cognitive therapies of Beck and Ellis, therapy interventions that are guided by attribution theory regard such behavioral techniques as a means to the goal of cognitive change and not as the goal itself. Unlike classical behavior therapy in which behavioral change is the actual goal, cognitive approaches stress the informational aspect of behavioral changes. Beck *et al.* (1979) have the following to say on this topic:

> By helping the patient the therapist may demonstrate to the patient that his negative, overgeneralized conclusions were incorrect. Following specific behavior changes, the therapist may show the patient that he has, in fact, not lost the ability to function at his previous level ... (p. 118).

Therapeutic interventions that are guided by attribution theory can pursue two different goals. First, the therapist can attempt to 'reduce' the dysfunctional attributions of clients by collecting information that contradicts these attributions. A highly attractive client feels depressed because she attributes her momentary loneliness to her 'ugliness'. In the therapy one can look for information that suggests to her that she is not unattractive (by 'attacking' her unrealistic attributions). The second possibility, however, would consist in collecting data and information for an alternative attribution by building up a functional one (such as that she has isolated herself socially lately, and this is why she has not made any friends), and not by dismantling a dysfunctional attribution. Perhaps the therapist has sufficient knowledge about the life conditions of the client in order to, for example, put forward the hypothesis that she is at present not placing herself in situations in which she can get to know other persons. She could be assigned the homework of placing herself more frequently in such situations. If she then received more invitations, the 'functional' (situative) attribution would be supported.

In order to come to a decision about the method of change to be used, it is important to know the conditions that lead to unrealistic attributions. Kelley (1967) follows Heider (1958) and suspects that the following mechanisms could lead to unrealistic attributions:

> Like all other perceptual and cognitive systems, attribution processes are subject to error.... (these) errors can be traced to instances in which, *first*, the relevant situation is ignored, *second*, egocentric assumptions are made, *third*, the relevant effects have affective significance for the observer and *fourth*, the surrounding situation is misleading. (p. 219)

These four possibilities will now be illustrated.

(1) If unrealistic attributions are made because relevant information (in a new situation) is ignored, it would be sensible to collect these data. A young college student, for example, has doubts about his ability to complete his course because he needs more time to prepare his work at the university than he did at school. A 'therapeutic' homework in which he had to ask his colleagues at the university for situation-relevant information might be of use to him. This would maybe make him realize that the increased time necessary for preparation is due to the

circumstances at the university and not due to his lack of ability, as probably most of his colleagues will report similar experiences.

(2) Individuals may possess sufficient information for a realistic attribution but draw false conclusions from this data because of, for example, 'egocentric assumptions'. In this case, attribution therapy would not consist in collecting new attribution-relevant information, but must uncover and correct the errors that are produced by 'data interpretation' and analysis (e.g., through egocentric assumptions). For example, if a depressive client is of the opinion that she must be appreciated by *all* people who are important to her in order to feel likable, it could be suggested that probably nobody could attain this goal, and that she can regard the previous affection that she has experienced as sufficient proof of her personal worth.

(3) If, however, emotional (self-enhancing) mechanisms maintain a false attribution, the therapist must reckon with (affective) 'resistances' to the change in attribution. A student who attributes every one of her failures during her university studies to unfair examiners, and thereby fails to try out new preparation strategies, responds with anxiety and anger when the therapist suggests that she is also responsible for her previous failures. Before attribution-relevant information can be collected in this case, the aversive emotional consequences of an internal attribution for own failure must be analyzed and maybe reduced.

One set of antecedents and consequences of the desire to protect the self from (negative) information that is relevant to one's own ability has been outlined by Berglas and Jones (1978; Jones and Berglas, 1978; see also Snyder and Smith, 1982; for a summary) while analyzing so-called self-handicapping strategies. Berglas and Jones (1978) suggest that certain 'undesirable' behaviors and (neurotic) emotional experiences might appear to the actor to have positive implications; for instance, a student who does not sleep the night before taking an exam, or gets drunk or terribly anxious before an exam, or deliberately does not study for it might be creating a self-serving excuse for a potential failure. If the student were to fail, he could readily attribute failure to these external impediments which are unrelated to his abilities and maintain the image that he could pass his exam if he would only try hard enough, or get enough sleep, or if he was less anxious. In addition, the individual would have ample reason to attribute a possible success to especially high ability, because success occurred *in spite of* a 'handicapping' cause (see Kelley, 1973). The active selection of performance-inhibiting settings (i.e., behaviors, emotions, or drugs) in order to protect the self from the negative implications of failure attributed to low ability is called 'self-handicapping'.

Berglas and Jones (1978) suggest that self-handicapping should be especially attractive to individuals who believe that they are relatively high in ability but have severe doubts about the correctness of this judgment. For them, failure might seriously threaten their self-concept (and, the impression they believe to be making on others), and they might, therefore, arrange excuses before attempting a task (use self-handicapping strategies) in order to maintain their high ability perceptions in the face of possible failure.

Individuals who are certain about their either high or low ability estimates, should be much less prone to use self-handicapping. Those who are certain about their (high) abilities would not consider revising their self-concept following failure and hence would not need 'protection' from failure; and individuals with low self perceptions have 'nothing to lose' and will, therefore, feel no need to use self-handicapping.

Berglas and Jones also speculate about the mechanisms that lead individuals to relatively high ability perceptions and high uncertainty about their estimates. They suggest that non-contingent reinforcement might be one of the antecedents of ability percepts that subsequently lead to self-handicapping. Individuals who receive high rewards regardless of their actions, for instance, because of their beauty or because of luck or social status, might believe that they could also have attained this position through own effort and/or ability. However, they cannot be sure that this is so.

In two experiments, Berglas and Jones (1979) found support for their assumption that non-contingent reinforcement can lead individuals to use self-handicapping strategies. Subjects who were praised and reinforced for solutions at unsolvable tasks (non-contingent reinforcement) chose to use self-handicapping (i.e., take a drug that was introduced as interfering with performance in a second stage of the experiment) much more often than subjects who had worked on solvable tasks (contingent reinforcement).

These arguments and empirical findings point to the fact that under certain circumstances, a therapist might need to 'emotionally prepare' a client before they can get them to gather information relevant to their self-attributions.

(4) That misleading information in new situations can lead to dysfunctional responses is reflected in the design of a therapy program for people who are afraid of flying developed by Lufthansa, the West German airline (see Liersch, 1983). It is assumed that persons who are afraid of flying make a series of incorrect attributions and evaluate completely flying procedures, such as the retraction of the landing flaps, as a sign of technical difficulties. Therefore in normal therapy, these individuals

are precisely informed about the different phases of flight, and they learn to identify single noises and to trace these back to 'normal' flight procedures. It is anticipated that fear will decrease when the various stimuli (noises and movements during flight) are more realistically processed and interpreted.

As well as informational methods, operant and vicarious learning techniques can also be used for changing attributions. An individual who spends a lot of time together with persons who suffer from the same problem (e.g., several 'underachievers' who form a leisure-time group) may be positively influenced by persons who are more successful in the corresponding field by adopting their attributions through, for example, model learning. If a client's reference group reinforces the dysfunctional attributions (e.g., parents), attributions may best be modified by using operant methods. In addition, Section 10.4.3. will show that indirect attributional communications from the therapist can also be responsible for the formation and alteration of the client's causal attributions under certain conditions.

10.4.2. Changing attributions through operant methods, persuasion, and vicarious learning

Although the basic premises of attribution theory (see Chapter 2) suggest that the rational scientific testing of dysfunctional attributions with information presents the most obvious method for reattribution, procedures that have less to do with cognitive 'insight processes' can also be used. Not every attribution and attributional change is the product of extensive rational information processing. Causal attributions can also be adopted uncritically from other persons or expressed randomly and maintained through positive consequences. In some reattribution trainings (see Chapter 8), for example, operant methods of attributional change are used with success. Andrews and Debus (1978) induced failure in their subjects and then asked them to express attributions. They verbally reinforced the participants when they expressed the desired causal attributions. Such *operant techniques* can also be used in cognitive therapies by, for example, verbally reinforcing clients when they make the attributions that the therapist wants, or by setting up programs with the clients in which undesired (causal) internal dialogues are followed by negative reinforcement (see also Cautela, 1966; Meichenbaum, 1977).

Reattribution programs (Chapter 8) and clinical practice have shown that *imitation processes* (vicarious learning, see Bandura, 1977a) can also bring out attributional changes. Zoeller *et al.* (1983) found that subjects who had observed a stimulus person who made attributions for the outcome of his action after failing a criterion task subsequently gave similar explanations for their own failures. In the literature on cogntive therapies (see, e.g., Ellis and Grieger, 1977), it is pointed out that the therapist should act as a model for the client by avoiding the verbalization of unrealistic and irrational evaluations during the therapy session (such as to talk about themselves as being a 'complete failure' or a 'complete success'). In the same manner, the 'attribution therapist' should personally make the same causal attributions for a particular situation that they wish to suggest to the client, and, if possible, verbalize them in the therapy session.

As well as the therapist, other individuals who have already positively altered a problematic behavior that the client wishes to work on may also serve as models. The success of self-help groups may well be in part determined by the fact that patients learn functional attributions from other group members. Clients can also be exposed to attribution-relevant information and experiences through various media such as video recordings or literature. The successful application of such technologies has been described by Zoeller *et al.* (1983) and Wilson and Linville (1982, 1985), and it is common practice in cognitive therapies to influence cognitions through 'bibliotherapy' (self-help books) (see, e.g., Ellis and Harper, 1975; Lazarus and Fay, 1976). For example, Waters (1979) produced picture stories for children in which they could learn to make functional causal explanations through models who show suitable cognitions (many of which are attributions).

Furthermore, attributions can also be altered through *persuasion*. It can be suggested to a client who feels depressed after a failure that they can feel better about the failure if it is attributed to external factors. One could explain what is known about the relation between attributions and emotions to this client in order to motivate them to reduce their dysfunctional (attributional) internal dialogues by suggesting that this will soon lead to an improved emotional state. Causal perceptions could also be changed if the therapist verbalizes the desired attribution when the client talks about a relevant event. When clients make undesired attributions (e.g., 'I have been unsuccessful because of my low ability'), the therapist can paraphrase the desired attribution (e.g., 'You didn't make enough effort ...'). When clients know how dysfunctional emotions and responses relate to unrealistic attributions, they can test which consequences accompany realistic attributions. Furthermore, the client can be asked to record causal cognitions between therapy sessions. These recordings can be used to determine when 'disadvantageous' attributions are made, which can also indicate to the client that they should change their internal dialogue.

10.4.3. Changing attributions through indirect communication

Meyer and coworkers (see Chapter 4), as well as clinical practice, have shown that the opinions of other persons about the causes of an event can also influence the attributions a person makes about their own behavior. Furthermore, the opinions about the causes of the behavior of an actor can at times be communicated indirectly by another person (an observer). Such 'indirect' communications are also relevant for therapy, as they constitute important aspects of the therapists' behavior. These include, for example, interpersonal emotions (whether the therapist is annoyed about the failures of the client, or whether they show sympathy), helping behavior (whether the therapist helps the client or leaves them alone to solve the task), task assignment (whether the client is given easy or hard homework), and evaluative behavior (praise or blame).

Emotions. In almost all approaches to therapy, the 'emotional relationship' between the therapist and the client is considered to be very important. Beck and coworkers (1979) stress that the therapist's emotional expressions to clients can also contain important (cognitive) communications.

> It is generally therapeutic for the therapist to express, *judiciously* feelings such as concern, appreciation, warmth, and encouragement. Moreover, it is sometimes therapeutic if he sometimes acknowledges some of his own 'negative' feelings, such as disappointments, frustrations, irritations. However, he must exercise caution in how much of his own feelings he expresses toward the depressed patient. He must realize that a genuine expression of feeling on his part may be misinterpreted by the patient. (p. 52)

As interpersonal emotions have a central status in therapy, an understanding of how attributions are communicated through affects is important if we want to change causal attributions 'therapeutically'. It would indeed be harmful to try to persuade a client to make attribution 'x' instead of attribution 'y' for a success if, at the same time, the therapist's expressive emotional behavior shows that the therapist explains the success with attribution 'y'.

Meyer (1984), Rustemeyer (1984), and Weiner *et al.* (1982) have shown that the expression of some emotions, which at first sight appear to be socially desirable and therapeutically helpful, could contain negative cognitive messages for the 'receiver'. In contrast, supposedly 'unfriendly' interpersonal affects contain positive cognitive communications. Individuals who received pity reactions ('friendly' response) from others after their own failures came to the conclusion that they were perceived as having low ability. If the person is shown anger by an evaluating person after the failure, the person feels that they are perceived by this other as sufficiently able to obtain a future success by applying increased effort.

Likewise, the therapist's positive emotions regarding the client's successes contain important (indirect) attributional communications. A therapist who shows 'surprise' and 'amazement' when the client has achieved an important goal, may thereby communicate that they had not anticipated the success and therefore attributes it to chance and not the client's ability. If the therapist only showed contentment at the success or acknowledged it without any particular response, the client could conclude that the success was anticipated and would not be attributed to chance.

Task assignment.   The research by Meyer and coworkers described in Chapter 4 reveals that, alongside emotions, the assignment of tasks of varying levels of difficulty can also contain attribution-relevant information in a social context. This is particularly important, as a significant part of current work in clinical psychology and especially behavior therapy consists of developing various therapeutic homework for the clients. This applies to both individual and group therapies.

The experiments on the effects of task assignments that were described in Chapter 4 allow us to speculate that a client who is assigned very simple therapeutic homework will conclude that the therapist perceives them as being relatively disturbed, weak, and frail. However, if the patient is given a difficult task that requires effort, the individual may experience that they are perceived as largely able to solve their own problems through personal effort. Without making any reference to the corresponding attributional considerations, Ellis (1983) points out that some behavior therapy techniques could have disadvantageous 'philosophical implications' for the clients, as they could be interpreted as being extremely easy tasks. For example, the cautious procedures in systematic desensitization (Wolpe, 1958), during which the client has to imagine approaching a feared object while in a relaxed state, may appear to the client to be extremely simple, but very time-consuming and laborious. The client might therefore conclude that they really have serious problems and disorders (because the method of treatment chosen is so complicated), and that the therapist perceives them to be rather incompetent with regard to the problem (they are only allowed to imagine the danger, and not to encounter it). For this reason, Ellis proposes that it is preferable to apply 'difficult' behavior therapy techniques, such as flooding, instead of systematic desensitization. By placing the client directly in the anxiety-producing situation and leaving them there until the anxiety is overcome, the therapist teaches the client that they *can* cope with and change the anxiety.

Praise and blame.   Evaluative behaviors by the therapist, such as praise after success and blame after failure, can also influence the clients' attributions for the own behavioral outcomes. By praising the client after success, the therapist may communicate that they attribute the client's success less to high ability and more to the client's high effort. This can in turn lead the client to feel reinforced in their low estimation of their personal ability. These low ability perceptions may then lead to the behavior that was praised not being repeated in the future. Hence, if the therapist responds to the client's positive experience (success) in a non-evaluative and neutral manner, this may under some circumstances be preferable and may improve the probability that the respective behavior will be performed again. Likewise, as the experiments described in Chapter 4 have further shown, blame after failure may indicate to the client that they have previously not attained their goal because of a lack of effort and not because of a lack of ability. Hence, again, blame following failure may in some cases have more positive implications for the client than 'tactfully' ignoring failure.

For a patient with a low self-concept of personal ability, 'blame' may contain a 'surprising' positive communication about the failure; namely, that the therapist evaluates the client as being relatively capable. This 'message' may lead the client to persist in working toward the goal. These 'apparently' paradoxical effects of praise and blame' (Meyer, 1984) are particularly important for clinical psychology because (popular and simplistic) versions of the clinical application of classical learning theory in behavior therapy attribute a solely positive function to praise after success (the probability of the behavior is increased) and a negative function to blame after failure (blame should reduce the probability of the behavior occuring).

Helping behavior.   While the expression of emotions, the assignment of tasks, and sanctions are only aspects of therapy, the client may regard the entire process of therapy as a help in solving personal problems. Clinical experiences show this acts as a 'deterrent' for many persons seeking treatment. In some cases, initial resistances are explained by assuming that the client has difficulties in admitting their need for help and therapy, because this would imply admitting an inability to resolve personal problems through personal effort. The slogan put out by the women's liberation movement, 'Help makes helpless', also points out the possible negative consequences of providing help.

Yet again, the experiments by Meyer (see Chapter 4) shed light on the ambiguity or the possible dangers of some forms of therapeutic assistance. The experiments are concerned with a special segment of helping behavior, namely the consequences of *unsought* help for the receiver of help, and can, therefore, not be related directly to all (therapeutic) helping situations. However, if they are transferred to the problem areas of clinical psychology and psychotherapy, the findings on the consequences of helping indicate that a therapist who gives a client unrequested help or advice also conveys that the therapist estimates the client to be not capable enough to reach their goals through personal effort. The various therapeutic 'assistance aids' that are used in behavior therapy may also contain such negative implications for the clients. For example, a smoker may think that they cannot stop smoking through personal willpower after several therapy sessions in which complicated self-control techniques have been taught. However, clinical psychologists have also recognized the possible negative consequences of help by now and then describing therapy as 'helping people to help themselves'. In addition, Beck *et al.* (1979) explicitly point out that therapists must proceed with great care when giving help:

> The clinically depressed patient often has a strong impulse to seek help from others in carrying out everyday activities. This wish for assistance ... generally exceeds the patient's realistic needs for help. Although help often gives the patient some temporary emotional relief, it can reinforce the patient's dependency and lack of self confidence. (p. 183)

In summary, it can be maintained that certain therapeutic interventions (task assignments, praise and blame, helping, and the expression of emotions) can provide the client indirectly with attributionally relevant information. It is possible that these forms of behavior and reacting are applied by therapists without their negative consequences being known or taken into account. Inexperienced therapists might assume that it is generally desirable to show sympathy or pity to a client, to help, to praise after success, and to assign light tasks. This can particularly lead to negative consequences when the client considers the therapist to be a competent judge of the client's condition and abilities and is consequently disposed to adopt the therapist's opinion. In addition, indirect communications can be evaluated as being particularly 'honest', and because of this, the client may place great importance on them. Indirect communications are possibly perceived as not being 'censored' by the therapist's tactical strategies, but are evaluated as an expression of 'what the therapist "really" thinks about my condition, but won't tell me openly'.

If these speculations are correct, some widespread therapeutic techniques might contain harmful elements. This would be particularly alarming against the background of the fact that indirect communications of attributions or perceptions of ability cannot always be influenced consciously; as can be seen, for example, in the communication of emotions (Izard, 1977; Scherer, 1986). Even if one knows that it might not be correct to show sympathy to a particular client, one might well do this unintentionally through intonation or facial expression when actually experiencing this emotion. In addition, it is questionable whether a therapist who strategically influences their indirect communications will appear to be credible for the client, or whether they will perhaps be considered unnatural and 'posed'.

Naturally, the research work presented above does not imply that praise, help, or sympathy and pity should always be avoided. On the one hand, we have already stressed that it is not always desirable to convey a high concept of personal ability to the client. In contrast, individuals who damage themselves through unrealistic persistence may well profit from being indirectly informed by their therapists that their abilities have limitations. On the other hand, the therapist's sympathy may provide the client with a positive report that will compensate for its eventual negative implications. For example, the sympathy of the therapist could convey to the client that they also have the right to be weak and is nevertheless considered important and taken seriously.

10.4.5. Changing attributions through changing moods

It has already been indicated in Section 7.6. that recent research has demonstrated that it is not only the cognitive processes that influence emotional states, but that emotional states can also influence cognitive variables that are attributionally relevant (see Bower, 1981). For instance, it was found that individuals tend to recall information better when they are in a mood state that is similar to the mood state they experienced when they learned the list of items than when they are in a different emotional state. The clinical implications of these findings are obvious. Suppose the therapeutic goal is to analyze the veridicality of the attribution for a recent social rejection that a depressed client presents to the therapist (e.g., 'I am totally unattractive'). The therapist might decide to consider consistency information regarding this attribution and ask the client to recall how often they had been rejected or accepted socially in the past. The research findings described above would suggest that —while in the state of depression — the client would recall more mood-congruent events (i.e., social failures, as these can be assumed to be linked to 'bad' moods) than events that are incongruent with their mood (i.e., social successes that were linked to 'good' moods). As a consequence, it might be helpful or even necessary to change the depressed clients' mood in order to obtain access to the information needed to check the validity of their attribution (i.e., past social successes). Therefore, from a cognitive view of therapy, it might also, under specific conditions, be valuable to change a client's emotional state before attempting to change their cognitions.

10.5.   GENERAL GOALS OF ATTRIBUTION THERAPY

As in every other form of therapy, the basic goal of attributionally based cognitive therapy is to change dysfunctional responses such as anxiety, depressive states, or self-destructive behavior in a positive direction. The most elegant way to achieve this change consists in the modification of causal cognitions through the 'scientific' testing of the thoughts that bring about dysfunctional responses. Above and beyond the easing of specific emotional problems, attribution therapy could, however, also 'help people to help themselves' by conveying to persons the ability to apply independently methods for testing dysfunctional and/or unrealistic cognitions in future problem situations (see Walen, DiGuiseppe and Wessler, 1980). Training clients to be their own therapists consists — in a similar manner to the therapy models of Beck and Ellis — in teaching them methods by which they can identify their own dysfunctional thoughts (attributions). In addition, in the therapy the client should learn to regard these cognitions as 'working hypotheses' that require scientific testing. A long-term goal of attribution therapy should be to encourage the client not to stick dogmatically to certain hypotheses but to be aware of the provisional nature of their hypotheses about the causal structure of the environment, and to be prepared to carry out experiments when causal cognitions lead to dysfunctional consequences.

Furthermore, clients should be encouraged *not* to avoid negative experiences in areas of high personal importance, but to see them as helpful sources of information for (long-term) personal decisions. Accordingly, clients could be encouraged through, for example, open communication with their fellows and through the study of relevant literature, to collect as much data as possible on potentially problematic areas of life. Therapy that is guided by attribution theory would then lead the clients to become, as Mahoney expresses it, their own 'personal scientists' (Mahoney, 1977b). Emotional techniques can also be used in this therapy in order, for example, to reduce the anxieties that bring about the avoidance of information gathering. However, it is also important not to let personal negative emotions prevent the collecting of relevant information on dysfunctional cognitions. For example, Meyer (1983) points out that a (unrealistically) low self-concept of ability possesses the character of a self-stabilizing system. If one considers oneself to be of low ability, one will prefer to choose easy tasks and avoid the learning experiences that would accompany the processing of harder tasks. Because high effort might appear to be useless when perceived ability is low, one shows less persistence and experiences a higher probability of failure. This 'stabilizes' the self-concept of low ability, and thus triggers negative self-evaluative affects.

These considerations make it clear that under certain circumstances one must carry out unknown activities despite negative feelings in order to subject one's erroneous assumptions to an empirical testing (e.g., to make a great effort to work on a difficult task which is accompanied by anxiety and has a low probability of success).

10.6. DEMANDS ON THE THERAPIST

As we already mentioned in Chapter 2, the basic theoretical positions of theories imply demands on individuals who apply these models in clinical psychology. A consequence of the signficance of the 'scientific procedure' in attribution therapy and of the goal of training the clients to be their own 'personal scientists' is that the therapist should have sound command of philosophy of science and scientific techniques such as experimental design and statistical procedures. At the same time, therapists must be able to 'translate' these in a plausible and understandable way into the everyday language and concepts of their clients. It would be helpful for the therapist to possess intelligence, an ability to abstract, and a critical distance to their personal convictions and opinions: similar qualities to those that we expect from scientists. Furthermore, therapists need to be able to deliver problem-relevant information to their clients. They should be 'professionals' in the prognosis and description of psychological disorders, and able, for example, to explain to clients that reactive depressions generally disappear after a while, and that phobias can be particularly reduced when the client places themself in the particular anxiety arousing situation

In order to serve as a source of information for the client, the therapist must not only possess relevant information but also be able to convey credibility. This credibility can probably be attained through an objective, task-oriented, competent, and reality-oriented approach to therapy. This orientation might imply that the therapist avoids signalling to the client that it is an important goal for them to be especially liked by the client and to convey 'good feelings' to them. Because these 'desires' of the therapist might threaten their credibility when wanting to present information to the client. The relationship between the attribution therapist and the client might therefore in many aspects be similar to the relationships between lawyers, teachers, and other professionals and their clients and students. Emotional dynamics and transference relationships between therapists and clients that are emphasized by the psychoanalytic approach would not be central from an attributional point of view. It is consistent with the image of the attribution therapist that they are sometimes — as in other therapies — actively directive and take on the role of a teacher who tests what progress the client has made with the 'scientific method of analysis' as an instrument for dealing with unrealistic cognitions. The therapist should at times convey scientific information, for example, the connections between thinking, feeling, and behavior. However, they should also create an atmosphere in which the client gains the necessary motivation and courage to test their cognitions, carry out experiments, and experience failure. It would also be desirable if the therapist were to be a model for the scientific approach, in other words, not to formulate an assumption in the therapy session in a fanatical, dogmatic, and absolutistic manner, but carefully and probablistically, and to clarify which data they are using to come to which causal conclusion. The therapist must — as demanded by Beck et al. (1979) — form a functioning team together with the client in order to test hypotheses scientifically.

As attribution theories use 'common sense' concepts, the client does not have to understand a complicated system during the therapy, as is the case with psychoanalysis or learning theory, in order to grasp how their difficulties come about and can be treated. Beck (1976) expresses this in the following way:

> Man has the key to understanding and solving his psychological disturbances with the scope of his own awareness. He can correct the misconceptions producing his emotional disturbances with the same problem-solving apparatus that he has been accustomed to using at various stages in his development. (p. 3)

Chapter 11

Conclusions

This volume has attempted to present a relatively comprehensive system for the analysis of phenomena from clinical psychology and therapy that is based on attribution theory. It has been shown that attribution theory and research has identified cognitive determinants of disorders of behavior and emotion, such as depression, anger, and motivationally determined performance deficits. In addition, the techniques for changing causal attributions that have been derived from attribution theory have proved to be effective for modifying behavior. Finally, we were able to show that the linking together of theoretical approaches to the antecedent conditions of attributions with approaches to the consequences of attributions enables us to make predictions about the conditions of situation-appropriate (functional) and situation-inappropriate (dysfunctional) responses.

Furthermore, this book has shown that a large number of therapeutic techniques can be derived from attribution research. These techniques and the considerations on which they are based are consistent with the theory and practice of the most influential present-day therapy procedures, namely cognitive behavior therapy, especially Beck's Cognitive Therapy and Ellis' Rational-Emotive Therapy.

The present approach to the analysis of problems in clinical psychology and therapy is derived from basic experimental research in psychology and therefore differs from many of the current 'schools' of therapy that have grown out of therapeutic practice. We can mention here the Rogers' Client-Centered Therapy (1961), Perls' Gestalt Therapy (1969), or the Cognitive Therapy from Beck (1976) and Ellis (1962). On the other hand, the present approach also shows parallels to these forms of therapy (especially to the cognitive therapies from Beck and Ellis).

This shows that research in general psychology and practice-related therapeutic models do not have to stand in isolation but can complement and profit from one another. This results in implications for both basic research in attribution theory and for the theory and practice of cognitive behavior therapy.

Implications for attribution research. First of all, the possibility of treating problems in clinical psychology within an attributional framework documents the breadth of the validity of attribution conceptions. Although other social psychological theories beside attributional models have been related to questions in clinical psychology, such as Festinger's (1957) cognitive dissonance theory, or Brehm's theory of (1966) reactance, they have never covered such a broad range as the attributional approach (see Försterling, 1987). Reactance and dissonance approaches can only describe and explain isolated clinical phenomena and special therapeutic techniques (see, for a summary, Brehm, 1976; Weary and Mirels, 1982).

Beyond this, the attributional analyses of motivationally determined performance deficits, helplessness, anger, and depression have received support from the fact that cognitive therapy theories (Beck; Ellis; see Chapter 10) arrive at very similar findings in therapeutic practice using non-experimental procedures.

The present integration of attribution models with the theories of cognitive therapies can in turn stimulate clinical attribution research. Researchers in the field of clinical attribution psychology can derive working hypotheses from the experiences of cognitive therapists and stimulate their research activity. Thus, the experiences gained within the practice of cognitive therapy indicate which types of disorder can be analyzed and treated within a cognitive framework. Because of the similarities between these two theoretical positions, one can conclude that forms of disorders that are successfully treated with cognitive therapy procedures can also be analyzed with attribution theory and possibly modified with reattribution techniques.

In addition to the reciprocal stimulations and expansions that theoretical models can receive through being compared with one-another, such comparisons also have implications for the validity of the respective approaches. We have shown in Chapter 10 that the trust in the validity of an understanding of a phenomenon grows when various positions (using different methods) arrive at matching statements on the phenomenon (e.g., depression). The comparison of the (cognitive) analyses and therapy of psychological disorders by attribution theory and the cognitive therapy theories has revealed that both approaches come to very similar conclusions for a number of clinical phenomena. We hope that this finding will contribute to a better understanding of some clinical phenomena such as reactive depression or anger problems.

Furthermore, the application of attribution theories to questions in clinical psychology has provided indicators for possible further developments in attributional theory. By looking for the attributional determinants of functional and dysfunctional responses (a 'typical' question in clinical psychology), we were able to propose the hypothesis that, in a given situation, the probability of functional responses increases if the individual makes realistic causal attributions in the situation, and that unrealistic causal attributions lead to comparatively dysfunctional responses. The 'verdicality' of attributions is defined by using the antecedent conditions of attributions (covariation information).

With this, the previously mostly unrelated research directions of attribution theories (on antecedent conditions; S → C) are linked to attributional models (of the consequences of attributions; C → R) in the model presented in Chapter 9 (see also Försterling and Rudolph, 1988). This integration points to a 'type' of possible future research in the field of attribution psychology, namely, investigations that deal with the *linking* of features of the situation and responses (S ←→ R) depending on the attributional representations of the situation (C).

In order to pursue, for example, the question in which situations (S), a response (R; e.g., anger) that is brought about by a particular attribution (C; e.g., controllability) is functional, one must first develop taxonomies of situations (see Kelley, 1983). Compared with the comprehensive studies on the characteristics of attributionally guided *responses* (see Chapter 5 to 7), there are, however, very few indications within the framework of attribution research for meaningful ways of categorizing situations. The present volume has pointed out the potential utility of the Kelley model (the principle of covariation) for such a taxonomy of situations.

A further implication for attribution research relates to the dimensional properties of attributions (see Chapter 3) on the one hand, and the investigation of consequences on the other. Until now, attributional research has in no way considered all the relevant classification possibilities of causal descriptions to behavioral prediction. There is, for example, as yet no research into the question whether depressives and nondepressives differ in their use of proximal and distal causes.

Implications for clinical psychology and cognitive therapies in particular. The fact that attribution theories show such strong similarities with the theory and practice of current forms of therapy provides a support for the theoretical assumptions of these approaches to therapy. As attribution approaches have been dominant in motivational and social psychology for the last twenty years and subjected to differentiated empirical testing, they have, in contrast to the cognitive therapy theories, a construct system at their disposal that has been tested by empirical (experimental) research. In addition, experimental paradigms have been developed from attribution research which — due to the above-mentioned similarities between the theories — have also been able to test hypotheses from the cognitive therapies empirically (see Försterling, 1985b). For this reason, attributional conceptions can provide cognitive therapies with a relatively unified theoretical and conceptual frame of reference and widen the possibilities of empirically testing their hypotheses.

In contrast to cognitive therapy theories that have not provided a differentiated model of the formation of the thoughts that they consider to be responsible for dysfunctional responses, attribution theories are concerned with just such antecedent conditions of (causal) cognitions. This is why attributional considerations can cast light on the conditions of emergence and the possibilities of changing the dysfunctional cognitions with which cognitive therapies are involved. It can thus provide the preconditions for cognitive measures of prevention: Because in order to prevent the occurence of dysfunctional cognitions, it is naturally important to know the conditions under which they come into being.

Some limitations of the present approach. Although the present possibilities for clinical diagnosis and intervention that are based on attribution theory have been successfully applied for changing behavior in laboratory studies, it is of course in no way shown that 'attributional therapy' is actually effective. Naturally, research work is necessary in order to evaluate the therapeutic interventions derived from the considerations presented here.

In addition, we naturally do not assume that causal attributions represent the sole conditions for all psychological disorders. Therefore it would be advantageous to specify which disorders of behavior and experience are mostly, partly, or in no way determined by attributions. Only such research could help decide when and to what extent therapy should concern itself with the alteration of attributions (see also Chapter 10). In a series of small investigations (Försterling, 1984, in preparation), it could be shown, for example, that potentially dysfunctional responses such as depression, anger, a lack of persistence, or anxiety, are not only characterized by specific patterns of attribution, but also by the degrees of importance that persons attach to the situations that are relevant for the respective responses. These findings already point to cases in which clients could not, or could only partially, be helped by attribution therapy: namely, when, for example, an individual attaches an excessive importance to a failure and consequently feels depressive. In such a case, therapy might preferably not consist in changing the attribution for failure, but in changing the importance of the event for the individual. This should especially be attempted if the corresponding causal attributions that relate to the feelings of depression are realistic.

References

Abramson, L. Y., Garber, J., and Seligman, M. E. P. (1980). Learned helplessness: An attributional analysis. In J. Garber and M. E. P. Seligman (eds), *Human helplessness: theory and applications*, New York: Academic Press, pp. 3–34.

Abramson, L. Y., and Sackheim, H. A. (1977). A paradox in depression: Uncontrollability and self-blame. *Psychological Bulletin*, **84**, 835–51.

Abramson, L. Y., Seligman, M. E. P., and Teasdale, J. D. (1978). Learned helplessness in humans. *Journal of Abnormal Psychology*, **87**, 49–74.

Affleck, G., Tennen, H., Croog, S., and Levine, S. (1987). Causal attribution, perceived benefits, and morbidity after a heart attack: A 8-year study. *Journal of Consulting and Clinical Psychology*, **55**, 29–35.

Alloy, L. B., and Abramson, L. Y. (1979). Judgments of contingency in depressed and non-depressed students: sadder but wiser? *Journal of Experimental Psychology: General*, *108*, 441–485.

Alloy, L. B., and Ahrens, A. H. (1987). Depression and pessimism for the future: Biased use of statistically relevant information in predictions for self versus others. *Journal of Personality and Social Psychology*, **52**, 366–378.

Alloy, L. B., and Tabachnik, N. (1984). Assessment of covariation by humans and animals: The joint influence of prior expectations and current situational information. *Psychological Review*, **91**, 112–149.

Alloy, L. B., Peterson, C., Abramson, L. Y., and Seligman, M. E. P. (1984). Attributional style and the generality of learned helplessness. *Journal of Personality and Social Psychology*, **46**, 681–68.

Anderson, C. A. (1983). Motivational and performance deficits in interpersonal settings: The effect of attributional style. *Journal of Personality and Social Psychology*, **45**, 1136–1147.

Anderson, C. A., Horowitz, L. M., and French, R. de S. (1983). Attributional style of lonely and depressed people. *Journal of Personality and Social Psychology*, **45**, 127–36.

Anderson, C. A., and Jennings, D. L. (1980). When experiences of failure promote expectancies of success. The impact of attributing failure to ineffective strategies. *Journal of Personality*, **48**, 393–407.

Andrews, G. R., and Debus, R. L. (1978). Persistence and the causal perception of failure: Modifying cognitive attributions. *Journal of Educational Psychology*, **70**, 154–66.

Antaki, C., and Brewin, C. (1982). (eds) *Attributions and psychological change: Applications of attributional theories to clinical and educational practice.* London: Academic Press.

Arkin, R. M., Appleman, A. J., and Burger, J. M. (1980). Social anxiety, self-presentation, and the self-serving bias in causal attribution. *Journal of Personality and Social Psychology*, **38**, 23–35.

Arkin, R. M., Detchon, C. S., and Maruyama, G. M. (1981). Causal attributions of high and low achievement motivation college students for performance on examinations. *Motivation and Emotion*, **5**, 139–52.

165

Arkin, R. M., Detchon, C. S., and Maruyama, G. M. (1982). Roles of attribution, affect, and cognitive interference in test anxiety. *Journal of Personality and Social Psychology*, **43**, 1111–1124.

Arkin, R. M., and Maruyama, G. M. (1979). Attribution, affect, and college performance. *Journal of Educational Psychology*, **71**, 85–93.

Arnold, M. (1960). *Emotion and personality*. Vol 1. New York: Columbia University Press.

Atkinson, J.W. (1957). Motivational determinants of risk-taking behavior. *Psychological Review*, **64**, 359–372.

Atkinson, J. W. (1964). *An introduction to motivation*. Princetown, N.J.: Van Nostrand.

Averill, S. R. (1983). Studies on anger and aggression: Implications for theories of emotion. *American Psychologist*, **38**, 1145–60.

Bandura, A. (1977a). *Social learning theory*. Englewood Cliffs, N. J.: Prentice Hall.

Bandura, A. (1977b). Self-efficacy: Toward a unifying theory of behavioral change. *Psychological Review*, **2**, 191–215.

Bandura, A. (1981). Self-referent thought: A developmental analysis of self-efficacy. In J. H. Flavell and L. Ross (eds). *Social cognitive development: Frontiers and possible futures*. Cambridge, UK: Cambridge University Press. pp. 200–239.

Bandura, A. (1982). Self-efficacy mechanism in human agency. *American Psychologist*, **37**, 122–147.

Bar-Tal, D. (1978). Attributional analysis of achievement-related behavior. *Review of Educational Research*, **48**, 259–271.

Beck, A. T. (1967). *Depression: Clinical, experimental and theoretical aspects*. New York: Harper and Row.

Beck, A. T. (1976). *Cognitive therapy and the emotional disorders*. New York: International Universities Press.

Beck, A. T., and Shaw, B. F. (1977). Cognitive approaches to depression. In A. Ellis and R. Grieger (eds). *Handbook of rational-emotive therapy*. New York: Springer. pp. 309–326.

Beck, A. T., Ward, C. H., Mendelsohn, M., Mock, J., and Erbaugh, J. (1961). An inventory for measuring depression. *Archives of General Psychiatry*, **4**, 561–571.

Beck, A. T., Rush, A. J., Shaw, B. F., and Emery, G. (1979). *Cognitive therapy of depression*. New York: Guilford.

Bem, D. J. (1972). Self-Perception theory. In L. Berkowitz (ed.), *Advances in experimental social psychology*, Vol. 6, New York: Academic Press, pp. 1–62.

Berglas, S., and Jones, E. E. (1978). Drug choice as a self-handicapping strategy in response to non-contingent success. *Journal of Personality and Social Psychology*, **36**, 405–417.

Bierhoff, H. W. (1982). Determinanten hilfreichen Verhaltens (Determinants of helping behavior). *Psychologische Rundschau*, **33**, 289–304.

Bindra, D. (1980). Cognition: It's origin and future in psychology. In J. R. Royce and L. P. Mos (eds). *Annals of Theoretical Psychology* Vol. 1, New York: Plenum Press. pp. 1–29.

Block, J., and Lanning, K. (1984). Attribution therapy requestioned: A secondary analysis of the Wilson–Linville study. *Journal of Personality and Social Psychology*, **46**, 705–708.

Bower, G. H. (1981). Mood and memory. *American Psychologist*, **36**, 129–148.

Brehm, J. (1966). *A theory of psychological reactance*. New York: Academic Press.

Brehm, S. S. (1976). *The application of social psychology to clinical practice*. Washington, London: Hemisphere.

Brewin, C. R. (1982). Adaptive aspects of self-blame in coping with accidental injury. In C. Antaki and C. R. Brewin (eds). *Attributions and psychological change. Applications of attributional theories to clinical and educational practice*. London: Academic Press pp. 119–133.

Brewin, C. R. (1984). Perceived controllability of life-events and willingness to prescribe psychotropic drugs. *British Journal of Social Psychology*, **23**, 285-287.

Brewin, C. R. (1985). Depression and causal attributions: What is their relation? *Psychological Bulletin*, **98**, 297-309.

Brockner, I., and Swap, W. C. (1983). Resolving the relationships between placebos, misattribution, and insomina: An individual-difference perspective. *Journal of Personality and Social Psychology*, **45**, 32-42.

Brown, J. (1984). Effects of induced mood on causal attributions for success and failure. *Motivation and Emotion*, **8**, 343-353.

Buckert, U., Meyer, W.-U., and Schmalt, H. D. (1979). The effects of difficulty and diagnositicity on choice among tasks in relation to achievement motivation and perceived ability. *Journal of Personality and Social Psychology*, **37**, 1172-1178.

Bulman, R. J., and Wortman, C. B. (1977). Attributions of blame and coping in the "real world': Severe accident victims react to their lot. *Journal of Personality and Social Psychology*, **35**, 351-363.

Carlston, D. E., and Shovar, N. (1983). Effects of performance attributions on others' perceptions of the attributor. *Journal of Personality and Social Psychology*, **44**, 515-525.

Carroll, J. S., and Payne, J. W. (1976). The psychology of the parole decision process: A joint application of attribution theory and information processing psychology. In J. S. Carroll and J. W. Payne (eds.), *Cognition and social behavior*. Hillsdale, N. J.: Erlbaum. pp. 13-32.

Cautela, J. R. (1966). Treatment of compulsive behavior by covert sensitization. *Psychological Record*, **16**, 33-41.

Chapin, M., and Dyck, D. G. (1976). Persistence and childrens' reading behavior as a function of N-length and attribution retraining. *Journal of Abnormal Psychology*, **85**, 511-515.

Covington, M. V., and Omelich, C. L. (1984). An empirical examination of Weiner's critique of attributional research. *Journal of Educational Psychology*, **76**, 1214-1225.

Coyne, J. C., and Gotlib, I. H. (1983). The role of cognition in depression: a critical appraisal. *Psychological Bulletin*, **94**, 472-505.

Crandall, V. C., Katkovsky, W., and Crandall, V. J. (1965). Children's beliefs in their own control of reinforcement in intellectual academic achievement situations. *Child Development*, **36**, 91-109.

Davison, G. C. (1966). Differential relaxation and cognitive restructuring in therapy with a paranoid schizophrenic or paranoid state. Paper presented at the 74th annual meeting of the American Psychological Association.

Davison, G. C., and Neale, J. M. (1978). *Abnormal Psychology. An experimental clinical approach*. New York: Wiley.

Davison, G. C., and Valins, S. (1969). Maintenance of self-attributed and drug-attributed behavior change. *Journal of Personality and Social Psychology*, **1**, 25-33.

Deci, E. L. (1975). *Intrinsic motivation*. New York: Plenum Press.

DeCharms, R. (1968). *Personal causation*. New York: Academic Press.

Dewey, J. (1895). The theory of emotion. *Psychological Review*, **1**, 553-569.

Diener, C. I., and Dweck, C. S. (1978). An analysis of learned helplessness: continuous changes in performance, strategy and achievement cognitions following failure. *Journal of Personality and Social Psychology*, **36**, 451-462.

Ducasse (1926). On the nature and observability of causal relation. *Journal of Philosophy*, 57-68.

Dweck, C. S. (1975). The role of expectations and attributions in the alleviation of learned helplessness. *Journal of Personality and Social Psychology*, **31**, 674-685.

Dweck, C. S., and Repucci, N. D. (1973). Learned helplessness and reinforcement responsibility in children. *Journal of Personality and Social Psychology*, **25**, 109-116.

Eimer, M. (1987). *Konzeptionen von Kausalität (Conceptions of causality).* Bern: Huber.

Einhorn, H. J., and Hogarth, R. M. (1986). Judging probable cause. *Psychological Bulletin,* **99**, 3–19.

Eiser, J. R., Van der Pligt, J. L., Raw, M., and Sutton, S. R. (1985). Trying to stop smoking: Effects of perceived addiction, attributions for failure, and expectancy of success. *Journal of Behavioral Medicine,* **8**, 321–341.

Ellis, A. (1962). *Reason and emotion in psychotherapy.* Secaucus, N.J.: Citadel Press.

Ellis, A. (1973). *Humanistic psychotherapy.* New York: McGraw-Hill.

Ellis, A. (1977). *Anger: How to live with and without it.* Secaucus, N. J.: Citadel Press.

Ellis, A. (1983). The philosophic implications and dangers of some popular behavior therapy techniques. In M. Rosenbaum, C. M. Franks and Y. Jaffe (eds.). *Perspectives on behavior therapy in the eighties* New York: Springer. pp. 138–151.

Ellis, A. (1984). The essence of RET. *Journal of Rational-Emotive Therapy,* **2**, 19–25.

Ellis, A., and Abrahms, E. (1978). *Brief psychotherapy in medical and health practice.* New York: Springer.

Ellis, A., and Grieger, R. (eds) (1977). *Handbook of rational-emotive therapy.* New York: Springer.

Ellis A., and Harper, R. A. (1975). *A new guide to rational living.* Englewood Cliffs, N.J.: Prentice Hall.

Ellis, A., and Knaus, P. (1977). *Overcoming procrastination.* New York: Institute for Rational Living.

Epiktet (edition 1984). *Handbüchlein der Moral und Unterredungen* (A brevier on morals and discourses). Alfred Kröner Verlag: Stuttgart.

Falbo, T., and Beck, R. C. (1979). Naive psychology and the attributional model of achievement. *Journal of Personality,* **47**, 185–195.

Feather, N. T. (ed.) (1982). *Expectations and actions. Expectancy-value models in psychology.* Hillsdale, N.J.: Lawrence Erlbaum Associates.

Festinger, L. A. (1954). A theory of social comparison processes. *Human Relations,* **7**, 117–140.

Festinger, L. A. (1957). *A theory of cognitive dissonance.* Evanston, Ill.: Row, Peterson.

Fincham, F. D. (1983). Clinical applications of attribution theory: Problems and prospects. In M. Hewstone (ed.) *Attribution theory: Social and functional extensions.* Oxford: Blackwell. pp. 187–203.

Fincham, F. D. (1985 a). Attributions in close relationships. In J. Harvey and G. Weary (eds) *Attribution: Basic issues and applications.* New York, Academic Press. pp. 203–234.

Fincham, F. D. (1985 b). Attribution processes in distressed and nondistressed couples: 2. Responsibility for marital problems. *Journal of Abnormal Psychology,* **94**, 183–190.

Fincham, F. D., Beach, S. R., and Baucom, D. H. (1987) Attribution processes in distressed and nondistressed couples: 4. Self-partner attribution differences. *Journal of Personality and Social Psychology,* **52**, 739–748.

Fincham, F. D., and O'Leary, K. D. (1983). Causal inferences for spouse behavior in maritally distressed and non-distressed couples. *Journal of Social and Clinical Psychology,* **1**, 42–57.

Folkes, V. S. (1978). *Causal communication in the early stages of affiliative relationships.* Unpublished doctoral dissertation, University of California, Los Angeles.

Fontaine, G. (1974). Social comparison and some determinants of expected personal control and expected performance in a novel situation. *Journal of Personality and Social Psychology,* **29**, 487–496.

Försterling, F. (1980 a). Attributional aspects of cognitive behavior modification: A theoretical approach and suggestions for techniques. *Cognitive Therapy and Research,* **4**, 27–37.

Försterling, F. (1980 b). A multivariate analysis of perceived causes for success and failure. *Archiv für Psychologie*, **133**, 45–52.

Försterling, F. (1980c). Kognitive Verhaltenstherapie: Abgrenzung und Gegenüberstellung der verschiedenen Schulen (Cognitive behavior therapy: Demarcations and comparisons of the various schools). In W. Schulz and M. Hautzinger (eds), *Klinische Psychologie und Psychotherapie*, Kongreßbericht der Deutschen Gesellschaft für Verhaltenstherapie und der Gesellschaft für wissenschaftliche Gesprächstherapie, Band 1; DGVT: Berlin.

Försterling, F. (1983). Interdependencies of different depressogenic cognitions. *Rational Living*, **18**, 13–16.

Försterling, F. (1984). Importance, causal attributions, and the emotion of anger. *Zeitschrift für Psychologie*, **192**, 25–32.

Försterling, F. (1985a). Attributional retraining: A review. *Psychological Bulletin*, **98**, 495–512.

Försterling, F. (1985b). Rational-emotive therapy and attribution theory: An investigation of the cognitive determinants of emotions. *British Journal of Cognitive Psychotherapy*, **3**, 12–25.

Försterling, F. (1986). Attributional conceptions in clinical psychology. *American Psychologist*, **41**, 275–285.

Försterling, F. (1987). Sozialpsychologische Begründung von Therapieverfahren: Eine attributionstheoretische Perspektive (Socialpsychological explanations of the therapy process: An attributional perspective). In J. Schultz-Gambard (ed.), *Handbuch der angewandten Sozialpsychologie*, Beltz. pp. 321–330.

Försterling, F. (in preparation). Das Konzept der persönlichen Wichtigkeit (The concept of personal importance).

Försterling, F., and Groeneveld, A. (1983). Ursachenzuschreibung für ein Wahlergebnis: Eine Überprüfung von Hypothesen der Attributionstheorie in einer Feldstudie anhand der niedersächsischen Kommunalwahlen 1981 (Explanation of election results: A test of attribution hypotheses in a field study based on the communal elections, 1981, in Lower Saxony) *Zeitschrift für Sozialpsychologie*, **14**, 262–269.

Försterling, F., and Rudolph, U. (1988). Situations, attributions and the evaluation of behavior. *Journal of Personality and Social Psychology*, **54**, 225–232.

Försterling, F., and Schoeler, J. (1984). Importance and perceived ability as determinants for information search. *Archiv für Psychologie*, **136**, 333–342.

Försterling, F., and Weiner, B. (1981). Some determinants of task preference and the desire for information about the self. *European Journal of Social Psychology*, **11**, 399–407.

Forsyth, D. R. (1980). The function of causal attributions. *Social Psychology Quarterly*, **43**, 184–189.

Fowler, J. W., and Peterson, P. L. (1981). Increasing reading persistence and altering attributional style of learned helpless children. *Journal of Educational Psychology*, **73**, 251–260.

Frank, J. D. (1973). *Persuasion and healing (Rev. edn)*. Baltimore: The John Hopkins University Press.

Frieze, I., Bar-Tal, D., and Carroll, J. S. (eds). (1979). *New approaches to social problems: Applications of attribution theory*. San Francisco: Jossey Bass.

Funke, U. (1987). Effekte einer therapeutischen Modifikation subjektiver Krankheitsursachen und Kontrollannahmen am Beispiel Migräne (The effects of a therapeutic modification of subjective reasons for illness with reference to migraine). In C. Bischoff, and H. Zenz (eds.) *Krankheitsbilder, Therapievorstellungen und Arzt-Patient-Beziehungen*. Bern: Huber.

Gatting-Stiller, I., Gerling, M., Stiller, K., Voss, B., and Wender, I. (1979). Änderung der

Kausalattribuierung und des Ausadauerverhaltens bei mißerfolgsmotivierten Kindern durch Modellernen (Altering causal attributions and persistence of children with fear of failure by means of modelling). *Zeitschrift für Entwicklungspsychologie und Pädagogische Psychologie*, **11**, 312–321.

Gerling, M., Petry-Sheldrick, A., and Wender, I. (1981). Zur Modellierung von Attributionen: Effekte zusätzlicher Erfolgserwartungen und affektiver Anreize (Modelling attributions: Efects of additional success expectations and emotional incentives). *Zeitschrift für Entwicklungspsychologie und Pädagogische Psychologie*, **13**, 312–321.

Golin, S., Sweeney, P. D., and Schaeffer, D. E. (1981). The causality of causal attributions in depression: A cross-lagged panel correlational analysis. *Journal of Abnormal Psychology*, **90**, 14–22.

Graham, S. (1984). Communicating sympathy and anger to black and white children: The cognitive (attributional) consequences of affective cues. *Journal of Personality and Social Psychology*, **47**, 40–54.

Grimm, K. H. (1980). Ursachenerklärungen in Leistungssituationen: Eine Untersuchung zum Kelley'schen Kovariationsprinzip. (Causal attributions in achievement situations: An investigation regarding Kelley's covariation principle). Unpublished doctoral dissertation, Universität Bielefeld.

Grimm, L. G., and Yarnold, P. R. (1984). Performance standards and the type A behavior pattern. *Cognitive Therapy and Research*, **8**, 59–66.

Haisch, J., Rduch, G., and Haisch, I. (1985). Längerfristige Effekte attributionstherapeutischer Maßnahmen bei Übergewichtigen: Auswirkungen eines Attributionstrainings auf Abnehmerfolg und Abbrecherquote bei einem 23wöchigen Gewichts-Reduktions-Programm (Longterm effects of attributional interventions in overweight persons ...) *Psychotherapie, Psychosomatik und Medizinische Psychologie*, **35**, 133–140.

Hanusa, B. H., and Schulz, R. (1977). Attributional mediators of learned helplessness. *Journal of Personality and Social Psychology*, **35**, 602–611.

Hatfield, E., Walster, G. W., and Piliavin, J. A. (1978). Equity theory and helping relationships. In L. Wispe (ed.), *Altruism, sympathy, and helping*. New York: Academic Press. pp. 115–139.

Harvey, J. H., and Galvin, K. S. (1984). Clinical implications of attribution theory and research. *Clinical Psychology Review*, **4**, 15–33.

Harvey, J. H., Ickes, W. J., and Kidd, R. F. (eds). (1976). *New directions in attribution research*. Vol. 1, Hillsdale, N. J.: Erlbaum.

Harvey, J. H., Ickes, W. J., and Kidd, R. F. (eds). (1978). *New directions in attribution research*. Vol. 2, Hillsdale, N. J.: Erlbaum.

Harvey, J. H. Ickeds, W. J., and Kidd, R. F. (eds). (1981). *New directions in attribution research*. Vol. 3, Hillsdale, N. J.: Erlbaum.

Harvey, J. H., and Weary, G. (1981). *Perspectives on attributional processes*. Dubuque, IA: Wm C. Brown.

Hautzinger, M. (1985). Kritische Lebensereignisse, soziale Unterstützung und Depressivität bei älteren Menschen (Critical life events, social support, and depression in the aged). *Zeitschrift für Klinische Psychologie*, **14**, 27–38.

Heckhausen, H. (1980). *Motivation und Handeln*. (Motivation and action). Berlin: Springer.

Heckhausen, H., and Kuhl, J. (1985). From wishes to action: the dead ends and short cuts on the long way to action. In M. Frese and J. Sabini (eds.), *Goal-directed behavior: Psychological theory and research on action*. Hillsdale, N. J.: Erlbaum. pp. 134–160.

Heider, F. (1958). *The psychology of interpersonal relations*. New York: Wiley.

Heider, F. (1978). Wahrnehmung und Attribution (Perception and attribution). In D. Görlitz, W.-U. Meyer, and B. Weiner (eds). *Bielefelder Symposium über Attribution*. Stuttgart: Klett. pp. 13–18.

Herkner, W. (1980). *Attribution: Psychologie der Kausalität* (Attribution, psychology of causality). Bern: Hans Huber.

Hewstone, M., and Jaspars, J. (1987). Covariation and causal attribution: A logical model of the intuitive analysis of variance. *Journal of Personality and Social Psychology*, **53**, 663–672.

Helmke, A. (1983). Prüfungsangst: Ein Überblick über neuere theoretische Entwicklungen und empirische Ergebnisse (Test anxiety: A review of the recent theoretical developments and experimental results). *Psychologische Rundschau*, **34**, 193–211.

Hilton, D. J., and Slugoski, B. R. (1986). Knowledge-based causal attribution: The abnormal conditions focus model. *Psychological Review*, **93**, 75–88.

Hiroto, D. S. (1974). Locus of control and learned helplessness. *Journal of Experimental Psychology*, **102**, 187–193.

Horowitz, L. M., French, R., and Anderson, C. A. (1982). The prototype of a lonely person. In L. Peplau and D. Perlman, (eds.), *Loneliness: A sourcebook of current theory, research, and therapy*. New York: Wiley-Interscience.

Hume, D. (1938). *An abstract of treatise of human nature*. London: Cambridge University Press. (Original work published 1740).

Ickes, W. J., and Kidd, R. F. (1976). An attributional analysis of helping behavior. In J. H. Harvey, W. J. Ickes, and R. F. Kidd (eds). *New directions in attribution research*, Vol. 1. Hillsdale, N.J.: Erlbaum Press. pp. 311–334.

Ickes, W. J., and Layden, M. A. (1978). Attributional styles. In J. H. Harvey, W. J. Ickes, and R. F. Kidd (eds). *New directions in attribution research*, Vol. 2, Hillsdale, N.J.: Erlbaum. pp. 121–152.

Izard, C. E. (1977). *Human emotions*. New York: Plenum Press.

Jacobson, N. S., McDonald, W. D., Follette, W. C., and Berly, R. A. (1985). Attributional processes in distressed and nondistressed married couples. *Cognitive Therapy and Research*, **9**, 35–50.

Janoff-Bulman, R. (1979). Characterological versus behavioral self-blame: Inquiries into depression and rape. *Journal of Personality and Social Psychology*, **37**, 1798–1809.

Janoff-Bulman, R., and Brickman, P. (1982). Expectation and what people learn from failure. In N. T. Feather (ed.). *Expectations and actions: expectancy-value models in psychology*. Hillsdale, N.J.: Lawrence Erlbaum Associates. pp. 207–237.

Jaspars, J. F. M. (1983). The process of attribution in common sense. In M. R. C. Hewstone (ed.), *Attribution theory: Social and functional extensions*, Oxford, UK: Basil Blackwell, pp. 28–44.

Jaspars, J., Fincham, F. D., and Hewstone, M. (eds) (1983). *Attribution theory and research: Conceptual, developmental and social dimensions*. London: Academic Press.

Johnson, M. H., and Magaro, P. A. (1987). Effects of mood and severety on memory processes in depression and mania. *Psychological Bulletin*, **101**, 28–40.

Jones, E. E. (1980). Strategies in the shaping of competence attributions. Paper presented at the Bielefelder Symposium über Attribution.

Jones, E. E., and Berglas, S. (1978). Control of attributions about the self through self-handicapping strategies: The appeal of alcohol and the role of under-achievement. *Personality and Social Psychology Bulletin*, **2**, 200–206.

Jones, E. E., and Davis, U. E. (1965). From acts to dispositions: The attribution process in person perception. In L. Berkowitz (ed.). *Advances in experimental social psychology*, Vol. 2, New York, Academic Press. pp. 219–266.

Jones, E. E., and McGills, D. (1976). Correspondent inferences and the attribution cube: A comparative appraisal. In J. H. Harvey, W. J. Ickes, and R. F. Kidd (eds.), *New directions in attribution research*, Vol. 1, Hillsdale, N. J.: Erlbaum. pp. 389–420.

Jones, E. E., and Nisbett, R. E. (1971). *The actor and the observer: Divergent perceptions of the causes of behavior.* New York, General Learning Press.

Jones, E. E., Rock, L., Shaver, K. G., Goethals, G. R., and Ward, L. M. (1968) Pattern of performance and ability attribution: An unexpected primacy effect. *Journal of Personality and Social Psychology*, **10**, 317–340.

Kammer, D. (1983a). Eine Untersuchung der psychometrischen Eigenschaften des deutschen Beck Depressionsinventars (BDI) (Research on the psychometric qualities of the German version of the Beck Depression Inventory). *Diagnostica*, **24**, 48–60.

Kammer, D. (1983b). Depression, attributional style, and failure generalization. *Cognitive Therapy and Research*, **7**, 413–424.

Kammer, D. (1984). Die Kausaldimension der Generalität: Vorauslaufende Bedingungen für das Zustandekommen globaler und spezifischer Attributionen (The causal dimension of generality: Prerequisites for the formation of global and specific attributions). *Zeitschrift für Experimentelle und Angewandte Psychologie*, **31**, 48–62.

Kammer, D. and Stiensmeier-Pelster, J. (1988). Erfassung des depressiven Attributionsstils: Erfahrungen mit einer deutschen Form des ASQ. (Assessment of depressogenic attributional style: Experiences with a German version of the ASQ). In G. Krampen (ed.) *Diagnostik von Kausalattributionen und Kontrollüberzeugungen*. (The diagnosis of causal attributions and beliefs about control). Göttingen, Hogrefe.

Kant, I. (1982). Critique of pure reason. (W. Schwarz Translation). Aalen, FRG Scienta Verlag. (Original work published 1781)

Kelley, H. H. (1967). Attribution theory in social psychology. In D. Levine (ed.). *Nebraska Symposium on Motivation*. Lincoln, NB: University of Nebraska Press. pp. 192–238

Kelley, H. H. (1971). *Attribution in social interaction.* Morristown, N.J.: General Learning Press.

Kelley, H. H. (1972). *Causal Schemata and the attribution process.* Morristown, N.J.: General Learning Press.

Kelley, H. H. (1973). The process of causal attributions. *American Psychologist*, **28**, 107–128.

Kelley, H. H. (1976). Recent research in causal attribution. Paper presented at the Western Psychological Association, Los Angeles, 1976.

Kelley, H. H. (1979). *Personal relationships: Their structure and processes.* Hillsdale, N.J.: Erlbaum.

Kelley, H. H. (1983a). Perceived causal structures. In J. Jaspars, F. D. Fincham and M. Hewstone (eds). *Attribution theory and research: Conceptual, developmental and social dimensions*. London: Academic Press. pp. 343–369.

Kelley, H. H. (1983b). The situational origins of human tendencies: A further reason for the formal analysis of structures. *Personality and Social Psychology Bulletin*, **9**, 8–30.

Kelley, H. H., and Michela, J. (1980). Attribution theory and research. *Annual Review of Psychology*, **31**, 457–501.

Kelly, G. A. (1955). *The psychology of personal constructs.* New York: W. W. Norton.

Kendall, P. C., and Korgeski, G. P. (1979). Assessment and cognitive-behavioral interventions. *Cognitive Therapy and Research*, **3**, 1–21.

Klinger, E. (1978). Modes of normal conscious flow. In K. S. Pope and J. L. Singer (eds) *The Stream of conciousness: Scientific investigations into the flow of human experience.* New York: Plenum. pp. 225–258.

Korzybski, A. (1933). *Science and sanity.* Lancaster, Pa.: Lancaster Press.

Krahe, B. (1984). The practice of scientific research and the reality of naive psychology: a contribution to the discussion of methods of attribution research. *Zeitschrift für Sozialpsychologie*, **15**, 180–193.

Krampen, G. (ed.) (1988). *Diagnostik von Kausalattributionen und Kontrollüberzeugungen.* (The diagnosis of causal attributions and beliefs about control). Göttingen: Hogrefe.

Krantz, S. E., and Rude, S. (1984). Depressive attributions: Selection of different causes or assignment of dimensional meanings? *Journal of Personality and Social Psychology,* **47,** 193–203.

Krug, S. (1983). Motive-change programs: possibilities and limitations. *Zeitschrift für Entwicklungspsychologie und Pädagogische Psychologie,* **15,** 317–346.

Krüger, J., Möller, H., and Meyer, W.-U. (1983). Allocation of tasks of varying difficulty: influences on achievement evaluation and affects. *Zeitschrift für Entwicklungspsychologie und Pädagogische Psychologie,* **15,** 280–291.

Kruglanski, A. W. (1975). The endogenous-exogenous partition in attribution theory. *Psychological Review,* **82,** 387–406.

Kuhl, J, (1983). *Motivation, Konflikt und Handlungskontrolle.* (Motivation, conflict and action control). Berlin: Springer.

Kun, A., and Weiner, B. (1973). Necessary versus sufficient causal schemata for success and failure. *Journal of Research in Personality,*7, 197–207.

Kyle, S. O., and Falbo, T. (1985). Relationships between marital stress and attributional preferences for own and spouse behavior. *Journal of Social and Clinical Psychology,* **3,** 339–351.

Lau, R. R., and Russell, D. (1980). Attributions in the sports pages. *Journal of Personality and Social Psychology,* **39,** 29–38.

Lazarus, A. A., and Fay, A. (1976). *I can if I want to.* New York: Morrow.

Lazarus, R. S. (1966). *Psychological stress and the coping process.* New York: McGraw-Hill.

Lazarus, R. S. (1984). On the primacy of cognition. *American Psychologist,* **39,** 124–129.

Lewin, K., Dembo, T., Festinger, L., and Sears, P. S. (1944). Level of aspiration. In J. McV. Hunt (ed.). *Personality and the behavior disorders,* Vol. 1, New York: Ronald Press. pp. 333–378.

Liebhart, E. H. (1978). Perceived autonomous changes as determinants of emotional behavior. In D. Görlitz, W. -U. Meyer, and B. Weiner (eds), *Bielefelder Symposium über Attribution.* Stuttgart: Klett. pp. 107–138.

Liersch, G. (1983). Fear of flying is not necessary. *Management Wissen,* **6,** 48–50.

Mahoney, M. J. (1974). *Cognition and behavior modification.* Cambridge, Mass.: Ballinger.

Mahoney, M. J. (1977a). Reflections on the cognitive learning trend in psychotherapy. *American Psychologist,* **32,** 5–13.

Mahoney, M. J. (1977b). Personal science: A cognitive learning therapy. In A. Ellis, and R. Grieger (eds), *Handbook of rational-emotive therapy.* New York: Springer. pp. 352–366.

Maier, S. F. (1970). Failure to escape traumatic electric shock: Incompatible skeletal motor responses or learned helplessness? *Learning and Motivation,* **1,** 157–169.

Maier, S. F. and Seligman, M. E. P. (1976). Learned helplessness: Theory and evidence, *Journal of Experimental Psychology,* **105,** 3–46.

Mandler, G. F., and Sarason, S. B. (1952). A study of anxiety and learning. *Journal of Abnormal and Social Psychology,* **47,** 166–173.

Marc Aurel (edition 1973). *Selbstbetrachtungen* (Reflections). Stuttgart: Alfred Kröner Verlag.

Maslow, A. H. (1954). *Motivation and Personality.* New York: Harper and Row.

McArthur, L. A. (1972). The how and what of why: Some determinants and consequences of causal attributions. *Journal of Personality and Social Psychology,* **22,** 171–193.

McClelland, D. C., Atkinson, J. W., Clark, R. W., and Lowell, E. L. (1953). *The achievement motive.* New York: Appleton-Century-Crofts.

McHugh, M., Beckman, L., and Frieze, I. H. (1979). Analyzing alcoholism. In I. Frieze, D. Bar-Tal and J. S. Carroll (eds). *New approaches to social problems*. San Francisco: Jossey Bass. pp. 168–208.

McMahan, I. D. (1973). Relationship between causal attributions and expectancy of success. *Journal of Personality and Social Psychology*, **28**, 108–115.

Medway, F. J., and Venino, G. R. (1982). The effects of effort-feedback and performance patterns on children's atributions and task persistence. *Contemporary Educational Psychology*, **7**, 26–34.

Meichenbaum, D. A. (1977). *Cognitive behavior modification: An integrative approach*. Morristown, N.J.: General Learning Press.

Meyer, J. P. (1980). Causal attribution for success and failure: A multivariate investigation of dimensionality, formation and consequences. *Journal of personality and Social Psychology*, **38**, 704–718.

Meyer, J. P., and Koelbl, S. L. M. (1982). Students' test performances: Dimensionality of causal attributions. *Personality and Social Psychology Bulletin*, **8**, 31–36.

Meyer, N. E., and Dyck, D. G. (1986). Effects of reward schedule parameters and attribution retraining on children's attributions and reading persistence. *Bulletin of the Psychometric Society*, **24**, 65–68.

Meyer, W. -U. (1973). *Leistungsmotiv und Ursachenerklärung von Erfolg und Mißerfolg* (Achievement motive and causal explanations for success and failure). Stuttgart: Klett.

Meyer, W. -U. (1976). Leistungsorientiertes Verhalten als Funktion von wahrgenommener eigener Begabung und wahrgenommener Aufgabenschwierigkeit (Achievement-oriented behavior as a function of self-perceived ability and perceived task difficulty). In H. D. Schmalt & W. -U. Meyer (eds.), *Leistungsmotivation und Verhalten* (Achievement motivation and behavior), Stuttgart: Klett. pp. 101–135.

Meyer, W. -U. (1978). Der Einfluß von Sanktionen auf Begabungsperzeptionen (The influence of sanctions on perceptions of ability). In D. Görlitz, W. -U. Meyer, and B. Weiner (eds), *Bielefelder Symposium über Attribution*. Stuttgart: Klett Cotta. pp. 71–87.

Meyer, W. -U. (1982). Indirect communication about perceived ability. *Journal of Educational Psychology*, **74**, 888–897.

Meyer, W. -U. (1983). Das Konzept von der eigenen Begabung als ein sich selbst stabilisierendes System (The self-concept of ability as a self-stabilizing system). *Zeitschrift für Personenzentrierte Psychologie und Psychotherapie*, **2**, 21–30.

Meyer, W. -U. (1984). *Das Konzept von der eigenen Begabung* (The self concept of ability). Bern: Hans Huber.

Meyer, W. -U. (1988). Die Rolle von Überraschung im Attributionsprozeß. (The role of surprise in the process of attribution.) *Psychologische Rundschau*, in press.

Meyer, W. -U., Folkes, V. S., and Weiner, B. (1976). The perceived informational value and affective consequences of choice behavior and intermediate difficulty task selection. *Journal of Research in Personality*, **10**, 410–423.

Meyer, W. -U. and Schmalt, H. D. (1978). Die Attributionstheorie. In D. Frey (ed.). *Kognitive Theorien in der Sozialpsychologie*. Bern: Hans Huber. pp. 98–136.

Meyer, W. -U., Bachman, M., Biermann, U., Hempelmann, M., Plöger, F. -O., and Spiller, H. (1979). The informational value of evaluative behavior: Influences of praise and blame on perceptions of ability. *Journal of Educational Psychology*, **71**, 259–265.

Michela, J. L., and Wood, J. V. (1986). Causal attributions in health and illness. In P. C. Kendall (ed.). *Advances in cognitive-behavioral research, Vol. 5*. New York: Academic Press. pp. 179–235.

Michotte, A. E. (1946). *La perception de la causalite*, Paris: J. Frin.

Mill, J. S. (1872). *A system of logic*. (8th edn). London: Longmans, Green, Reader and Dyer.

Miller, I. W., and Norman, W. H. (1979). Learned helplessness in humans: A review and attribution theory model. *Psychological Bulletin*, 86, 93–118.

Miller, R. L., Brickman, P., and Bolen, D. (1975). Attribution versus persuasion as a means for modifying behavior. *Journal of Personality and Social Psychology*, 31, 430–441.

Miller, W. R., and Seligman, M. E. P. (1974). Depression and learned helplessness in man. *Journal of Abnormal Psychology*, 84, 228–238.

Neisser, U. (1966). *Cognitive Psychology*. New York, Appleton Century Crofts.

Nisbett, R. W. and Wilson, T. D. (1977). Telling more than we can know: Verbal reports on mental processes. *Psychological Review*, 84, 231–259.

Nisbett, R. E., Borgida, E., Crandall, R., and Reed, H. (1976). Popular induction: Information is not necessarily informative. In J. S. Carroll and J. W. Payne (eds). *Cognition and social behavior*. Hillsdale, N. J.: Erlbaum. pp. 113–259.

Novaco, R. W. (1975). *Anger control: The development and evaluation of an experimental treatment*. Lexington: Lexington Books.

Orvis, B. R., Cunningham, J. D., and Kelley, H. H. (1975). A closer examination of causal inference: The role of consensus, distinctiveness, and consistency information. *Journal of Personality and Social Psychology*, 32, 605–616.

Overmier, J. B., and Seligman, M. E. P. (1967). Effects of inescapable shock upon subsequent escape and avoidance learning. *Journal of Comparative and Physiological Psychology*, 63, 28–33.

Passer, M. W. (1977). *Perceiving the causes of success and failure revisited: A multi-dimensional scaling approach*. Unpublished Dissertation, University of California, Los Angeles.

Pavlov, I. P. (1927). *Conditioned reflexes*. London: Oxford University Press.

Peplau, L. A., Russell, D., and Heim, M. (1979). The experience of loneliness. In I. H. Frieze, D. Bar-Tal and J. Carroll (eds). *New approaches to social problems*. San Francisco: Jossey-Bass. pp. 53–78.

Perls, F. (1969). *Gestalt therapy verbatim*. Lafayette, CA.: Real People Press.

Peterson, C., and Seligman, M. E. P. (1984). Causal explanations as a risk factor for depression: Theory and evidence. *Psychological Review*, 91, 347–374.

Peterson, C., Semmel, A., von Baeyer, C., Abramson, L. Y., Metalski, G. I., and Seligman, M. E. P. (1982). The attributional style questionnaire. *Cognitive Therapy and Research*, 6, 287–299.

Phares, E. J. (1957). Expectancy changes in skill and chance situations. *Journal of Abnormal and Social Psychology*, 54, 339–342.

Piaget, J. (1954). *Das moralische Urteil beim Kinde*. Zürich: Goldman, Rascher.

Piliavin, I. M., Rodin, J., and Piliavin, J. A. (1969). Good samaritanism: An underground phenomenon. *Journal of Personality and Social Psychology*, 13, 289–299.

Pruit, D. J., and Insko, C. A. (1980). Extension of the Kelley attribution model: The role of comparison-object consensus, target-object consensus, distinctiveness, and consistency. *Journal of Personality and Social Psychology*, 39, 39–58.

Quattrone, G. A. (1985). On the congruity between internal states and action. *Psychological Bulletin*, 98, 3–40.

Raimy, V. (1975). *Misunderstandings of the self: Cognitive psychotherapy and the misconception hypothesis*. San Francisco, Ca.: Jossey Bass.

Reisenzein, R. (1983). The Schachter theory of emotion: Two decades later. *Psychological Bulletin*, 94, 239–264.

Reisenzein, R. (1986). A structural equation analysis of Weiner's attribution-affect model of helping behavior. *Journal of Personality and Social Psychology*, 50, 1123–1133.

Rescorla, R. A. (1988). Pavlovian conditioning: It's not what you think it is. *American Psychologist*, 43, 151–160.

Rest, S., Nierenberg, R., Weiner, B., and Heckhausen, H. (1973). Further evidence concerning the effects of perceptions of effort and ability on achievement evaluation. *Journal of Personality and Social Psychology*, **28**, 187–191.

Rizley, R. (1978). Depression and distortion in the attribution of causality. *Journal of Abnormal Psychology*, **87**, 32–48.

Rogers, C. R. (1961). *On becoming a person*. Boston: Houghton, Mifflin.

Rosenbaum, R. M. (1972). *A dimensional analysis of the perceived causes of success and failure*. Unpublished dissertation. University of California, Los Angeles.

Ross, L. (1977). The intuitive psychologist and his shortcomings: Distortions in the attribution process. In L. Berkowitz (ed) *Advances in experimental social psychology*. Vol. 10, Orlando: Academic Press. pp. 173–220.

Ross, L., Rodin, J., and Zimbardo, P. G. (1969). Toward an attribution therapy: The reduction of fear through induced cognitive-emotional misattribution. *Journal of Personality and Social Psychology*, **12**, 279–288.

Ross, M., and Olson, J. M. (1981). An expectancy-attribution model of the effects of placebos. *Psychological Review*, **88**, 408–437.

Rotter, J. B. (1954). *Social learning and clinical psychology*. Englewood Cliffs, N.J.: Prentice Hall.

Rotter, J. B. (1966). Generalized expectancies for internal versus external control of reinforcement. *Psychological Monographs*, **80**, (Whole No. 60).

Rotter, J. B. (1982). Social learning theory. In N. T. Feather (ed.). *Expectations and actions: Expectancy-value models in psychology*. Hillsdale, N. J.: Erlbaum. pp. 244–260.

Russell, B. (1950). *The conquest of happiness*. New York: Pocket Books.

Russell, D. (1982). The Causal Dimension Scale: A measure of how individuals perceive causes. *Journal of Personality and Social Psychology*, **42**, 1137–1145.

Rustemeyer, R. (1984). Selbsteinschätzung eigener Fähigkeit — vermittelt durch die Emotionen anderer Personen (Self-estimation of own ability — mediated through the emotions of others). *Zeitschrift für Entwicklungspsychologie und Pädagogische Psychologie*, **16**, 149–161.

Schachter, S., and Singer, J. E. (1962). Cognitive, social, and physiological determinants of emotional states. *Psychological Review*, **69**, 379–399.

Scherer, K. R. (1986). Vocal affect expression: A review and model for future research. *Psychological Bulletin*, **99**, 143–165.

Schulte-Tölle, W. (1975). *Psychiatrie*. Berlin: Springer.

Schunk, D. H. (1981). Modeling and attributional effects on children's achievement: A self-efficacy analysis. *Journal of Educational Psychology*, **73**, 93–105.

Schunk, D. H. (1982). Effects of effort attributional feed-back on children's perceived self-efficacy and achievement. *Journal of Educational Psychology*, **74**, 548–556.

Schunk, D. H. (1983). Ability versus effort attributional feedback. Differential effects on self-efficacy and achievement. *Journal of Educational Psychology*, **75**, 848–856.

Schunk, D. H. (1984). Sequential attributional feedback and children's achievement behaviors. *Journal of Educational Psychology*, **76**, 1159–1169.

Schuster, B., Försterling, F., and Weiner, B. (in press). Perceiving the causes of success and failure: A cross-cultural examination of attributional concepts. *Journal of Cross Cultural Psychology*.

Schütz, A. (1967). *Collected papers I. The problem of social reality*. The Hague: Martinus Nijhoff.

Seligman, M. E. P. (1975). *Helplessness: On depression, development, and death*. San Francisco: W. H. Freeman.

Seligman, M. E. P. (1981). A learned helplessness point of view. In L. P. Rehm (ed.). *Behavior therapy for depression*. Present status and future directions. New York: Academic Press. pp. 123–141.

Seligman, M. E. P. and Maier, J. F. (1967). Failure to escape traumatic shock. *Journal of Experimental Psdychology*, **74**, 1–9.

Seligman, M. E. P., Abramson, L. Y., Semmel, A., and von Baeyer, C. (1979). Depressive attributional style. *Journal of Abnormal Psychology*, **88**, 242–247.

Skinner, B. F. (1953). *Science and human behavior*. New York: Macmillan.

Smith, D. (1982). Trends in counseling and psychotherapy. *American Psychologist*, **37**, 802–809.

Smith, E. R., and Miller, F. (1983). Mediation among attributional inferences and comprehension processed: Initial findings and general methods. *Journal of Personality and Social Psychology*, **44**, 492–505.

Snyder, C. R., and Smith, T. W. (1982). Symptoms as self-handicapping strategies: The virtues of old wine in a new bottle. In G. Weary and H. L. Mirels (eds) *Integrations of clinical and social psychology*. New York: Oxford University Press. pp. 104–127.

Spiolberger, C. D. (1966). *Anxiety and behavior*. New York: Academic Press.

Steinsmeier, J., Kammer, D., Pelster, A., and Niketta, A. (1983). Attributionsstil und Bewertung als Risikofaktoren der depressiven Reaktion (Attributional style and evaluation as risk-factors for depressive reactions). *Diagnostica*, **31**, 300–311.

Storms, M. D., and McCaul, K. D. (1976). Attribution processes and emotional exacerbation of dysfunctional behavior. In J. H. Harvey, W. J. Ickes and R. F. Kidd (eds). *New directions in attribution research*. Vol. 1, Hillsdale, N. J.: Erlbaum Press. pp. 143–164.

Storms, M. D., and Nisbett, R. E. (1970). Insomnia and the attribution process. *Journal of Personality and Social Psychology*, **16**, 319–328.

Strong, S. R. (1978). Social psychological approach to psychotherapy research. In S. Garfield, and A. E. Bergin (eds). *Handbook of psychotherapy and behavior therapy*. New York: Wiley.

Taylor, S. E. (1983). Adjustment to threatening events: A theory of cognitive adaptation. *American Psychologist*, **38**, 1161–1173.

Taylor, S. E. and Fiske, S. T. (1981). Getting inside the head: methodologies for process analysis in attribution and social cognition. In J. H. Harvey, W. J. Ickes, and R. F. Kidd (eds). *New directions in attribution research*. Vol. 3, Hillsdale, N. J.: Erlbaum. pp. 459–524.

Thomae, H. (1986). Introduction In F. L. Halisch and J. Kuhl (eds.). *Motivation, intention, and volition*. Berlin: Springer.

Thompson, S. C., and Kelley, H. H. (1981). Judgments of responsibility for activities in close relationships. *Journal of Personality and Social Psychology*, **41**, 469–477.

Tomkins, S. S. (1962). *Affect, imagery, and conciousness (Vol. 1): The positive affects*. New York: Springer.

Trope, Y. (1975). Seeking information about one's ability as a determinant of choice among tasks. *Journal of Personality and Social Psychology*, **32**, 1004–1013.

Trope, Y. (1979). Uncertainty reducing properties of achievement tasks. *Journal of Personality and Social Psychology*, **37**, 1505–1518.

Trope, Y., and Brickman, P. (1975). Difficulty and diagnosticity as determinants of choice among tasks. *Journal of Personality and Social Psychology*, **31**, 918–926.

Valins, S., and Nisbett, R. E. (1971). *Some implications of the attribution processes for the development and treatment of emotional disorders*. Morristown, N.J.: General Learning Press.

Valle, V. A. (1974). *Attributions of stability as a mediator in the changing of expectations*. Unpublished doctoral dissertation, University of Pittsburgh.

Valle, V. A. (1979). An attributional analysis of consumer behavior. In I. Frieze, D. Bar-Tal and I. S. Carroll (eds). *New approaches to social problems*. San Franscisco: Jossey Bass. pp. 109–129.

Walen, S. R., Di Giuseppe, R., and Wessler, R. (1980). *A practitioner's guide to Rational-*

Emotive Therapy. New York: Oxford University Press.

Waters, V. (1979). *Color us rational*. New York: Institute for Rational Living.

Weary, G., and Mirels, H. L. (eds) (1982). *Integrations of clinical and social psychology*. New York: Oxford University Press.

Weiner, B. (1972). *Theories of motivation*. Chicago: Markham.

Weiner, B. (1975). "On being sane in insane places." A process (attributional) analysis and critique. *Journal of Abnormal Psychology*, **84**, 433–441.

Weiner, B. (1979). A theory of motivation for some classroom experiences. *Journal of Educational Psychology*, **71**, 1–29.

Weiner, B. (1980a). *Human Motivation*. New York: Holt Rinehart and Winston.

Weiner, B. (1980b). A cognitive (attribution) — emotion action model of motivated behavior: An analysis of judgments of help-giving. *Journal of Personality and Social Psychology*, **39**, 186–200.

Weiner, B. (1980c). May I borrow your class notes? An attributional analysis of help-giving in an achievement-related context. *Journal of Educational Psychology*, **72**, 676–681.

Weiner, B. (1982a). An attributionally based theory of motivation and emotion: Focus, range, and issues. In N. T. Feather (ed.). *Expectations and actions: Expectancy-value models in psychology*. Hillsdale, N. J.: Lawrence Erlbaum. pp. 163–204.

Weiner, B. (1982b). The emotional consequences of causal attributions. In M. Clark, and S. T. Fiske (eds). *Affect and cognition: 17th Annual Carnegie symposium on cognition*. Hillsdale, N. J. Erlbaum. pp. 185–209.

Weiner, B. (1985a). "Spontaneous" causal search. *Psychological Bulletin*, **79**, 74–84.

Weiner, B. (1985b). An attributional theory of emotion and motivation. *Psychological Review*, **92**, 548–573.

Weiner, B. (1986). *An attributional theory of motivation and emotion*. New York: Springer.

Weiner, B., Kun, A., and Benesh-Weiner, M. (1979). The development of mastery, emotions and morality from an attributional perspective. *Minnesota Symposium on Child Development*. Vol. 13, Hillsdale, N. J.: Erlbaum. pp. 103–130.

Weiner, B., and Litman-Adizes, T. (1980). An attributional, expectancy-value analysis of learned helplessness and depression. In J. Garber and M. E. P. Seligman (eds). *Human Control*. New York: Academic Press. pp. 35–57.

Weiner, B., Nierenberg, R., and Goldstein, M. (1976). Social learning (locus of control) versus attributional (causal stability) interpretation of expectancy of success. *Journal of Personality*, **44**, 52–68.

Weiner, B., and Potepan, P. A. (1970). Personality characteristics and affective reactions toward exams of superior and failing college students. *Journal of Educational Psychology*, **61**, 144–151.

Weiner, B., Russel, D., and Lerman, D. (1978). Affective consequences of causal ascriptions. In J. H. Harvey, W. J. Ickes and R. F. Kidd (eds), *New directions in attribution research*. Vol. 2, Hillsdale, N. J.: Erlbaum. pp. 59–90.

Weiner, B., Russell, D., and Lerman, D. (1979). The cognition-emotion process in achievement-related contexts. *Journal of Personality and Social Psychology*, **37**, 1211–1220.

Weiner, B., and Sierad, J. (1975). Misattribution for failure and enhancement of achievement strivings. *Journal of Personality and Social Psychology*, **31**, 415–421.

Weiner, B., Frieze, I. H., Kukla, A., Reed, L., Rest, S., and Rosenbaum, R. M. (1971). *Perceiving the causes of success and failure*. New York: General Learning Press.

Weiner, B., Heckhausen, H., Meyer, W. U., and Cook, R. E. (1972). Causal ascriptions and achievement behavior: A conceptual analysis of effort and reanalysis of locus of control. *Journal of Personality and Social Psychology*, **21**, 239–248.

Weiner, B., Graham, S., Stern, P., and Lawson, M. E. (1982). Using affective cues to infer causal thoughts. *Developmental Psychology*, **18**, 278–286.

Weiner, B., Graham, S., Taylor, S., and Meyer, W. -U. (1983). Social cognition in the classroom. *Educational Psychologist*, **18**, 109–124.

Weiner, B., Amirkhan, J., Folkes, V. S., and Verretto, J. A. (1987). Attributional analysis of excuse giving: Studies of a naive theory of emotion. *Journal of Personality and Social Psychology*, **52**, 316–324.

Weiner, B., and Kukla, A. (1970). An attributional analysis of achievement motivation. *Journal of Personality and Social Psychology*, **15**, 1–20.

Wessler, R. A., and Wessler, R. L. (1980). *The principles and practice of rational-emotive therapy*. San Francisco: Jossey-Bass.

Whalen, C. K., and Henker, B. (1976). Psychostimulants and children: A review and analysis. *Psychological Bulletin*, **83**, 1113–1130.

Wilson, T. D., and Linville, P. W. (1982). Improving the academic performance of college freshmen: Attribution therapy revisited. *Journal of Personality and Social Psychology*, **42**, 367–376.

Wilson, T. D. and Linville, P. W. (1985). Improving the performance of college freshmen with attributional techniques. *Journal of Personality and Social Psychology*, **49**, 287–293.

Wimer, S., and Kelley, H. H. (1982). An investigation of the dimensions of causal attribution. *Journal of Personality and Social Psychology*, **43**, 1142–1162.

Wine, J. (1980). Cognitive-attentional theory of text-anxiety. In I. G. Sarason (ed.), *Test-anxiety: Theory, research and applications*. Hilldale, N. J.: Erlbaum. pp. 349–385.

Wine, J. (1982). Evaluation anxiety. A cognitive-attentional construct. In H. W. Krohne and L. Laux (ed.), *Achievement, stress, and anxiety*. Washington: Hemisphere. pp. 207–219.

Wolpe, J. (1958). *Psychotherapy by reciprocal inhibition*. Stanford: Stanford University Press.

Wong, P. T. P., and Weiner, B. (1981). When people ask "Why" questions, and the heuristics of attributional search. *Journal of Personality and Social Psychology*, **40**, 650–663.

Wortman, C. B., and Brehm, J. W. (1975). Responses to uncontrollable outcomes: An integration of reactance theory and the learned helplessness model In L. Berkowitz, (ed.) *Advances in experimental social psychology*. Vol. 8, New York: Academic Press. pp. 277–336.

Zajonc, R. B. (1980). Feeling and thinking, preferences need no inferences. *American Psychologist*, **35**, 151–175.

Zajonc, R. B. (1984). On the primacy of affect. *American Psychologist*, **39**, 117–123.

Zimmer, D. (1981). *Die Vernunft der Gefühle: Ursprung, Natur und Sinn menschlicher Gefühle* (The reason of emotions: Source, nature and meaning of human emotions). München: R. Piper & Co.

Zoeller, C. J., Mahoney, G., and Weiner, B. (1983). Effects of attribution training on the assembly task performance of mentally retarded adults. *American Journal of Mental Deficiency*, **4**, **88**, 109–112.

Author Index

181

Subject Index

185